Company's Coming®

Home for the Holidays

Photo Legend inset front cover:

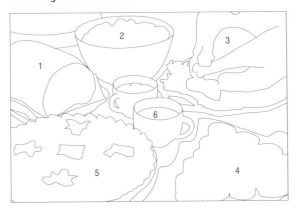

1. Christmas Bread, page 72
2. Sautéed Sprouts, page 146
3. Wild Rice And Herb Stuffing, page 32
4. Crab Wrap 'N' Roll, page 44
5. Peach Blueberry Pie, page 129
6. Refreshing Cranberry Tonic, page 57

Home for the Holidays
Copyright © Company's Coming Publishing Limited

First Printing October 2002

National Library of Canada Cataloguing in Publication

Paré, Jean
          Home for the holidays / Jean Paré.

(Special occasion series)
Includes index.
ISBN 1-895455-98-7

          1. Christmas cookery. I. Title.

TX739.2.C45P373 2002   641.5'68   C2002-902339-4

Published by
COMPANY'S COMING PUBLISHING LIMITED
2311 - 96 Street
Edmonton, Alberta, Canada T6N 1G3
Tel: 780.450.6223 Fax: 780.450.1857
www.companyscoming.com

Company's Coming is a registered trademark owned by
Company's Coming Publishing Limited

Colour separations, printing, and binding by
Friesens, Altona, Manitoba, Canada
Printed in Canada

Pictured at left:

Top: Peanut Butter Bites, page 88
Centre: Grasshopper Squares, page 86
Centre Right: Rum And Butter Balls, page 84
Bottom Left: Ambrosia Orange Cookies, page 85

Home for the Holidays was created thanks to the dedicated efforts of the people and organizations listed below.

COMPANY'S COMING PUBLISHING LIMITED

Author	Jean Paré
President	Grant Lovig
Production Manager	Derrick Sorochan
Design Director	Jaclyn Draker
Publishing Coordinator	Shelly Willsey

The Recipe Factory

Research & Development Manager	Nora Prokop
Editor	Laurel Hoffmann
Editorial Assistant	Rendi Dennis
Associate Editor	Sarah Campbell
Copy Editor	Debbie Dixon
Proofreaders	Audrey Dahl
	Connie Townsend
	Audrey Whitson
Food Editor	Lynda Elsenheimer
Associate Food Editor	Suzanne Hartman
Researcher	Sheila Hradoway
Test Kitchen Supervisor	Jessica Pon
Test Kitchen Staff	Lori Bateman
	James Bullock
	Ellen Bunjevac
	Janice Ciesielski
	Sandra Clydesdale
	Pat Yukes
Photographer	Stephe Tate Photo
Assistant Photographer	John McDougall
Photo Editor	Sherri Cunningham
Food Stylists	Allison Dosman
	Leah Duperreault
Prep Kitchen Coordinator	Audrey Smetaniuk
Prep Kitchen Staff	Cathy Anderson
	Dana Royer
Prop Stylists	Paula Bertamini
	Snezana Ferenac
Nutrition Analyst	Margaret Ng, B.Sc., M.A., R.D.

Our special thanks to the following businesses for providing extensive props for photography.

Anchor Hocking Canada	Michael's The Arts And Crafts Store
Bernardin Ltd.	Pfaltzgraff Canada
Browne & Co. Ltd.	Pyrex
Cherison Enterprises Inc.	Regal Greetings & Gifts
Corningware	Sears Canada
Dansk Gifts	Stokes
Linens 'N Things	The Bay

Table of Contents

Foreword

I just love Christmas! It's always been my favourite time of the year. The season to celebrate the spirit of giving, strengthen family ties and renew old friendships. It's a time to be thankful for all we hold dear.

There seems to be something magical about the holiday season that touches us all. And where does this enchantment come from? Well, certainly, there's magic in the wonderful traditions and folklore that surround the season. Many of the customs I grew up with are familiar favourites: decorating the Christmas tree, waiting for Santa Claus and attending church and school concerts. I even remember finding a lump of coal in my stocking on one or two occasions (along with some candy, because Santa was forgiving!).

We love to recreate some of our own favourite childhood memories by passing on these ageless traditions to our children and grandchildren. As you might imagine, in my family, cooking became a special and important tradition begun by my mother. Her energy was limitless as she bustled in the kitchen on Christmas Day, enthusiastically preparing not just one but two feasts for us to enjoy at lunch and dinner. While she cooked, Dad would take the rest of us down to our store to pick out toys, groceries and candy. Once our arms were laden with food and gifts, we drove a few miles out of town to visit a family who couldn't afford to celebrate Christmas. We followed this tradition of goodwill for many years.

Yes, Christmas is a special time to remember. It's also a busy time. Indeed, more often than not, I notice that as the days count down, everyone seems more rushed. There are cards to write, gifts to buy and holiday activities to plan—and of course, family and guests to feed. This book holds a wonderful collection of recipes for any holiday occasion and also features fun crafts, as well as party and decorating ideas the whole family will enjoy. With the turn of every page, you will find interesting ways to help make your Christmas season memorable.

Maybe you would like to spend more time with family. Start a new tradition—make a day out of decorating your tree, your home and even your yard. Invite neighbours, family and friends to join in the celebration and be sure to include some of the ideas from our section on hosting a **Tree-Trimming Party.**

Create wonderful memories for your children with the craft projects in our **Christmas is for Kids** section. Their energy is boundless this time of year, and busy hands can help to pass the time. Christmas only happens once a year, so why not take the time to make a gingerbread log cabin? Children love to create such delicious decorations, and even adults will find it entertaining.

Maybe your idea of the Christmas spirit includes a gesture of goodwill to others. Think about a family food drive or spending an evening knocking on a few neighbourhood doors to say "Merry Christmas." We've included some simple home-cooked gifts you can take along with you in **Gifts for the Host.**

As Christmas Day grows nearer, most of us begin planning the evening feast. If the family has decided to congregate at your home for a traditional Christmas dinner, that probably means you need to cook a turkey. You'll find inspiration in our section **Know Your Turkey** dedicated to this traditional main course—from selecting, to thawing, cooking and carving the perfect turkey. When the feast is over and the guests have left, you'll find inspiration to cook yet again with some delicious and economical leftover recipe ideas.

But Christmas is also a time to explore new ways to celebrate with family and friends, and maybe even create a few traditions of your own. Think about creating your own special tradition by including a few of the global flavours in your Christmas menu. You'll find an excellent selection of recipe ideas in **International Buffet.**

Not everyone celebrates the holiday season in the same way, so we've assembled a variety of menus to suit any get-together from small quiet evenings to larger festive parties.

Finally, the tree is brought down and the last ornament packed away, but the magic lives on in precious Christmas memories—a reminder of the warmth and love that surrounds the season. I'm especially proud to see that some of the special traditions that I grew up with are now those of my children and grandchildren. It's my hope that you will also find something special inside *Home for the Holidays* that will make your own celebrations memorable.

From everyone here at Company's Coming to you and your loved ones, we wish you all the best of the holiday season. Have a Merry Christmas!

Jean Paré

Each recipe has been analyzed using the most up-to-date version of the Canadian Nutrient File from Health Canada, which is based on the United States Department of Agriculture (USDA) Nutrient Data Base. If more that one ingredient is listed (such as "hard margarine or butter"), then the first ingredient is used in the analysis. Where an ingredient reads "sprinkle", "optional", or "for garnish", it is not included as part of the nutrition information.

Margaret Ng, B.Sc. (Hon), M.A.
Registered Dietitian

Tree-Trimming Party

Bring the holiday season to life with an invitation for family

and friends to join in this fun Christmas tradition.

Include a handicraft project in your celebrations

to make it an event to remember!

Cookie Hangers

The idea of cookie hangers has been around for a number of years. Create a theme with certain shapes or colours.
Personalize them with the names of your family and friends (see page 192). Use your imagination!
Or invite a group over to help make your tree hangers—it would be nice to let each guest take one home too.
Have a batch of Butter Cookie Dough (below) and Gingerbread Cookie Dough (below) already chilling.

BUTTER COOKIE DOUGH

Shortening, softened	1/2 cup	125 mL
Butter (not margarine), softened	1/2 cup	125 mL
Finely grated lemon peel	2 tsp.	10 mL
Granulated sugar	2 cups	500 mL
Egg whites (large)	4	4
Container of lemon (or plain) yogurt	4 1/2 oz.	125 mL
All-purpose flour	5 1/2 cups	1.4 L
Baking powder	1 tsp.	5 mL
Baking soda	1 tsp.	5 mL
Salt	1/2 tsp.	2 mL

Large straw, for making hole

Butter Cookie Dough: Beat shortening, butter and lemon peel together in large bowl. Gradually beat in sugar. Add egg whites. Beat well. Beat in yogurt on lowest speed until combined.

Combine next 4 ingredients in separate large bowl. Add to butter mixture. Stir until just moistened and forms a ball. Divide dough into 4 portions. Cover each portion with plastic wrap. Chill for at least 3 hours.

Roll out 1 portion of dough on lightly floured surface to 1/4 inch (6 mm) thickness. Cut out desired shapes using cookie cutters. Arrange on greased cookie sheets. Make hole near top of each cookie, using straw. Repeat with remaining portions of dough. Bake in 350°F (175°C) oven for about 8 minutes until edges are just golden. Let stand on cookie sheets for 5 minutes before removing to wire racks to cool.

GINGERBREAD COOKIE DOUGH

Hard margarine (or butter), softened	3/4 cup	175 mL
Granulated sugar	1/2 cup	125 mL
Brown sugar, packed	1/2 cup	125 mL
Large egg	1	1
Fancy (mild) molasses	1 cup	250 mL
White vinegar	2 tbsp.	30 mL
All-purpose flour	5 cups	1.25 L
Ground ginger	2 tsp.	10 mL
Ground cinnamon	1 tsp.	5 mL
Baking soda	1 1/2 tsp.	7 mL
Salt	3/4 tsp.	4 mL
Ground cloves	1/4 tsp.	1 mL
Ground allspice	1/4 tsp.	1 mL
Ground nutmeg	1/4 tsp.	1 mL

Large straw, for making hole

Gingerbread Cookie Dough: Cream margarine and both sugars together in large bowl. Beat in egg. Add molasses and vinegar. Beat well.

Stir next 8 ingredients together in medium bowl. Add to molasses mixture. Mix until well combined. Divide dough into 4 portions. Cover each portion with plastic wrap. Chill for at least 3 hours.

Roll out 1 portion of dough on lightly floured surface to 1/4 inch (6 mm) thickness. Cut out desired shapes using cookie cutters. Arrange, 1 inch (2.5 cm) apart, on ungreased cookie sheets. Make hole near top of each cookie, using straw. Repeat with remaining portions of dough. Bake in 375°F (190°C) oven for about 10 minutes until firm and edges are browned. Let stand on cookie sheets for 5 minutes before removing to wire racks to cool.

TO DECORATE:

Edible coloured glitter (optional)
Coloured fine sugar (optional)
Royal Icing, page 19 (optional)
Gold and silver dragées (optional)
Ribbon (or string), cut into 8 inch (20 cm) lengths

Sprinkle glitter and/or fine sugar on cookies while still warm. Decorate cooled cookies with icing and dragées. Thread ribbons through holes in cookies. Tie to make loops. Each recipe makes about thirty-six 3 inch (7.5 cm) cookie hangers.

Pictured on page 12/13.

Spiced Apple Potpourri Balls

Poh-puh-REE can also be used in a bowl by itself as a room fragrance.

Medium apples, with peel, cut in half, cored and very thinly sliced	2	2
Lemon juice	1/4 cup	60 mL
Medium oranges, quartered lengthwise, seeded and thinly sliced	3	3
Sprigs of fresh rosemary	5	5
Strips of lemon zest	1/2 cup	125 mL
Whole green cardamom	1/4 cup	60 mL
Whole cloves	1/4 cup	60 mL
Whole allspice	1/4 cup	60 mL
Coarsely chopped cinnamon bark	1 cup	250 mL
Strips of Christmas fabric (optional), for potpourri in a bowl		
Clear acrylic balls (3 inch, 7.5 cm, size), with vent holes	6	6
Ribbons (8 inch, 20 cm, each, in length)	6	6
Christmas decorations, for top of ball	6	6
Glue gun		

Toss apple slices and lemon juice together in medium bowl. Drain. Arrange in single layer on lightly greased baking sheet. Arrange orange slices in single layer on separate lightly greased baking sheet. Bake in 200°F (95°C) oven, with door ajar, for 1 1/2 hours, switching positions of pans at halftime. Turn oven off. Close door. Let stand for several hours until completely dry. Cool.

Spread rosemary and lemon zest on separate ungreasd baking sheet. Bake in 200°F (95°C) oven for 30 minutes. Turn over. Bake, with door slightly ajar, for 8 minutes until dry. Spread on paper towel to cool. Remove and discard stems from rosemary.

Combine next 4 ingredients in large bowl. Add apple, orange, rosemary and lemon zest. Toss. Add fabric only if using potpourri in a bowl for room fragrance. Makes 8 cups (2 L) potpourri.

Place 3/4 cup (175 mL) potpourri in bottom half of 1 acrylic ball. Put ball together. Thread 1 length of ribbon through loop on top. Tie. Glue 1 decoration around loop. Repeat with remaining supplies. Makes 6 balls.

Pictured on page 13.

Cone Ornament

Decorate these ornaments with colours complementary to the scheme of other decorations on your tree.

6 styrofoam balls (2 inch, 5 cm, size)
6 sugar ice cream cones
Small paring knife

Glue gun
6 Christmas decorations

12 ribbons (8 inch, 20 cm, length, each)

Shape styrofoam ball so bottom fits just below rim of cone.

Glue decorations onto round side of ball. Gently set into cone to check placement. Glue shaped end of ball into cone.

Glue 1 end of each of 2 pieces of ribbon to either side of cone. Tie in bow. Repeat with remaining supplies. Makes 6 ornaments.

Pictured on page 12.

Heart And Fruit Garland

*Make more garlands and tie together
to make longer garland.*

Fishing line (3 – 3 1/2 feet, 0.9 – 1.07 m, length)
1 long sewing needle
4 grapevine mini heart wicker decorations
6 kumquats
12 fresh cranberries

Knot fishing line at 1 end. Thread other end through needle. Thread through 1 heart, 1 kumquat, 4 cranberries, 1 kumquat. Repeat pattern, ending with heart. Knot other end of fishing line. Makes one 3 foot (0.9 m) long garland.

Pictured above and on page 12/13.

Candy Icicle Garland

*Make more garlands and tie together
to make longer garland.*

3 tbsp. (50 mL) pure white rolled fondant

Icing (confectioner's) sugar, for dusting
Wooden pick (or small straw)

Hole punch
24 pieces of wrapped candy
3 – 3 1/2 feet (0.9 – 1.07 m) white pearl string
    (1/8 inch, 3 mm, size)

Keep fondant in resealable plastic bag to prevent drying out. Divide into nine 1 tsp. (5 mL) portions. Roll each portion into ball.

To make icicles: Place 1 ball on working surface lightly dusted with icing sugar. Roll into 4 inch (10 cm) rope, making 1 end pointed. Twist rope around wooden pick. Remove pick. Poke hole in thick end of rope using wooden pick. Hole needs to be big enough for pearl string. Lay flat. Repeat with remaining balls of fondant. Let stand for at least 1 day to dry completely.

Punch hole through wrapping at both ends of candy. Knot 1 end of pearl string, making a loop to hang on tree. Thread other end through 1 icicle, then through 3 wrapped candies. Repeat pattern, ending with icicle. Knot other end of pearl string, making a loop to hang on tree. Makes one 3 foot (0.9 m) long garland.

Pictured on page 12/13.

Photo Legend next page:

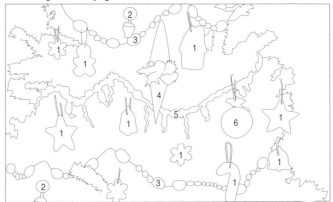

1. Cookie Hangers, page 9
2. Candy Cane Topiary, page 14
3. Heart And Fruit Garland, this page
4. Cone Ornament, page 10
5. Candy Icicle Garland, this page
6. Spiced Apple Potpourri Balls,
    page 10

Candy Cane Topiary

These trendy little decorations are easy to make.

12 styrofoam balls (1 inch, 2.5 cm, size)
6 terra cotta pots (1 inch, 2.5 cm, size)
6 cinnamon sticks (4 inch, 10 cm, each, in length)
6 paper clips
Glue gun

18 miniature candy canes, broken into small pieces
6 ribbons (6 inch, 15 cm, length, each)

Glue 1 styrofoam ball into pot. Gently push 1 cinnamon stick into middle of ball. Push second styrofoam ball onto top of cinnamon stick. Straighten paper clip at 1 end, leaving hook at other end. Push and glue straight end into top of second ball.

Divide and glue candy pieces onto both styrofoam balls. Tie ribbon into bow around rim of pot. Glue to secure. Repeat with remaining supplies. Makes 6 topiaries.

Picture on page 12.

Sugared Snowflakes

Crispy, sweet and colourful. Hang on the Christmas tree or from the ceiling to enjoy their delicate prettiness, or pile on a plate for munching. They will last for years if handled and packed carefully.

Small flour tortillas (6 inch, 15 cm, size)	10	10
Water		
Foil		
Scissors		
Sharp knife		
Cooking oil	1 tbsp.	15 mL
Coloured fine sugar (available at grocery stores in cake decoration section; wider variety of colours and brands at craft stores)	2 tbsp.	30 mL
Gold thread (or ribbon)		

Wet each tortilla by running hand under water and then rubbing over surface of tortilla. Stack. Tightly cover with foil. Heat in 350°F (175°C) oven for 10 minutes. Keep tortillas covered with damp cloth and keep warm to maintain pliability.

Fold tortilla in half. Fold in half again. Cut out decorative edge along curved side, using scissors. Make small cut-outs along straight edges.

Cut out designs in area between straight edges, using tip of knife. Open tortilla.

Brush both sides of tortilla with cooking oil. Place on baking sheet. Repeat with remaining tortillas, arranging in single layer on baking sheets. Bake on centre rack in 350°F (175°C) oven for 10 to 15 minutes, turning at halftime, until crisp and golden. Sprinkle icing sugar over tortillas. Tie gold thread through 1 hole of each snowflake. Makes 10 snowflakes.

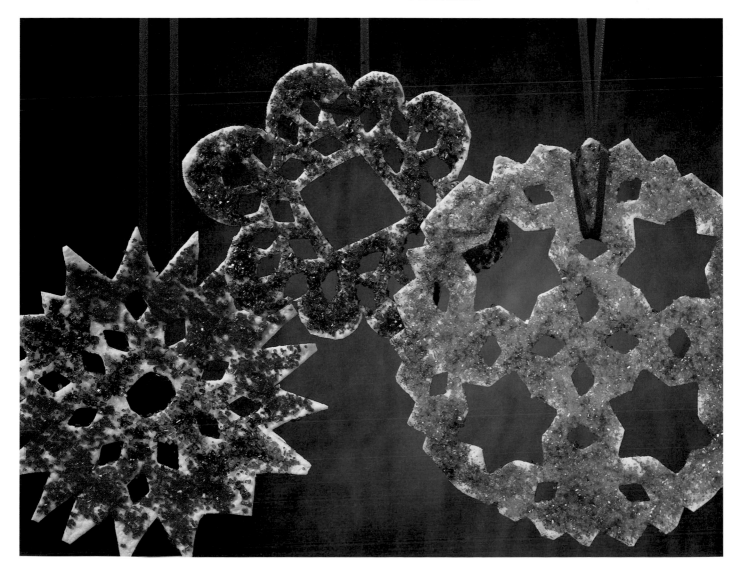

Christmas is for Kids

Children are so excited during this magical time of year.
Why not focus that energy on some fun crafts
to keep them busy? These projects can be
adapted to suit almost any age group.

Gingerbread Log Cabin

*"Deep in the woods you will find a log cabin.
It is the home of the friendly woodcutter and his family..."*

BASE
Foamcore board (20 × 24 inches, 50 × 60 cm)
Piece of heavy-duty aluminum foil (22 × 26 inches,
   55 × 65 cm)
Masking tape

LOG CABIN
Piece of brown paper (or other heavier paper),
   18 × 24 inch (45 × 60 cm) size
Scissors
Gingerbread Cookie Dough, page 9
Sharp knife

5 recipes of Royal Icing (white), about 10 cups (2.5 L),
   page 19

ASSORTED CANDY FOR DECORATING CABIN
50 candy sticks, 2 different patterns, for roof
24 square pink candies, for edges of roof
12 round Christmas candies, for peak of roof
15 cinnamon sticks, for corners of house, chimney and
   above door
156 chocolate sticks with mint filling (such as Ovation),
   for walls and chimney
2 miniature candy canes, for inside and outside of door
1 mint patty, placed above door as wreath
1 foil-covered Santa, to stick out chimney

SUGAR POND
Piece of parchment paper
   (10 × 10 inches, 25 × 25 cm)

Granulated sugar	1/2 cup	125 mL
Water	2 tbsp.	30 mL

3 – 4 drops of blue food colouring
20 stone-shaped candies

TREES
3 – 4 drops of green food colouring
2 regular-sized pointed ice-cream cones
2 miniature pointed ice-cream cones

PATH/FENCE
2 cups (500 mL) hard candies (such as Jolly
   Rancher), coarsely chopped
72 small pretzels
20 stone-shaped hard candies

Base: Cover board with foil. Tape underneath to secure.

To enlarge pattern: Mark brown paper into 1 inch
(2.5 cm) squares. Transfer pattern to grid, matching lines
within each square. Cut out patterns.

Log Cabin: Roll out 1/3 of dough on lightly floured surface
to 1/4 inch (6 mm) thickness. Lay front wall pattern on top.
Cut out, using tip of knife. Carefully transfer to lightly
greased baking sheet. Repeat using remaining dough
and patterns. Place smaller patterns on separate lightly
greased baking sheet. Bake in 375°F (190°C) oven for 8 to
10 minutes for larger pieces and 5 to 7 minutes for smaller
pieces until edges are beginning to brown. Let stand on
baking sheets for 10 minutes before removing to wire racks
to cool completely.

LOG CABIN PATTERN

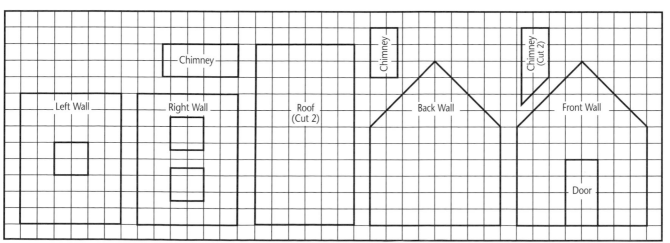

Chimney — Left Wall — Right Wall — Roof (Cut 2) — Chimney — Back Wall — Chimney (Cut 2) — Front Wall — Door

41 inches (103 cm)

14 inches (25 cm)

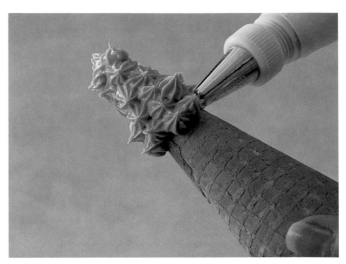

Spread 3 cups (750 mL) icing over base. Keep slightly uneven to look like snow. Cover remaining icing with damp cloth until ready to use. Stand front wall in desired position on base. Generously spread icing up and down side edges. Place side walls in place. Hold for 1 minute to "glue." Add back wall in similar manner. Once all walls are up, allow icing to dry completely before assembling roof. Assemble roof and chimney in same manner, following photo on page 19, allowing icing to dry completely before decorating. This will use about 1 cup (250 mL) icing.

Trees: Colour 1 cup (250 mL) icing with green food colouring. Pipe stars around ice cream cones. "Glue" trees around yard.

Decorate cabin with assorted candy. "Glue" in place with dabs of icing. This will use about 1 1/2 cups (375 mL) icing.

Sugar Pond: Place parchment paper on baking sheet. Put remaining 3 ingredients into small saucepan. Stir. Bring to a boil on medium-high, stirring occasionally. Boil, without stirring, until mixture reaches hard crack stage (300 to 310°F, 150 – 154°C) on candy thermometer or until small amount dropped into very cold water separates into hard, brittle threads. Sugar should not brown. Remove from heat. Pour onto parchment paper to form pond-like circle. Let stand until set. "Glue" pond in front yard, off to one side. "Glue" stone-shaped candies around edge of pond.

Path: Press chopped hard candies into icing from front edge of base in winding pattern leading up to front door. Any remaining candy pieces can be "glued" randomly onto trees.

Fence: "Glue" pretzels around outside of base and along both sides of path, alternating 1 up and 1 down.

Royal Icing

Use to decorate Cookie Hangers, page 9, and to construct the Gingerbread Log Cabin, page 17, and Good-To-Eat Popcorn Tree, page 21.

Icing (confectioner's) sugar	4 1/3 cups	1.1 L
Liquid albumen (such as Simply Egg Whites)	6 1/2 tbsp.	107 mL
Cream of tartar, just a pinch		

Sift icing sugar into medium bowl. Add albumen and cream of tartar. Beat until smooth and thickened. Add more icing sugar, 1 tsp. (5 mL) at a time, if necessary, until desired consistency. Cover with plastic wrap or damp cloth until ready to use. Makes 2 cups (500 mL).

Pipe remaining icing around edge of roof to look like icicles.

Jigsaw Puzzle Cookies

These are lots of fun with just one child or a whole gang. Vary the degree of difficulty depending on the age of the children.

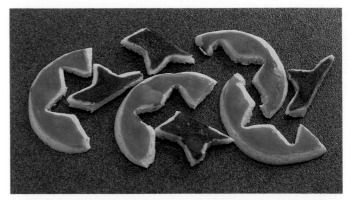

Butter Cookie Dough, page 9

EGG YOLK PAINT

Egg yolks (large)	4	4
Water	1 tsp.	5 mL

Food colouring (paste is best
  for more vibrant colours)
Sharp knife

Roll out 3 inch (7.5 cm) ball of dough on lightly floured surface to 1/4 inch (6 mm) thickness. Cut out desired shapes.

Transfer shapes to greased cookie sheet. Cut dough with 1 or 2 cookie cutters.

Egg Yolk Paint: Combine egg yolks and water in small dish using fork. Divide into several very small bowls. Add different food colouring to each bowl. Paint onto dough using fine brush. Use knife to cut shapes into puzzle pieces. Do not separate. Bake in 350°F (175°C) oven for 5 minutes. Remove from oven. Re-cut lines using tip of knife. Bake for 3 to 4 minutes until edges are barely browned. Remove to wire racks to cool completely.

Place cookies on solid work surface. Gently cut or break apart. Mix pieces up and have fun putting cookies back together!

Good-To-Eat Popcorn Tree

Decorate with a variety of different candies. Smaller individual trees can be made for children to decorate.

Stiff paper (16 × 16 inch, 40 × 40 cm, size)
Scotch tape
Waxed paper (16 × 16 inch, 40 × 40 cm, size)

Popped corn (about 1/3 cup, 75 mL, unpopped)	8 cups	2 L
Colourful fruit loops-type cereal	8 cups	2 L
Hard margarine (or butter)	1/2 cup	125 mL
Bag of miniature white marshmallows	14 oz.	400 g
Vanilla	2 tsp.	10 mL

Shoestring licorice, for decorating
Assorted candies, for decorating
Royal Icing, page 19

Fold stiff paper to make cone shape with 8 inch (20 cm) base. Tape along seam. Trim base to sit flat. (Cone should be about 14 inches, 35 cm, high.) Generously grease 1 side of waxed paper. Fold, greased side in, to make cone shape with 8 inch (20 cm) base. Tape along seam. Fit inside stiff paper cone.

Mix popped corn and cereal in extra-large bowl.

Melt margarine in large saucepan on medium-low. Add marshmallows. Stir until coated with margarine. Heat, stirring frequently to prevent scorching, until most marshmallows are melted. Remove from heat.

Add vanilla. Stir until smooth. Pour over popcorn mixture. Stir to coat.

"Glue" licorice and candies on tree using icing.

Spoon popcorn mixture into cone, packing lightly, but well, as you go. Let stand upright on flat surface until cool. Remove stiff paper cone. Peel off waxed paper cone.

Gifts for the Host

You'll be rewarded with smiles of delight
when you hand these tasty morsels to your host.

Nutty Pecan Logs

This impressive homemade candy has a nougat centre coated with caramel and nuts. You'll need strong arms to make these! Easy but pricey.

Jar of marshmallow crème	7 oz.	200 g
Vanilla	1 tsp.	5 mL
Almond flavouring	1/4 tsp.	1 mL
Icing (confectioner's) sugar	3 cups	750 mL
COATING		
Caramels (about 10 oz., 285 g)	40	40
Water	2 tbsp.	30 mL
Finely chopped pecans	1 1/2 cups	375 mL

Mix marshmallow crème, vanilla and almond flavouring in large bowl.

Add icing sugar, 1 cup (250 mL) at a time, until all sugar is absorbed and mixture is very thick and firm. Divide into 6 equal portions. Shape each portion into log, 1 inch (2.5 cm) in diameter. Arrange on ungreased baking sheets. Set in freezer.

Coating: Combine caramels and water in heavy medium saucepan. Heat on medium-low, stirring often, until smooth. Roll each log in caramel mixture until coated.

Immediately roll each log in pecans. Cover with plastic wrap or foil. Store in airtight container at room temperature for up to 4 weeks. For longer storage, cover with plastic wrap and freeze. Makes 6 logs, each cutting into about 10 slices, for a total of 60 slices.

1 slice: 74 Calories; 2.5 g Total Fat; 13 mg Sodium; 1 g Protein; 13 g Carbohydrate; trace Dietary Fibre

Pictured on page 24/25.

Test your candy thermometer before each use. Bring cold water to a boil. Candy thermometer should read 212°F (100°C) at sea level. Adjust recipe temperature up or down based on test results. For example, if your thermometer reads 206°F (97°C), subtract 6°F (43°C) from each temperature called for in recipe.

Candied Nuts

Nuts with sugar and spice in a thin fudge coating.

Granulated sugar	1 cup	250 mL
Milk	6 tbsp.	100 mL
Ground cinnamon	1 tsp.	5 mL
Mixed nuts (toasted, optional)	3 cups	750 mL
Vanilla	1/2 tsp.	2 mL

Combine sugar, milk and cinnamon in small heavy saucepan. Heat and stir until boiling. Cook on medium, without stirring, until mixture reaches firm ball stage (242 to 248°F, 117 to 120°C) on candy thermometer or until small amount dropped into very cold water forms a firm but pliable ball.

Stir nuts and vanilla into sugar mixture. Pour onto buttered baking sheet. Separate nuts using fork. Serve warm or cool. Store in airtight container for up to 1 week at room temperature. For longer storage, cover with plastic wrap and freeze. Makes 4 1/2 cups (1.1 L).

1/4 cup (60 mL): 184 Calories; 12 g Total Fat; 5 mg Sodium; 4 g Protein; 17 g Carbohydrate; 1 g Dietary Fibre

Pictured on page 25.

Photo Legend next page:

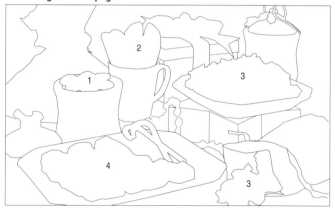

1. Chocolate-Coated Mint Patties, page 26
2. Mandarin Chocolate Biscotti, page 26
3. Candied Nuts, this page
4. Nutty Pecan Logs, above

Chocolate-Coated Mint Patties

Just as good as the store-bought patties, but better because you made them at home!

All-purpose flour	3 1/2 tbsp.	57 mL
Milk	6 tbsp.	100 mL
Icing (confectioner's) sugar	3 cups	750 mL
Peppermint flavouring	3/4 tsp.	4 mL
Milk (or dark) chocolate melting wafers (about 9 oz., 255 g)	1 1/3 cups	325 mL

Mix flour and milk in small saucepan until smooth. Heat and stir on medium until boiling and very thick. Remove from heat.

Add icing sugar and peppermint flavouring. Mix well. Let stand for 5 minutes. Turn out onto surface dusted with icing sugar. Knead until smooth, adding more icing sugar as necessary, until no longer sticky. Divide into 2 equal portions. Shape each portion into log, 1 inch (2.5 cm) in diameter. Cover with plastic wrap. Let stand at room temperature overnight. Cut into 1/4 inch (6 mm) slices, re-shaping as necessary. Place on ungreased baking sheets. Let stand, uncovered, for about 1 hour, turning at halftime, until dry.

Heat chocolate in small glass bowl over simmering water in small saucepan, stirring occasionally, until just melted. Dip patties into chocolate (see Tip, below), allowing excess to drip back into bowl. Place on foil or waxed paper-lined baking sheets. Make small swirl on top while chocolate is still soft if desired. Let stand at room temperature until firm. Makes about 5 dozen mint patties.

1 mint patty: 49 Calories; 1.3 g Total Fat; 4 mg Sodium; trace Protein; 9 g Carbohydrate; trace Dietary Fibre

Pictured on page 24.

For best results when dipping candies into chocolate, be sure the candy is at room temperature. Place candy on a fork or other similar utensil and lower candy into chocolate to cover completely. Lift, allowing excess chocolate to drip back into bowl.

Mandarin Chocolate Biscotti

Little bits of chocolate and orange peel are visible in these great dunkers in hot coffee.

Hard margarine (or butter), softened	1/2 cup	125 mL
Granulated sugar	1 cup	250 mL
Large eggs	3	3
Egg yolk (large)	1	1
Vanilla	1 tsp.	5 mL
All-purpose flour	4 cups	1 L
Baking powder	2 1/2 tsp.	12 mL
Salt	1/4 tsp.	1 mL
Large seedless mandarin oranges, peel reserved	2	2
Finely chopped reserved mandarin orange peel, white pith scraped off	1 1/2 tbsp.	25 mL
Milk chocolate candy bar, coarsely chopped (about 2/3 cup, 150 mL)	1	1
Egg white (large)	1	1
Water	1 tsp.	5 mL
Granulated sugar	1 tbsp.	15 mL

Cream margarine and first amount of sugar together in large bowl. Beat in eggs, egg yolk and vanilla.

Combine flour, baking powder and salt in medium bowl. Stir into egg mixture until thoroughly combined.

Separate oranges into sections. Cut each section into 3 or 4 pieces, reserving any juice. You should have about 1 cup (250 mL) orange pieces with juice. Mix into dough. Add orange peel and chocolate. Mix well. Turn dough out onto well-floured surface. Divide into 2 equal portions. Shape each portion into oval-shaped log, 1 inch (2.5 cm) in diameter and 11 inches (28 cm) long. Arrange 1 1/2 to 2 inches (3.8 to 5 cm) apart on large ungreased baking sheet.

Combine egg white and water in small bowl. Brush over logs. Sprinkle second amount of sugar over top. Bake in 375°F (190°C) oven for 30 minutes until lightly browned. Let stand on baking sheet for 1 hour until cool. Diagonally cut each log into 1/2 inch (12 mm) slices. Lay slices flat on same baking sheet. Bake in 325°F (160°C) oven for 30 to 35 minutes, turning slices over at halftime, until crisp. Remove to wire racks to cool completely. Makes about 32 biscotti.

1 biscotti: 144 Calories; 4.8 g Total Fat; 94 mg Sodium; 3 g Protein; 23 g Carbohydrate; 1 g Dietary Fibre

Pictured on page 24.

Cranberry Mango Chutney

Deep red colour and chunky texture to this beautiful and festive gift. Serve with Cranberry Scones, page 64.

Can of sliced mango in syrup, chopped	14 oz.	398 mL
Bag of fresh (or frozen, thawed) cranberries	12 oz.	340 g
Chopped red pepper	1 cup	250 mL
Chopped onion	1 cup	250 mL
Brown sugar, packed	2/3 cup	150 mL
Dark raisins	1/2 cup	125 mL
Apple cider vinegar	1/4 cup	60 mL
Grated gingerroot (or 3/4 tsp., 4 mL, ground ginger)	1 tbsp.	15 mL
Yellow mustard seed	1 tsp.	5 mL
Dried crushed chilies	3/4 tsp.	4 mL
Ground coriander	1/2 tsp.	2 mL
Salt	1 tsp.	5 mL
Freshly ground pepper	1/4 tsp.	1 mL
Strip of lemon peel (4 inches, 10 cm, length)	1	1

Combine all 14 ingredients in large pot or Dutch oven. Bring to a boil on medium. Reduce heat to medium-low. Simmer, uncovered, for 50 to 60 minutes until thickened. Remove and discard lemon peel. Store in refrigerator for up to 4 weeks. Makes about 4 cups (1 L).

2 tbsp. (30 mL): 40 Calories; 0.1 g Total Fat; 75 mg Sodium; trace Protein; 10 g Carbohydrate; 1 g Dietary Fibre

Pictured on this page and on page 67.

Quick Rumtopf

Instead of taking months to make using fresh fruit, this only takes one week. Delicious to serve over ice cream or cake.

Can of sliced peaches in syrup, drained and syrup reserved, diced	14 oz.	398 mL
Can of sliced mango in syrup, drained and syrup reserved, diced	14 oz.	398 mL
Cans of mandarin orange segments (10 oz., 284 mL, each), drained and juice reserved	2	2
Can of pineapple tidbits, drained and juice reserved	19 oz.	540 mL
Dried cherries (see Note)	2 cups	500 mL
Amber rum	1 cup	250 mL
Reserved syrup and fruit juice	3 3/4 cups	925 mL
Granulated sugar	2 cups	500 mL

Combine peach, mango, orange, pineapple and cherries in large bowl. Spoon into large pitcher.

Pour rum over fruit mixture.

Stir reserved syrup, reserved fruit juice and sugar together in large saucepan. Heat, stirring occasionally, until boiling. Gently boil, uncovered, for 10 minutes. Cool for 1 hour. Pour over fruit mixture. Cover. Store in refrigerator for 1 week to blend flavours and up to 5 weeks. Makes about 9 cups (2.25 L).

1/2 cup (125 mL): 222 Calories; 0.7 g Total Fat; 4 mg Sodium; 1 g Protein; 48 g Carbohydrate; 2 g Dietary Fibre

Pictured below.

Note: Don't be disappointed when cherries and other fruit lose their colour. They still lend their flavour to the finished product.

Centre: Quick Rumtopf, this page
Bottom Left: Cranberry Mango Chutney, this page

Italian Panettone

Pronounced pan-uh-TOH-nee. Rich, fruit-filled and pine nut-studded sweet bread. Although traditionally done in a round dome shape, this can be baked in coffee cans or deep round pans. Very festive when glazed and decorated.

Milk	2 cups	500 mL
Butter (not margarine), cut into chunks	1/2 cup	125 mL
Large eggs	4	4
Granulated sugar	2/3 cup	150 mL
Finely grated orange peel	2 tsp.	10 mL
Aniseed, crushed (optional)	1 1/2 tsp.	7 mL
Salt	1 tsp.	5 mL
All-purpose flour	2 cups	500 mL
Instant yeast	1 tbsp.	15 mL
All-purpose flour	4 1/2–5 cups	1.1–1.25 L
Mixed glazed fruit, diced	2/3 cup	150 mL
Sultana raisins	1/2 cup	125 mL
Pine nuts, toasted (see Tip, page 100)	1/3 cup	75 mL
Sliced almonds, toasted (see Tip, page 100)	1/3 cup	75 mL
Large egg	1	1
Milk	1 tsp.	5 mL
GLAZE (optional)		
Lemon juice	1 tbsp.	15 mL
Icing (confectioner's) sugar	1/2–2/3 cup	125–150 mL

Red and/or green glazed cherries, for garnish
Almonds, for garnish

Heat milk and butter in small saucepan until butter is melted and mixture is hot. Remove from heat.

Beat first amount of eggs, granulated sugar, orange peel, aniseed and salt together in large bowl. Slowly whisk in hot milk mixture. Temperature of egg mixture should feel very warm but not hot.

Combine first amount of flour and yeast in small bowl. Mix into egg mixture until smooth.

Add second amount of flour, 1 cup (250 mL) at a time, stirring well and working in with hands, until sticky ball forms. Turn out onto floured surface. Knead dough, adding small amounts of remaining flour as necessary, until soft dough forms. Place dough in greased bowl, turning once to grease top. Cover with greased waxed paper and tea towel. Let stand in oven with light on and door closed for about 1 hour until doubled in bulk. Punch dough down. Turn out onto greased surface. Press or roll dough out to large rectangle.

Sprinkle with mixed fruit, raisins, pine nuts and almonds. Roll up, jelly roll-style. Knead, greasing work surface with cooking oil as dough becomes tacky, until fruit and nuts are well distributed and dough is elastic and no longer sticky. Divide into 2 portions. Form each portion into round shape. Place on greased baking sheet. Cover with greased waxed paper and tea towels. Let stand in oven with light on and door closed for about 45 minutes until doubled in size.

Beat egg and second amount of milk together in small cup using fork. Brush over tops of loaves. Bake in 350°F (175°C) oven for 45 to 50 minutes until golden brown and hollow sounding when tapped.

Glaze: Measure lemon juice into small bowl. Stir in icing sugar, 1 tbsp. (15 mL) at a time, adding more icing sugar or lemon juice, until barely pourable consistency. Drizzle over top centre of panettone, allowing some to run down sides.

Garnish with cherries and almonds when glaze has stopped moving but before becoming dry. Makes 2 loaves, each cutting into about 20 slices, for a total of about 40 slices.

1 slice: 158 Calories; 4.6 g Total Fat; 102 mg Sodium; 4 g Protein; 25 g Carbohydrate; 1 g Dietary Fibre

Pictured on page 29.

Variation: Form each portion into balls. Put into well-greased 2 1/4 lb. (1 kg) coffee can.

Italian Panettone, this page

Know Your Turkey

A golden turkey, roasted to tender perfection, is an established tradition at many Yuletide feasts. Here are a few guidelines on how to truss, thaw, cook and carve the perfect Christmas turkey. Recipes for stuffing, soups and next-day turkey delights are included.

Trussing the Turkey

Over the years, cooks have developed various ways to truss (or tie up) the turkey so that the legs and wings stay tucked into the sides, preventing overcooking and drying out. Is there a right way and a wrong way? We don't believe so, but, if you are going to carve your turkey at the table (see page 33), we'd like to recommend this method. Place cleaned bird on cutting board. Loosely stuff cavities in body and neck with stuffing if desired.

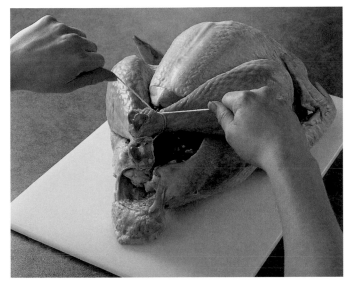

Loop centre of butcher's string (18 inches, 45 cm, long) 1 1/2 times around each leg. Bring string together and tie to secure.

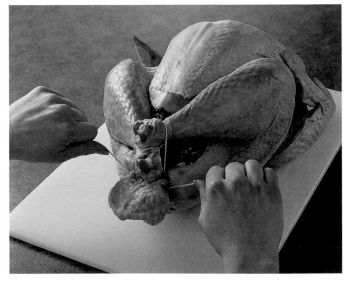

Bring ends down under tail. Tie to secure. Trim excess string.

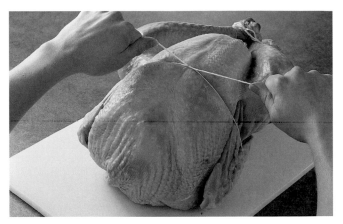

Turn turkey around. Work separate piece of string (30 inches, 75 cm, long) under turkey. Bring ends of string up and over turkey. Tie across breast to secure wings. Trim any excess string.

TURKEY COOKING GUIDE			
Oven temperature at 350°F (175°C)			
Weight		Unstuffed	Stuffed
6 – 8 lbs.	2.7 – 3.5 kg	2 1/4 – 3 1/4 hrs.	3 – 3 1/2 hrs.
8 – 10 lbs.	3.5 – 4.5 kg	2 3/4 – 3 hrs.	3 1/4 – 3 1/2 hrs.
10 – 12 lbs.	4.5 – 5.4 kg	3 – 3 1/2 hrs.	3 3/4 – 4 1/2 hrs.
12 – 16 lbs.	5.4. – 7 kg	3 3/4 – 4 3/4 hrs.	4 – 5 1/4 hrs.
16 – 22 lbs.	7 – 10 kg	4 1/2 – 5 1/4 hrs.	5 – 6 1/2 hrs.

❋ For unstuffed turkey — Use a meat thermometer to ensure that breast meat reaches an internal temperature of 185°F (85°C) and thigh meat reaches an internal temperature of 170°F (77°C).

❋ For stuffed turkey — Use a meat thermometer to ensure that breast meat reaches an internal temperature of 185°F (85°C) and thigh meat reaches an internal temperature of 180°F (82°C).

❋ If turkey is stuffed, temperature of stuffing should reach 165°F (74°C).

❋ Juices should run clear, leg should move easily and no pink should remain in meat.

❋ Cooking time can be affected by the starting temperature of the turkey, size of the turkey, size of oven, type of roasting pan, covered or uncovered, lid or foil cover, etc. but the times noted above should be a reasonable guideline. A fresh turkey that has never been frozen will take a bit longer than a frozen, thawed turkey. A meat thermometer reading is the best assurance of doneness.

TO STUFF OR NOT TO STUFF:

The question of whether or not to stuff the turkey is often asked these days. Food safety information indicates that the stuffing must be put into the cavity of the turkey just before cooking and removed immediately after the turkey is taken from the oven. We have provided two options: Wild Rice and Herb Stuffing, below, that is cooked separately in a casserole dish in the oven or can be cooked inside the cavity of the turkey, and Spicy Sausage And Bread Stuffing, page 148, that is cooked in a slow cooker.

Wild Rice And Herb Stuffing

Chewy with great nutty flavour.
Wonderful aroma of sage and other herbs.

Cans of condensed chicken broth (10 oz., 284 mL, each)	2	2
Water	2 cups	500 mL
Wild rice	1 1/2 cups	375 mL
Chopped onion	1 cup	250 mL
Chopped celery	1 cup	250 mL
Diced red pepper	2/3 cup	150 mL
Diced fresh mushrooms	1 cup	250 mL
Hard margarine (or butter)	1/4 cup	60 mL
Coarse dry bread crumbs	1 cup	250 mL
Pine nuts, chopped	1/2 cup	125 mL
Chopped fresh parsley (or 1 1/2 tsp., 7 mL, flakes)	2 tbsp.	30 mL
Chopped fresh mint leaves (or 1 1/2 tsp., 7 mL, dried)	2 tbsp.	30 mL
Chopped fresh thyme (or 1 1/2 tsp., 7 mL, dried)	2 tbsp.	30 mL
Chopped fresh sage (or 3/4 tsp., 4 mL, dried)	1 tbsp.	15 mL
Salt	1/2 tsp.	2 mL
Pepper	1/4 tsp.	1 mL

Bring broth and water to a boil in large saucepan.

Add rice. Stir. Cover. Bring to a boil on medium. Reduce heat to medium-low. Simmer for about 45 minutes until rice has just popped but is still slightly firm. Turn into large bowl.

Sauté onion, celery, red pepper and mushrooms in margarine in large frying pan for about 5 minutes until onion is soft.

Add remaining 8 ingredients. Stir until well combined. Add to rice. Stir. Transfer stuffing to well-greased 3 quart (3 L) baking dish. Cover. Bake in 350°F (175°C) oven for 30 to 60 minutes until heated through. Makes 8 cups (2 L).

1/2 cup (125 mL): 160 Calories; 6.7 g Total Fat; 416 mg Sodium; 7 g Protein; 20 g Carbohydrate; 2 g Dietary Fibre

Pictured on front cover and on this page.

Carving the Turkey

EQUIPMENT:

❋ A good quality carving knife is essential. An electric knife works well, but does not have the precision or control that a carving knife will have when guided by your hand. Be sure that the blade is sharp.

❋ Having a carving fork in the opposite hand helps to steady the turkey as you carve and to lift slices to serving platter.

❋ Always work on a clean cutting board, preferably one that has grooves to catch drippings.

BEFORE CARVING:

❋ Remove turkey from oven and roasting pan and let stand on cutting board for 10 to 15 minutes before carving.

❋ If turkey is stuffed, remove stuffing immediately and put into serving bowl after turkey is taken from oven. Keep warm.

CARVING AT THE TABLE:

Remove turkey from cutting board to platter. Remove strings. Have small cutting board at table beside platter to cut leg/thigh meat. Depending on number of guests, some people carve only from one side of turkey first and, if necessary, turn platter and work from other side.

Slice through skin, between leg and body, down to leg joint. Pull leg slightly away from body. Cut through joint closest to body. Cut meat from thigh and leg, making slices roughly parallel to bone. Remove tough tendons from leg meat.

Make horizontal cut just above wing, slicing through just to bone of rib cage.

Starting at 1 end of breast, cut off thin slices of meat. A slightly diagonal slant to the knife will give larger slices. Once you have sliced down to the bone, change angle of cut to remove more meat further down breast.

CARVING IN THE KITCHEN:

Follow same steps for removing and slicing leg.

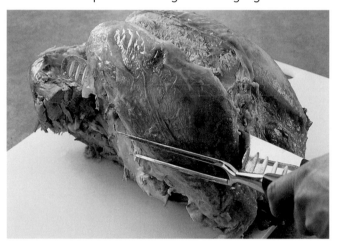

For breast meat, slice down along breastbone following the rib cage. Remove the entire breast from the body of the turkey and place on cutting board.

Slice breast across the grain into thin slices. Place on platter.

Turkey Fricassee

An elegant way to serve leftover turkey!
Serve in puff pastry patty shells.

Finely chopped onion	1/2 cup	125 mL
Finely chopped celery	1/2 cup	125 mL
Garlic cloves, minced (or 1/2 tsp., 2 mL, powder)	2	2
Hard margarine (or butter)	3 tbsp.	50 mL
All-purpose flour	2 tbsp.	30 mL
Milk	1 1/4 cups	300 mL
Chopped cooked turkey	1 1/2 cups	375 mL
Frozen peas	1 cup	250 mL
Jar of pimiento, drained and finely diced	2 oz.	57 mL
Chicken bouillon powder	2 tsp.	10 mL
Parsley flakes	1 1/2 tsp.	7 mL
Salt	1/2 tsp.	2 mL
Pepper	1/4 – 1/2 tsp.	1 – 2 mL

Sauté onion, celery and garlic in margarine in large saucepan until onion is soft.

Sprinkle flour over onion mixture. Stir well. Add milk. Heat and stir until boiling and thickened.

Add next 7 ingredients. Stir. Bring to a boil. Reduce heat. Simmer, uncovered, for about 3 minutes, stirring often, until peas are tender. Makes 2 3/4 cups (675 mL).

1/4 cup (60 mL): 174 Calories; 7.7 g Total Fat; 227 mg Sodium; 15 g Protein; 11 g Carbohydrate; 2 g Dietary Fibre

Pictured on page 35.

Honey Mustard Turkey Salad

A crunchy and hearty salad with a sweet dressing.

HONEY MUSTARD DRESSING

Finely chopped red onion	1/4 cup	60 mL
Red wine vinegar	1/4 cup	60 mL
Lemon juice	1/4 cup	60 mL
Dijon mustard	1/4 cup	60 mL
Liquid honey	1/4 cup	60 mL
Cooking oil	2 tbsp.	30 mL
Dillweed	1 tsp.	5 mL
Salt	1/2 tsp.	2 mL
Pepper	1/4 tsp.	1 mL
Chopped cooked turkey	4 cups	1 L
Shredded savoy cabbage	1 1/2 cups	375 mL
Sliced celery	1 cup	250 mL
Seedless red grapes, halved	25	25
Baby greens lettuce	3 1/2 cups	875 mL

Small bunches of red grapes, for garnish

Honey Mustard Dressing: Stir first 9 ingredients together in small bowl. Makes 1 1/4 cups (300 mL) dressing.

Combine turkey, cabbage, celery and halved grapes in large bowl. Drizzle dressing over salad. Toss to coat.

Arrange lettuce on serving platter or on individual salad plates. Top with turkey mixture.

Garnish with grape bunches. Makes 7 cups (1.75 L).

1 cup (250 mL): 246 Calories; 7.1 g Total Fat; 382 mg Sodium; 27 g Protein; 20 g Carbohydrate; 1 g Dietary Fibre

Pictured on page 35.

Top Right: Turkey Mixed Bean Soup, page 161
Centre & Centre Left: Turkey Fricassee, this page
Top Left & Bottom Right: Honey Mustard Turkey Salad, above

Top Left: Turkey Cristo Sandwich, page 161   Centre: Hot Turkey Sandwich, below   Top Right: Fresh Tomato Relish, page 93

Hot Turkey Sandwich

A meal unto itself—just add some vegetables or a salad.
Toast the bread for a crispier sandwich.

Cold leftover gravy	2 tbsp.	30 mL
White bread slice	1	1
Leftover Spicy Sausage And Bread Stuffing, page 149 (or other leftover stuffing)	3 tbsp.	50 mL
Sliced cooked turkey, to cover	2 oz.	57 g
Whole cranberry sauce, mashed	2 tbsp.	30 mL
White bread slice	1	1
Leftover gravy, thinned with a little hot water, if necessary	1/4 cup	60 mL
Pepper, sprinkle		

Spread first amount of gravy over first bread slice. Place on microwave-safe plate.

Scatter stuffing over gravy. Lay turkey over stuffing. Carefully spread cranberry sauce over turkey. Cover. Microwave on medium (50%) for 2 minutes, turning plate at halftime if microwave doesn't have turntable.

Lay second bread slice over cranberry sauce. Pour second amount of gravy over bread slice. Microwave, uncovered, on medium (50%) for 1 minute. Sprinkle pepper over top. Let stand for 1 minute. Makes 1 sandwich.

1 sandwich: 409 Calories; 11.3 g Total Fat; 1045 mg Sodium; 26 g Protein; 50 g Carbohydrate; 2 g Dietary Fibre

Pictured above.

Turkey Salad Wraps, below

Turkey Salad Wraps

A good way to use all the bits of turkey that seem to get bypassed for larger pieces.

Whole cranberry sauce	2/3 cup	150 mL
Salad dressing (or mayonnaise)	1/3 cup	75 mL
Large spinach (or flour) tortillas (about 10 inches, 25 cm), see Tip, this page	5	5
Large iceberg lettuce leaves	5	5
Slivered (or diced) cooked turkey	2 cups	500 mL
Medium tomato, seeded and diced	1	1
Ground rosemary	1/8 tsp.	0.5 mL
Dried sweet basil, crushed	1/8 tsp.	0.5 mL
Salt	1/4 tsp.	1 mL
Pepper, sprinkle		

Combine cranberry sauce and salad dressing in small bowl. Spread about 3 tbsp. (50 mL) down centre of each tortilla.

Lay 1 lettuce leaf over top of each cranberry mixture.

Toss remaining 6 ingredients together in medium bowl. Spoon about 1/2 cup (125 mL) down centre of each lettuce leaf. Fold 1 end of tortilla over filling and fold in sides, leaving top end open. Makes 5 wraps.

1 wrap: 375 Calories; 12.8 g Total Fat; 478 mg Sodium; 22 g Protein; 42 g Carbohydrate; 2 g Dietary Fibre

Pictured above.

To make folding tortillas easier, sprinkle some water onto each tortilla. Stack damp tortillas on foil. Enclose. Heat in 350°F (175°C) oven for about 20 minutes until warm or microwave tortillas individually, unwrapped, on high (100%) for 20 seconds.

Menu Suggestions

Large or small, mellow or festive, the Christmas season plays host
to a medley of social activities. These menu ideas are just some
of the ways you can mix and match recipes for
any occasion—the possibilities are endless.

Family Lunch

Spinach And Olive Braid, page 76

Burger Strata, page 80

Cream Of Mushroom Soup, page 156

Greek Pea Salad, page 138

Spice Coffee Cake, page 77

Late Night Supper

Rich Chicken Stew, page 127

Sautéed Sprouts, page 146

Eggnog Chantilly, page 103

or

Blackened Chicken Caesar Salad, page 138

Orange Couscous With Sultanas, page 150

Eggnog Fondue, page 102

Holiday Open House

Refreshing Cranberry Tonic, page 57

Hot Tea Wassail, page 60

Feta Spinach Mushroom Caps, page 43

Crab Wrap 'N' Roll, page 44

Candied Nuts, page 23

Chocolate-Coated Mint Patties, page 26

Butter Crunch, page 83

Chocolate Almond Cookies, page 84

Butterscotch Cookies, page 88

Caramel Nut Squares, page 91

Italian Panettone, page 28

Stuffed Ham Casserole, page 126

In From Outdoors

By-The-Fire Hot Chocolate, page 59

Warm Spiced Cranberry, page 60

Scotch Broth, page 154

Sweet Potato Biscuits, page 65

Rice Pudding, page 174

Celebrate-The-Holidays Teen Party

Fruit Slush, page 58

Spicy Sticky-Finger Wings, page 50

Holiday Whirls, page 50

Creamed Tahini Dip, page 54
(with fresh vegetables)

Butter Crunch, page 83

Butterscotch Cookies, page 88

Peanut Butter Bites, page 88

Toasted Popcorn Snack, page 91

Romantic Dinner

Two-Toned Buns, page 65

Shrimp Marinara Sauce, page 118

Ginger Honey-Glazed Beans, page 146

Eggnog Chantilly, page 103

Trim-The-Tree Treats

Rush Eggnog, page 56

Fruit Slush, page 58

Ricotta And Jalapeño Tarts, page 44

Crab Wrap 'N' Roll, page 44

Mustard Ranch Drumettes, page 50

Grasshopper Squares, page 86

Peanut Butter Bites, page 88

Ragged Chocolate Drops, page 89

Norwegiean Almond Pastry, page 174

Kid's Sleepover Brunch

Refreshing Cranberry Tonic, page 57

Doctored Oatmeal Porridge, page 75

The Big Breakfast, page 81

Two-Toned Buns, page 65

Finger Food Party

Rush Eggnog, page 56

Maple And Rye Gravlax, page 48

Old-Fashioned Bran Bread, page 71

Honey Mustard Sauce, page 92

Mustard Ranch Drumettes, page 50

Cocktail Shrimp-On-A-Pineapple, page 48

Grape Cheese Wreath, page 51

Gorgonzola Cheese Dip, page 54
(with fresh vegetables)

Spiced Plum Sauce, page 55

Spring Rolls, page 167

Toasted Popcorn Snack, 91

Kid's Sleepover Brunch

Refreshing Cranberry Tonic, page 57

Doctored Oatmeal Porridge, page 75

The Big Breakfast, page 81

Two-Toned Buns, page 65

Snowed-In Supper

Caramel Cider Tea, page 59

Holiday Whirls, page 50

Barley And Rice Pilaf, page 146

Paprika Stew With Zucchini Biscuits, page 119

Butterscotch Cookies, page 88

Pear And Ginger Pie, page 130

Progressive Supper

Organize a holiday progressive supper with friends or neighbours. Start with cocktails and appetizers at the first house, salad and bread at the second stop, the main course at the next, and dessert and coffee at the last. It's an easy way to share the cooking, plus you get to see everyone's holiday decorations!

Hot Tea Wassail, page 60

Spicy Sticky-Finger Wings, page 50

Mexican Christmas Salad, page 168

Christmas Bread, page 72

Cajun Chicken, page 111

Pineapple Fluff Cake, page 104

Quiet Christmas Eve

Refreshing Cranberry Tonic, page 57

Cornmeal Muffins, page 64

Creamy Seafood Sauce, page 117

Rice Pudding, page 174

Make-Ahead Christmas Morning

Rush Eggnog, page 56

Peanut Butter Dip, page 54
(with fresh fruit)

Breakfast Trifle, page 73

Blueberry Streusel French Toast, page 77

Cranberry Scones, page 64

Christmas Day Wrap-Up

Hot Mushroom Dip, page 51

Oriental Candied Pork, page 45

Horseradish Dipping Sauce, page 54

Rum And Butter Balls, page 84

Piña Colada Squares, page 82

Chocolate Raspberry Biscotti, page 106
(with coffee)

New Year's Eve Dinner

Candy Cane Bread, page 70

Cranberry Scones, page 64

Slaw Special, page 137

Stuffed Turkey Breast, page 121

Hot Carrot Ring, page 146

Broccoli With Lemon Cheese Sauce, page 142

Varenyky With Onion Butter, page 170

Pumpkin Chiffon Pie, page 130

Recipes

Celebrate the holiday season in style
with this festive collection of recipes.
Create some imaginative showpieces, such as the
Cocktail Shrimp-On-A-Pineapple, page 48,
or Candy Cane Bread, page 70, and uncover
some ideas for dressing up buffet trays
and punch bowls.

Appetizers

Feta Spinach Mushroom Caps

A very nice one-bite appetizer. Have them on hand in the freezer for unexpected company. Serve on a bed of shredded carrots.

Finely chopped onion	1/2 cup	125 mL
Garlic clove, minced (or 1/4 tsp., 1 mL, powder), optional	1	1
Hard margarine (or butter)	2 tsp.	10 mL
Box of frozen spinach, thawed, squeezed dry and finely chopped	10 oz.	300 g
Seasoned salt	1 tsp.	5 mL
Pepper, heavy sprinkle		
Crumbled feta cheese	1 cup	250 mL
Parsley flakes	1 tsp.	5 mL
Dried sweet basil	1/4 tsp.	1 mL
Dried whole oregano	1/4 tsp.	1 mL
Fresh medium mushrooms (about 1 lb., 454 g), cleaned and stems removed	40	40

Sauté onion and garlic in margarine in frying pan for about 3 minutes until onion is soft.

Add spinach, seasoned salt and pepper. Sauté for 3 to 4 minutes until spinach is tender. Drain. Turn into medium bowl. Cool completely.

Add cheese, parsley flakes, basil and oregano. Stir.

Pack about 2 tsp. (10 mL) filling in each mushroom cap. Arrange on ungreased baking sheet. Bake, uncovered, in 450°F (230°C) oven for 6 to 8 minutes until hot. To cook from frozen, bake for about 10 minutes until heated through. Makes 40 mushroom caps.

1 mushroom cap: 19 Calories; 1.2 g Total Fat; 82 mg Sodium; 1 g Protein; 1 g Carbohydrate; trace Dietary Fibre

Pictured on page 47.

Whole heated or partially cooked mushrooms will unavoidably "weep" a bit, so arrange on a bed of lettuce or shredded carrot to make a more attractive presentation for company.

Outer Ring: Ricotta And Jalapeño Tarts, below

Centre: Crab Wrap 'N' Roll, below

Ricotta And Jalapeño Tarts

A delicious little tart that invites your guests to stick around for the rest of the meal.

Jalapeño pepper, seeded and diced (see Note)	1	1
Sliced green onion	2 tbsp.	30 mL
Finely grated carrot	2 tbsp.	30 mL
Cooking oil	2 tsp.	10 mL
Salt	1/2 tsp.	2 mL
Dried whole oregano, crushed	1/4 tsp.	1 mL
Ricotta cheese	1 cup	250 mL
Large egg, fork-beaten	1	1
Unbaked mini-tart shells (or line small tart tins with your own pastry)	20	20

Sauté jalapeño pepper, green onion and carrot in cooking oil in frying pan for 2 to 3 minutes until soft.

Stir in salt and oregano. Cool.

Stir in cheese and egg. Divide among tart shells. Bake in 400°F (205°C) oven for 12 to 15 minutes until pastry is golden and filling is set. Serve warm. Makes 20 tarts.

1 tart: 75 Calories; 5.1 g Total Fat; 122 mg Sodium; 2 g Protein; 5 g Carbohydrate; trace Dietary Fibre

Pictured above.

Note: Wear gloves when chopping jalapeño peppers and avoid touching your eyes.

Crab Wrap 'N' Roll

These pretty spirals are a confetti of colours.

Can of crabmeat, drained, cartilage removed, flaked	4 1/4 oz.	120 g
Green onion, thinly sliced	1	1
Small roma (plum) tomato, seeded, finely diced and drained	1	1
Finely diced red pepper	2 tbsp.	30 mL
Cream cheese, softened	2 tbsp.	30 mL
Mayonnaise (not salad dressing)	2 tsp.	10 mL
Creamed horseradish	1/2 tsp.	2 mL
Celery seed	1/8 tsp.	0.5 mL
Salt, sprinkle		
Pepper, sprinkle		
Large red and/or green flour tortillas (about 10 inches, 25 cm), see Tip, page 37	2	2

Combine first 10 ingredients in medium bowl. Makes 1 1/3 cups (325 mL) filling.

Spread 1/2 of filling over each tortilla to within 1/2 inch (12 mm) of edge. Roll up tightly. Cover with plastic wrap. Twist ends to seal well. Chill overnight. Trim and discard 1 inch (2.5 cm) from each end. Cut each roll into 1 inch (2.5 cm) slices. Makes 2 rolls, each cutting into 8 slices, for a total of 16 slices.

1 slice: 35 Calories; 1.6 g Total Fat; 83 mg Sodium; 2 g Protein; 3 g Carbohydrate; trace Dietary Fibre

Pictured on front cover and above.

Itty-Bitty Crab Bits

The curry paste in these appetizers leaves a pleasant warmth in the back of the throat. Serve with plain yogurt to cool the palate! This recipe works best, and is quite fast, in a food processor. Mince the ingredients very fine if doing by hand. Serve with Creamed Tahini Dip, page 54.

White bread slice, torn into several pieces	1	1
Fresh parsley sprig, cut into 3 pieces	1	1
Finely grated gingerroot (or 1/4 tsp., 1 mL, ground ginger)	1 tsp.	5 mL
Green onion, cut into several pieces	1	1
Flake coconut	2 tbsp.	30 mL
Salt	1/2 tsp.	2 mL
Freshly ground pepper, sprinkle		
Can of crabmeat, drained and cartilage removed	4 1/4 oz.	120 g
Large egg, fork-beaten	1	1
Green curry paste	2 – 3 tsp.	10 – 15 mL
Lemon juice	1 1/2 tsp.	7 mL

COATING

Medium coconut	3 tbsp.	50 mL
Finely crushed soda crackers (3 to 4)	3 tbsp.	50 mL

Cooking oil, for deep-frying

Put first 7 ingredients into food processor. Pulse with on/off motion 3 to 4 times until coarsely chopped. Process for about 5 seconds until finely chopped.

Add crab, egg, curry paste and lemon juice. Pulse with on/off motion several times until evenly moistened. Shape into 3/4 inch (2 cm) balls.

Coating: Combine coconut and cracker crumbs in small bowl. Roll crab balls in coconut mixture to coat completely.

Deep-fry, in about 3 batches, in hot (375°F, 190°C) cooking oil for about 1 minute until golden. Place on paper towel to drain. Makes about 24 crab bits.

1 crab bit: 41 Calories; 3.6 g Total Fat; 95 mg Sodium; 1 g Protein; 1 g Carbohydrate; trace Dietary Fibre

Pictured on page 47.

To Make Ahead: Prepare crab bits and freeze. To reheat from frozen, do not thaw. Place on greased baking sheet. Bake in 350°F (175°C) oven for about 10 minutes until hot.

Oriental Candied Pork

Slices of meat with a chewy coating and tender inside. Serve with Spiced Plum Sauce, page 55.

MARINADE

Soy sauce	1/4 cup	60 mL
Brown sugar, packed	1/4 cup	60 mL
Hoisin sauce	3 tbsp.	50 mL
Liquid honey	2 tbsp.	30 mL
Apple cider vinegar	2 tbsp.	30 mL
Garlic clove, minced (or 1/4 tsp., 1 mL, powder)	1	1
Red food colouring	1 tsp.	5 mL
Pork tenderloin	1 lb.	454 g

Water

Marinade: Combine first 7 ingredients in small saucepan. Bring to a boil, stirring constantly, until brown sugar is dissolved. Pour into shallow glass dish. Cool.

Add pork to marinade. Turn to coat. Cover. Marinate in refrigerator overnight, or for up to 24 hours, turning once. Remove pork, reserving marinade. Pour marinade into medium saucepan. Bring to a boil. Heat and stir for 3 minutes.

Place pork on rack in roasting pan containing about 1/2 inch (12 mm) water. Roast in 275°F (140°C) oven for 2 hours, adding more water if needed. Generously brush pork several times with marinade. Cool before cutting into 1/4 inch (6 mm) slices. Makes about 40 slices.

1 slice: 30 Calories; 0.7 g Total Fat; 164 mg Sodium; 3 g Protein; 3 g Carbohydrate; trace Dietary Fibre

Pictured on page 53.

Photo Legend next page:

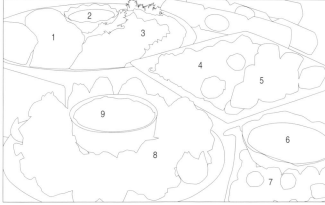

Maple And Rye Gravlax

Traditionally a Scandinavian delicacy of raw salmon cured in sugar mixture. Canadianized here with maple flavouring and rye whiskey. Requires 3 days curing time, so plan ahead. Serve very thinly sliced with Old-Fashioned Bran Bread, page 71, and Honey Mustard Sauce, page 92.

Fresh salmon fillet, with skin, blotted dry	1 1/2 lbs.	680 g
Cheesecloth, enough to wrap salmon in double thickness		
Rye whiskey	3 tbsp.	50 mL
Coarse sea salt	3 tbsp.	50 mL
Brown sugar, packed	3 tbsp.	50 mL
Maple flavouring	1 tsp.	5 mL
Pepper	1/4 tsp.	1 mL
Fresh dill sprigs, to cover		
Fresh rosemary sprigs, to cover		

Lay salmon, skin side down, on cheesecloth.

Drizzle whisky over top of salmon. Sprinkle with sea salt.

Stir brown sugar, maple flavouring and pepper together in small cup until evenly coloured. Spread over sea salt.

Layer dill and rosemary sprigs over top. Wrap cheesecloth around salmon. Set, skin side down, in shallow glass dish. Lay sheet of plastic wrap over cheesecloth. Do not seal. Place 3 unopened 28 oz. (796 mL) cans in pan that will fit inside glass dish. Place weighted pan on top of salmon. Chill, without turning, for 3 days. Unwrap cheesecloth. Remove dill and rosemary sprig. Very thinly slice salmon across grain on diagonal removing fish from skin. Tightly cover any uncut gravlax with plastic wrap. Chill for up to 5 days. Serves 6.

1 serving: 250 Calories; 12.3 g Total Fat; 3605 mg Sodium; 23 g Protein; 7 g Carbohydrate; trace Dietary Fibre

Pictured on page 46.

Cocktail Shrimp-On-A-Pineapple

A spectacular way to present shrimp at a gathering.

SEAFOOD SAUCE		
Chili sauce	1/4 cup	60 mL
Ketchup	1/2 cup	125 mL
White vinegar	1 tsp.	5 mL
Granulated sugar	1 tsp.	5 mL
Prepared horseradish	3/4 tsp.	4 mL
Onion powder	1/8 tsp.	0.5 mL
Garlic powder	1/8 tsp.	0.5 mL
Salt	1/8 tsp.	0.5 mL
Water	2 cups	500 mL
White (or alcohol-free) wine	1/2 cup	125 mL
Bay leaves	2	2
Chopped celery, with leaves	1/4 cup	60 mL
Raw medium shrimp (about 1 1/2 lbs.,680 g), peeled and deveined, tails left intact	50	50
Ice water		
PINEAPPLE HOLDER		
Whole large pineapple (about 4 inches, 10 cm, in diameter)	1	1
Cocktail (or wooden or plastic) picks (4 inch, 10 cm, lengths)	50	50

Seafood Sauce: Combine first 8 ingredients in small bowl. Chill. Makes 3/4 cup (175 mL) sauce.

Combine water, wine, bay leaves and celery in large saucepan. Bring to a boil.

Add shrimp. Stir. Cover. Cook for 3 minutes until shrimp are pink and curled. Remove shrimp. Immerse shrimp in ice water until cold. Add more ice as needed to chill well. Drain. Blot dry. Discard liquid.

Pineapple Holder: Wash outside of pineapple and leaves under running water. Drain and pat dry. Cut thin slice from bottom to allow pineapple to sit flat. Using ruler and felt marker, measure and mark 5 lengthwise wedges, about 2 1/4 inches (5.6 cm) across, leaving about 3/4 inch (2 cm) in between each wedge. Cut each wedge at a 45° angle, slicing right to core. Remove cut out pineapple wedges (see Line Drawing, below). From bird's eye viewpoint, pineapple should resemble star shape. Slice off and discard outer skin from wedges. Cut pineapple into at least 50 bite-size pieces.

Thread 1 pineapple piece and 1 shrimp onto each cocktail pick. Poke about 10 filled picks into each wedge, shrimp-side out, filling in all empty spaces. Chill. Serve with Seafood Sauce. Makes 50 appetizers.

1 appetizer: 23 Calories; 0.3 g Total Fat; 76 mg Sodium; 3 g Protein; 2 g Carbohydrate; trace Dietary Fibre

Pictured on this page.

TRADITIONAL SHRIMP COCKTAIL: To present as a first course, arrange 6 shrimp per person on crushed ice in individual seafood cocktail glasses. If you don't have seafood cocktail glasses, make bed of lettuce on individual plates. Arrange about 6 shrimp per plate on top of lettuce and drizzle with Seafood Sauce. Serves 8.

Pictured on this page.

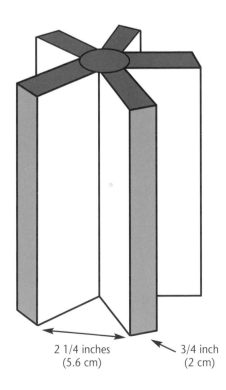

2 1/4 inches
(5.6 cm)

3/4 inch
(2 cm)

Cocktail Shrimp-On-A-Pineapple, page 48

Spicy Sticky-Finger Wings

Have plenty of napkins handy when you serve these yummy appetizers. Serve with Horseradish Dipping Sauce, page 54.

Chili sauce	2/3 cup	150 mL
Liquid honey	1/3 cup	75 mL
Indonesian sweet soy sauce	1/4 cup	60 mL
Prepared mustard	1 tbsp.	15 mL
Hot pepper sauce	1 tsp.	5 mL
Garlic powder	1/4 tsp.	1 mL
Whole chicken wings (about 18), split in half, tips discarded	3 lbs.	1.4 kg

Combine first 6 ingredients in small bowl.

Place chicken in shallow dish. Pour marinade over chicken. Stir to coat. Cover. Marinate in refrigerator for several hours or overnight, stirring several times. Turn out wings and marinade onto greased foil-lined 11 × 17 inch (28 × 43 cm) baking sheet. Arrange in single layer. Bake, uncovered, in 450°F (230°C) oven for 15 minutes. Stir and turn wings to coat with marinade. Bake for 10 minutes. Stir. Bake for about 10 minutes until completely coated with sticky sauce. Makes 36 wings.

1 wing: 64 Calories; 3.3 g Total Fat; 153 mg Sodium; 4 g Protein; 5 g Carbohydrate; trace Dietary Fibre

Pictured on page 52.

Mustard Ranch Drumettes

Great taste with just a hint of mustard. Use a hot, spicy mustard for more intense flavour. Serve with Gorgonzola Cheese Dip, page 54.

Ranch dressing	1 cup	250 mL
Grainy mustard	1/4 cup	60 mL
Mustard powder	1 tsp.	5 mL
Chicken drumettes (or whole wings, split in half, tips discarded)	3 lbs.	1.4 kg
Fine dry bread crumbs	1 1/3 cups	325 mL

Combine first 3 ingredients in small bowl.

Place chicken in shallow dish. Pour marinade over chicken. Stir to coat. Cover. Marinate in refrigerator for several hours or overnight, stirring several times. Remove chicken. Discard marinade.

Roll chicken in bread crumbs until completely coated. Arrange in single layer on greased foil-lined baking sheet. Bake, uncovered, in 425°F (220°C) oven for 15 minutes. Turn over. Bake for about 15 minutes until brown and crispy. Makes 24 drumettes or 36 wing pieces.

1 drumette: 149 Calories; 10.9 g Total Fat; 206 mg Sodium; 7 g Protein; 6 g Carbohydrate; trace Dietary Fibre

Pictured on page 46/47.

Holiday Whirls

These appetizers have the festive colours of red, white and green. Serve on a bed of mint leaves.

Block of cream cheese, softened	8 oz.	250 g
Crumbled feta cheese (about 8 oz., 225 g), room temperature	1 3/4 cups	425 mL
Chopped dried cranberries	1 cup	250 mL
Finely chopped fresh mint leaves (or green onion)	1/4 cup	60 mL
Large spinach tortillas (about 10 inches, 25 cm), see Tip, page 37	5	5

Cream both cheeses together in medium bowl until well mixed. Stir in cranberries and mint.

Spread about 1/2 cup (125 mL) cheese mixture on each tortilla to within 1/2 inch (12 mm) of edge. Roll up tightly, jelly roll-style. Cover each roll securely with plastic wrap. Chill for several hours or overnight. Trim and discard about 1 inch (2.5 cm) from ends of each roll. Cut each roll on diagonal into 1 inch (2.5 cm) slices. Makes 5 rolls, each cutting into 8 slices, for a total of 40 pieces.

1 piece: 65 Calories; 4 g Total Fat; 121 mg Sodium; 2 g Protein; 5 g Carbohydrate; 1 g Dietary Fibre

Pictured on page 47.

Grape Cheese Wreath

So pretty on a buffet table! Mild green peppercorn flavour with a slight sweet orange accent. Serve on buttery crackers with wedges of apple and other fruits.

WREATH		
Block of cream cheese, softened	8 oz.	250 g
Whole green peppercorns in brine, drained, slightly crushed	2 tsp.	10 mL
Rounds of Brie cheese (4 oz., 125 g, each), chilled and diced	2	2
FROSTING		
Block of cream cheese, softened	4 oz.	125 g
Frozen concentrated orange juice, thawed	1 tbsp.	15 mL
Icing (confectioner's) sugar	1 tsp.	5 mL
Finely grated orange zest	1/2 tsp.	2 mL
GARNISHES		
Red seedless grapes, halved, approximately	3	3
Chopped fresh parsley	1/4 cup	60 mL
Long piece of orange peel	1	1

Wreath: Beat cream cheese and peppercorns together in large bowl until fluffy.

Stir Brie cheese into cream cheese mixture. Beat for about 2 minutes until combined. Cover. Chill for several hours or overnight. Form into log about 1 1/2 inches (3.8 cm) in diameter. Join ends to form ring on serving plate. Flatten edges with knife if desired. Cover. Chill.

Frosting: Beat cream cheese, concentrated orange juice, icing sugar and orange zest together in small bowl until smooth. Spread on ring.

Garnishes: Decorate ring using grapes and parsley. Tie orange peel into bow and place on ring. Serves about 20.

1 serving: 111 Calories; 10.1 g Total Fat; 137 mg Sodium; 4 g Protein; 1 g Carbohydrate; trace Dietary Fibre

Pictured on page 53.

Hot Mushroom Dip

Hot and spicy from the cheese with a definite mushroom and onion presence. Great make-ahead appetizer. Can also be served cold but will become thicker.

Finely chopped onion	1 cup	250 mL
Garlic clove, minced (or 1/4 tsp., 1 mL, powder), optional	1	1
Chopped fresh white mushrooms	3 cups	750 mL
Hard margarine (or butter)	2 tbsp.	30 mL
Block of cream cheese, room temperature, cut into 8 pieces	8 oz.	250 g
Seasoned salt	1/2 tsp.	2 mL
Dill weed	1/2 tsp.	2 mL
Pepper, heavy sprinkle		
Mayonnaise (not salad dressing)	1/2 cup	125 mL
Grated Monterey Jack With Jalapeño cheese	1 1/2 cups	375 mL
Fresh mushroom slices, for garnish	7	7
Fresh chives (or sliced green onion), for garnish	1 tbsp.	15 mL

Sauté onion, garlic and mushrooms in margarine in large frying pan for about 10 minutes until liquid from mushrooms has evaporated and mushrooms are golden. Remove from heat.

Add next 4 ingredients. Stir until cream cheese is melted.

Add mayonnaise and Monterey Jack cheese. Mix well. Spread in shallow baking dish or glass pie plate.

Garnish with mushrooms and chives. Cover and chill for up to 2 days if desired. Bake in 350°F (175°C) oven for about 30 minutes until heated through. Makes 2 1/2 cups (625 mL).

2 tbsp. (30 mL): 131 Calories; 12.5 g Total Fat; 153 mg Sodium; 3 g Protein; 2 g Carbohydrate; trace Dietary Fibre

Pictured on page 52/53.

Buffet Platters

* Arrange items in relation to shape of plate or platter.
* Cut bite size or at least similar in size.
* As you fill the plate, maintain symmetrical balance, that is, repeat on one side what you did on the other.
* Alternate light and dark items for visual balance.
* Use paper napkins or doilies to add background colour.
* Garnish with parsley sprigs, fresh herbs, carrot/tomato roses or radish flowers.

Deli Platter

Thin slices of deli roast beef, rolled
Thin slices of Black Forest (or other) ham,
  rolled into cone shapes
Thin slices of peppered (or other) salami, folded into fan
Thin slices of farmer's sausage, rolled with thin slices
  of process Cheddar cheese
Thin slices of mozzarella cheese
Assortment of pickles and olives
Assortment of hard cheeses, cut into sticks

Fold 1 slice of salami in half. Fold in half again. Set 'fan' on platter with final fold up.

Pictured at right:

Top Left: Hot Mushroom Dip, page 51
Top Right: Spiced Plum Sauce, page 55,
  with Oriental Candied Pork, page 45
Bottom Left: Spicy Sticky-Finger Wings, page 50,
  with Horseradish Dipping Sauce, page 54
Bottom Right: Grape Cheese Wreath, page 51

Creamed Tahini Dip

A smooth dip with the distinctive taste of sesame seeds.
Good with Itty-Bitty Crab Bits, page 45.

Tahini	1/3 cup	75 mL
Indonesian sweet soy sauce	1 tbsp.	15 mL
Lemon juice	2 tsp.	10 mL
Whipping cream	3/4 cup	175 mL
Roasted sesame seeds	1/2 tsp.	2 mL

Combine tahini, soy sauce and lemon juice in small bowl.

Beat whipping cream in medium bowl until soft mounds form but don't stay in peaks.

Fold in tahini mixture and sesame seeds. Chill for at least 1 hour. Makes 1 1/2 cups (375 mL).

2 tbsp. (30 mL): 87 Calories; 8.5 g Total Fat; 52 mg Sodium; 2 g Protein; 2 g Carbohydrate; 1 g Dietary Fibre

Pictured on page 47.

Gorgonzola Cheese Dip

A creamy dip that is great with Mustard Ranch Drumettes, page 50, and vegetables.

Sour cream	1 cup	250 mL
Crumbled Gorgonzola cheese, softened	1/3 cup	75 mL
Block of cream cheese, softened, cut into 4 pieces	4 oz.	125 g
Dried chives	1 1/2 tsp.	7 mL
White vinegar	1 tsp.	5 mL
Prepared horseradish	1 tsp.	5 mL
Onion salt	3/4 tsp.	4 mL

Fresh chives, sliced, for garnish

Beat first 7 ingredients together in medium bowl until smooth and fluffy.

Garnish with chives. Makes about 1 1/2 cups (375 mL).

2 tbsp. (30 mL): 81 Calories; 7.3 g Total Fat; 163 mg Sodium; 2 g Protein; 2 g Carbohydrate; trace Dietary Fibre

Pictured on page 46.

Horseradish Dipping Sauce

A distinct tangy flavour in this dipping sauce.
Serve with meatballs, sausages, ham or
Spicy Sticky-Finger Wings, page 50.

Mayonnaise (not salad dressing)	1/4 cup	60 mL
Creamed horseradish	3 tbsp.	50 mL
Ketchup	2 tbsp.	30 mL
Prepared mustard	2 tsp.	10 mL
Worcestershire sauce	1/4 tsp.	1 mL

Combine all 5 ingredients in small bowl. Cover. Chill until ready to serve. Makes about 1/2 cup (125 mL).

2 tbsp. (30 mL): 117 Calories; 11.5 g Total Fat; 211 mg Sodium; 1 g Protein; 3 g Carbohydrate; trace Dietary Fibre

Pictured on page 52/53.

Peanut Butter Dip

Creamy smooth blend of peanut butter and orange flavours.
Good with fresh fruit, celery and peppers.

Smooth peanut butter	1/2 cup	125 mL
Prepared orange juice	3 tbsp.	50 mL
Corn syrup	1 1/2 tbsp.	25 mL
Frozen whipped topping, thawed	1 cup	250 mL

Stir first 3 ingredients together in small bowl until smooth.

Fold in whipped topping until blended well. Makes 1 1/3 cups (325 mL).

1 tbsp. (15 mL): 53 Calories; 4 g Total Fat; 31 mg Sodium; 2 g Protein; 3 g Carbohydrate; trace Dietary Fibre

Pictured on page 55.

To keep your bowl from moving while using an electric hand mixer, place a dampened, folded tea towel underneath.

Cranberry Cheese

A pretty and festive spread that can be moulded to any shape you desire. Serve with crackers or melba toast.

Grated sharp white Cheddar cheese, room temperature	2 cups	500 mL
Block of cream cheese, room temperature	4 oz.	125 g
Dried cranberries, coarsely chopped	1/4 cup	60 mL

Beat Cheddar cheese and cream cheese together in medium bowl until smooth.

Mix in cranberries. Press into ungreased 1 1/2 cup (375 mL) mould or large cookie cutter, packing well to avoid air spaces. Cover with plastic wrap. Chill for at least 3 hours until firm. Loosen in mould. Invert onto serving plate. Serves 6 to 8.

1 serving: 242 Calories; 20.5 g Total Fat; 309 mg Sodium; 12 g Protein; 4 g Carbohydrate; 1 g Dietary Fibre

Pictured below.

Spiced Plum Sauce

This sauce has a nice heat that lingers and a slight honey sweetness. Serve with Oriental Candied Pork, page 45.

Can of prune plums in heavy syrup, pits removed	14 oz.	398 mL
Liquid honey	1/4 cup	60 mL
White vinegar	2 tbsp.	30 mL
Chili sauce	1 tbsp.	15 mL
Cornstarch	2 tsp.	10 mL
Dried crushed chilies	1/4 – 1/2 tsp.	1 – 2 mL

Measure all 6 ingredients into blender. Process until almost smooth. Pour into medium saucepan. Bring to a boil. Reduce heat to medium-low. Simmer, uncovered, for about 10 minutes, stirring occasionally, until thickened slightly. Cool. Makes 1 1/2 cups (375 mL).

2 tbsp. (30 mL): 51 Calories; 0.1 g Total Fat; 26 mg Sodium; trace Protein; 13 g Carbohydrate; trace Dietary Fibre

Pictured on page 53.

Left: Cranberry Cheese, above
Right: Peanut Butter Dip, page 54

Beverages

Left: Rush Eggnog, below

Rush Eggnog

A quick and easy way to spruce up store-bought eggnog.

Eggnog	4 cups	1 L
Milk	2 cups	500 mL
Liquor of your choice (such as brandy, Irish whiskey or rum)	1/2 – 3/4 cup	125 – 175 mL
Whipping cream	1 cup	250 mL

Measure eggnog, milk and liquor into punch bowl. Stir.

Beat whipping cream in medium bowl until stiff peaks form. Add to eggnog mixture. Stir gently. Chill until ready to serve. Makes 7 cups (1.75 L).

1 cup (250 mL): 331 Calories; 18 g Total Fat; 127 mg Sodium; 9 g Protein; 25 g Carbohydrate; 0 g Dietary Fibre

Pictured above.

Centre: Refreshing Cranberry Tonic, below

Right: Cool Coffee Nog, below

Refreshing Cranberry Tonic

This cool, tart drink will quench your thirst.
Float orange slices and whole cranberries in tonic.

Fresh (or frozen) cranberries, chopped	4 cups	1 L
Granulated sugar	2 cups	500 mL
Water	4 cups	1 L
Prepared orange juice	1 1/2 cups	375 mL
Lemon juice	1/2 cup	125 mL
Tonic water (or club soda or water)	6 cups	1.5 L

Combine cranberries, sugar and water in large pot or Dutch oven. Bring to a boil on medium-high, stirring occasionally. Reduce heat to medium-low. Simmer, uncovered, for about 10 minutes until cranberries are soft. Pour through fine sieve or double thickness of cheesecloth over large punch bowl. Discard solids.

Add remaining 3 ingredients. Stir gently. Chill until ready to serve. Makes 13 1/2 cups (3.4 L).

1 cup (250 mL): 193 Calories; 0.1 g Total Fat; 6 mg Sodium; trace Protein; 50 g Carbohydrate; trace Dietary Fibre

Pictured on front cover and above.

Cool Coffee Nog

Pleasant, cool, creamy coffee flavour in this nog with a punch!
Serve with mint chocolate sticks.

Cold prepared strong coffee	4 cups	1 L
Coffee-flavoured liqueur (such as Kahlúa)	1/2 cup	125 mL
Chocolate-flavoured liqueur (such as Crème de Cacao)	1/4 cup	60 mL
Vanilla ice cream, softened	4 cups	1 L

Pour coffee into 2 quart (2 L) pitcher. Add both liqueurs and ice cream. Stir gently until smooth. Chill until ready to serve. Makes 6 2/3 cups (1.65 L).

1 cup (250 mL): 272 Calories; 10.8 g Total Fat; 81 mg Sodium; 3 g Protein; 30 g Carbohydrate; 0 g Dietary Fibre

Pictured above.

Variation: Omit vanilla ice cream. Use same amount of coffee or chocolate ice cream.

Variation: Omit chocolate-flavoured liqueur. Use same amount of orange-flavoured liqueur (such as Grand Marnier or Triple Sec).

Fruit Slush

Cloudy, lemon yellow, frozen slush with banana.
Very cold and refreshing. Serve with Ice Ring, this page.

Prepared orange juice	6 cups	1.5 L
Pineapple juice	3 cups	750 mL
Lemon juice	2/3 cup	150 mL
Granulated sugar	2 cups	500 mL
Small ripe bananas, puréed	4	4
Ginger ale	6 cups	1.5 L

Pour orange juice, pineapple juice and lemon juice into medium bowl. Add sugar. Stir until sugar is dissolved.

Add banana. Stir, using whisk, until combined well. Pour into airtight container. Freeze until firm.

Turn frozen mixture into large punch bowl at least 4 hours before serving. Add ginger ale just before serving. Stir. Makes 18 cups (4.5 L).

1 cup (250 mL): 205 Calories; 0.2 g Total Fat; 8 mg Sodium; 1 g Protein; 52 g Carbohydrate; 1 g Dietary Fibre

Pictured below.

Outside Ring: Fruit Slush, above   Centre: Ice Ring, this page

Ice Ring

A simple punch is transformed into a stunning show-stopper with this crystal creation of fruit and juice.
Use in Fruit Slush, this page.

Crushed ice	2 cups	500 mL
Seedless red grapes	2 cups	500 mL
Fresh cranberries	1 cup	250 mL
Sliced frozen mango	1/4 cup	60 mL
Star fruit, sliced	1	1
Fresh blueberries	1/4 cup	60 mL
Medium orange, sliced	1	1
Fruit punch	1 cup	250 mL
Mango juice	1 cup	250 mL

Put crushed ice into bottom of 12 cup (3 L) bundt pan. Arrange fruit on top of ice, sticking some star fruit and orange slices into ice to anchor fruit. Freeze, keeping level, for 1 hour.

Combine punch and juice in 2 cup (500 mL) liquid measure. Slowly pour juice mixture, in one spot, over fruit. To prevent fruit from floating, do not submerge fruit. Freeze, keeping level, for at least 8 hours. To unmould, run warm water over underside of bundt pan for a few seconds. Carefully remove ice ring. Gently place in prepared punch.

Left: By-The-Fire Hot Chocolate , below

Right: Caramel Cider Tea, below

By-The-Fire Hot Chocolate

Definite cinnamon flavour to this holiday hot chocolate.

Granulated sugar	1/2 cup	125 mL
Cocoa, sifted if lumpy	1/2 cup	125 mL
Milk (not skim)	6 cups	1.5 L
Cinnamon sticks (4 inch, 10 cm, lengths)	2	2
Large eggs	2	2
Vanilla	2 tsp.	10 mL

Miniature marshmallows, for garnish
Grated chocolate, for garnish

Combine sugar and cocoa in large saucepan. Slowly stir in milk. Add cinnamon sticks. Heat, uncovered, on medium for about 8 minutes, stirring occasionally, until steaming and very foamy.

Beat eggs and vanilla in small bowl using fork. Add 1/2 cup (125 mL) cocoa mixture to egg mixture. Stir. Remove and discard cinnamon sticks. Whisk egg mixture into cocoa mixture. Whisk vigorously for about 4 minutes until mixture is almost boiling and froth forms on top.

Ladle into mugs. Garnish with marshmallows and chocolate. Makes 6 cups (1.5 L).

1 cup (250 mL): 223 Calories; 5.5 g Total Fat; 152 mg Sodium; 12 g Protein; 35 g Carbohydrate; 2 g Dietary Fibre

Pictured above.

Caramel Cider Tea

Tea that tastes like apple pie—delicious and comforting.

Apple juice (or cider)	4 cups	1 L
Water	2 cups	500 mL
Brown sugar, packed	2 tbsp.	30 mL
Cinnamon stick (4 inch, 10 cm, length)	1	1
Orange pekoe tea bag	1	1
Whipped cream (or prepared dessert topping)	1 1/3 cups	325 mL
Thick caramel ice cream topping	3 tbsp.	50 mL
Ground cinnamon, sprinkle (optional)		
Cinnamon sticks (4 inch, 10 cm, lengths), optional	4	4

Heat apple juice, water, brown sugar and cinnamon stick in large saucepan until boiling. Remove from heat.

Add tea bag. Cover. Let steep for 5 minutes. Remove and discard tea bag and cinnamon stick. Ladle into 4 large mugs.

Top each with about 1/3 cup (75 mL) whipped cream.

Put ice cream topping into small resealable freezer bag. Cut tiny hole in 1 corner. Squeeze over whipped cream in zigzag pattern. Dust cinnamon over top. Add 1 cinnamon stick to each mug. Serves 4.

1 serving: 318 Calories; 13.8 g Total Fat; 88 mg Sodium; 1 g Protein; 50 g Carbohydrate; trace Dietary Fibre

Pictured above.

Cool Irish Coffee

A real treat. Dark mocha coffee with a white creamy layer on top. Sprinkle with edible brown glitter to dress up this drink.

Boiling water	2 tbsp.	30 mL
Instant coffee granules	2 tsp.	10 mL
Granulated sugar	1 tsp.	5 mL
Cold water	1 cup	250 mL
Vanilla ice cream	1/2 cup	125 mL
Irish whiskey	2 tbsp.	30 mL
Frozen whipped topping (or whipped cream), optional		

Stir boiling water into coffee granules in small bowl. Add sugar and cold water. Stir until sugar is dissolved.

Spoon ice cream into large mug. Add whiskey. Pour coffee mixture over ice cream mixture to fill mug. Makes 1 3/4 cups (425 mL).

Top with dollop of whipped topping. Serves 1.

1 serving: 230 Calories; 7.7 g Total Fat; 57 mg Sodium; 3 g Protein; 22 g Carbohydrate; 0 g Dietary Fibre

Pictured on page 61.

Variation: Omit cold water. Use 1 cup (250 mL) milk for a richer taste.

Warm Spiced Cranberry

Pretty amber colour with a rose hue. Not-too-sweet, fruity blend with a hint-of-cinnamon drink.

Cranberry cocktail	4 cups	1 L
Prepared orange juice	2 cups	500 mL
Lemon juice	1/2 cup	125 mL
Granulated sugar	1/4 cup	60 mL
Cinnamon sticks (4 inch, 10 cm, lengths)	2	2
Whole cloves	4	4
Ginger ale, room temperature	4 cups	1 L

Combine first 6 ingredients in large saucepan. Heat on low, stirring often, until simmering. Cover. Simmer for 15 minutes. Pour into warm punch bowl.

Add ginger ale. Stir. Makes about 10 cups (2.5 L).

1 cup (250 mL): 143 Calories; 0.1 g Total Fat; 10 mg Sodium; trace Protein; 36 g Carbohydrate; trace Dietary Fibre

Pictured on page 61.

Hot Tea Wassail

Pronounced WAHS-uhl. Norwegian for "be in good health." Made in the slow cooker. A nice blend of wine, tea, apple, lemon and spices.

Orange pekoe tea bags	4	4
Boiling water	6 cups	1.5 L
Large lemon, sliced 1/2 inch (12 mm) thick	1	1
Liquid honey	1/2 cup	125 mL
Dry red (or alcohol-free) wine	3 cups	750 mL
Cinnamon sticks (3 inch, 7.5 cm, lengths)	2	2
Small cooking apples (such as McIntosh), with skin, cored	3	3
Whole allspice	12	12
Whole cloves	12	12

Preheat slow cooker on Low until warm. Add tea bags. Pour boiling water over tea bags. Cover. Let steep for 10 minutes. Squeeze and discard tea bags.

Stir in lemon, honey, wine and cinnamon sticks.

Pierce skin on apples several times with tip of paring knife. Push allspice and cloves into slits of apples. Add to wine mixture. Cover. Heat on Low for 2 hours. Do not boil or may become bitter tasting. Strain and discard solids just before serving. Makes 9 3/4 cups (2.4 L).

1 cup (250 mL): 124 Calories; 0 g Total Fat; 7 mg Sodium; trace Protein; 20 g Carbohydrate; trace Dietary Fibre

Pictured on page 61.

Top: Cool Irish Coffee, this page
Left Centre: Hot Tea Wassail, above
Bottom Right: Warm Spiced Cranberry, this page

Breads & Quick Breads

Cherry Muffins

Mild almond flavour with a cherry surprise in the middle.

Hard margarine (or butter), softened	6 tbsp.	100 mL
Brown sugar, packed	1/3 cup	75 mL
Granulated sugar	1/3 cup	75 mL
Large egg	1	1
Milk	7/8 cup	200 mL
Maraschino cherry syrup	2 tbsp.	30 mL
Vanilla	1 tsp.	5 mL
All-purpose flour	2 cups	500 mL
Baking powder	1 tbsp.	15 mL
Salt	1/2 tsp.	2 mL
Maraschino cherries, blotted dry	12	12
Chopped pecans	1/3 cup	75 mL

Cream margarine and both sugars together in large bowl. Beat in egg. Add milk, cherry syrup and vanilla. Beat until mixed.

Combine flour, baking powder and salt in medium bowl. Add to margarine mixture. Stir until just moistened. Fill greased muffin cups 3/4 full.

Press 1 cherry into centre of batter in each muffin cup. Sprinkle with pecans. Bake in 400°F (205°C) oven for about 18 minutes until wooden pick inserted in centre of muffin comes out clean. Let stand in pan for 5 minutes before turning out onto wire rack to cool. Makes 12 muffins.

1 muffin: 233 Calories; 9 g Total Fat; 281 mg Sodium; 4 g Protein; 35 g Carbohydrate; 1 g Dietary Fibre

Pictured on page 63.

Gingerbread Muffins

The taste of Christmas and the comfort of home all in one muffin. Serve warm with butter.

Hard margarine (or butter), softened	1/2 cup	125 mL
Granulated sugar	1/2 cup	125 mL
Large eggs	2	2
Fancy (mild) molasses	2/3 cup	150 mL
Milk	1/4 cup	60 mL
All-purpose flour	2 1/2 cups	625 mL
Baking soda	1 tsp.	5 mL
Baking powder	1 tsp.	5 mL
Ground ginger	1 1/2 tsp.	7 mL
Ground cinnamon	1 tsp.	5 mL
Salt	1/2 tsp.	2 mL
Ground cloves	1/4 tsp.	1 mL

Cream margarine and sugar together in large bowl. Beat in eggs, 1 at a time, beating well after each addition. Add molasses and milk. Beat until mixed.

Combine remaining 7 ingredients in medium bowl. Add to margarine mixture. Stir until just moistened. Fill greased muffin cups 3/4 full. Bake in 375°F (190°C) oven for about 20 minutes until wooden pick inserted in centre of muffin comes out clean. Let stand in pan for 5 minutes before turning out onto wire rack to cool. Makes 12 muffins.

1 muffin: 274 Calories; 9.3 g Total Fat; 352 mg Sodium; 4 g Protein; 44 g Carbohydrate; 1 g Dietary Fibre

Pictured below.

Top Centre & Bottom Left: Cherry Muffins, page 62
Top Right: Gingerbread Muffins, this page

Cornmeal Muffins

Slightly sweet, cheesy corn-flavoured muffins.

Cooking oil	1/4 cup	60 mL
Granulated sugar	1/4 cup	60 mL
Large egg	1	1
Milk	1 cup	250 mL
Sour cream	1/4 cup	60 mL
Grated sharp Cheddar cheese	3/4 cup	175 mL
Yellow cornmeal	1 cup	250 mL
All-purpose flour	3/4 cup	175 mL
Baking powder	1 tbsp.	15 mL
Salt	1/2 tsp.	2 mL

Beat cooking oil, sugar and egg together in medium bowl until smooth. Add milk and sour cream. Stir in cheese.

Combine cornmeal, flour, baking powder and salt in separate medium bowl. Add to milk mixture. Stir until just moistened. Fill greased muffin cups 3/4 full. Bake in 400°F (205°C) oven for about 18 minutes until wooden pick inserted in centre of muffin comes out clean. Let stand in pan for 5 minutes before removing to wire rack to cool. Makes 12 muffins.

1 muffin: 188 Calories; 9 g Total Fat; 257 mg Sodium; 5 g Protein; 22 g Carbohydrate; 1 g Dietary Fibre

Pictured on page 67.

Fruit Tea Loaf

Moist and fruity. Very nice flavour with a hint of tea.

Strong prepared tea	1 cup	250 mL
Granulated sugar	1 cup	250 mL
Raisins	1/2 cup	125 mL
Chopped mixed glazed fruit	1/2 cup	125 mL
Hard margarine (or butter)	1/4 cup	60 mL
Large eggs	2	2
Vanilla	1 tsp.	5 mL
All-purpose flour	2 1/4 cups	550 mL
Baking powder	2 tsp.	10 mL
Salt	1/2 tsp.	2 mL

Heat first 5 ingredients in large saucepan, stirring occasionally, until simmering. Simmer, uncovered, for 3 minutes. Cool until saucepan feels warm to touch.

Beat eggs and vanilla together in small cup using fork. Stir into fruit mixture.

Add flour, baking powder and salt. Mix until just moistened. Turn into greased 9 x 5 x 3 inch (22 x 12.5 x 7.5 cm) loaf pan. Bake in 350°F (175°C) oven for about 50 minutes until wooden pick inserted in centre comes out clean. Let stand in pan for 10 minutes before turning out onto wire rack to cool. Cuts into 18 slices.

1 slice: 170 Calories; 3.5 g Total Fat; 151 mg Sodium; 3 g Protein; 33 g Carbohydrate; 1 g Dietary Fibre

Pictured on page 66.

Cranberry Scones

These are the perfect Christmas scones. Serve hot with butter and jam or Cranberry Mango Chutney, page 27.

All-purpose flour	2 cups	500 mL
Granulated sugar	1/4 cup	60 mL
Baking powder	4 tsp.	20 mL
Salt	1/2 tsp.	2 mL
Large egg	1	1
Hard margarine (or butter), melted	6 tbsp.	100 mL
Milk	2/3 cup	150 mL
Dried cranberries	1 1/2 cups	375 mL
TOPPING		
Milk	1 tbsp.	15 mL
Granulated sugar	1 tbsp.	15 mL

Combine flour, sugar, baking powder and salt in large bowl. Make a well in centre.

Beat egg in small bowl until frothy. Add margarine and milk. Mix. Pour into well. Add cranberries. Stir until just moistened. Turn out onto well-floured surface. Knead 8 to 10 times. Divide into 2 equal portions. Pat each into 6 inch (15 cm) circle. Arrange on greased baking sheet.

Topping: Brush tops with milk. Sprinkle with sugar. Score each circle into 6 wedges. Bake in 425°F (220°C) oven for about 15 minutes until risen and lightly golden. Makes 12 scones.

1 scone: 195 Calories; 6.7 g Total Fat; 304 mg Sodium; 4 g Protein; 31 g Carbohydrate; 3 g Dietary Fibre

Pictured on page 66/67.

Sweet Potato Biscuits

So yummy, everybody will want to eat their vegetables.

All-purpose flour	3 1/2 cups	875 mL
Brown sugar, packed	1/4 cup	60 mL
Flaxseeds	4 tsp.	20 mL
Baking powder	4 tsp.	20 mL
Baking soda	1/2 tsp.	2 mL
Salt	1 tsp.	5 mL
Milk	1 cup	250 mL
White vinegar	1 tbsp.	15 mL
Can of sweet potatoes, drained and mashed	19 oz.	540 mL
Cooking oil	1/2 cup	125 mL

Combine first 6 ingredients in large bowl. Make a well in centre.

Combine milk and vinegar in medium bowl. Let stand for 5 minutes.

Add sweet potato and cooking oil to milk mixture. Mix. Pour into well. Stir until dough forms soft ball. Turn out onto lightly floured surface. Pat out to 1 inch (2.5 cm) thick. Cut into 2 1/2 inch (6.4 cm) circles. Arrange on greased baking sheet. Bake in 400°F (205°C) oven for 20 minutes until risen and golden. Makes 16 biscuits.

1 biscuit: 216 Calories; 8 g Total Fat; 300 mg Sodium; 4 g Protein; 32 g Carbohydrate; 1 g Dietary Fibre

Pictured on page 66.

Two-Toned Buns

Serve these fun buns for the undecided on Christmas Day and wow your guests. Wonderful with Turkey Mixed Bean Soup, page 161.

Granulated sugar	1 tsp.	5 mL
Warm water	1/2 cup	125 mL
Active dry yeast	2 1/2 tsp.	12 mL
Granulated sugar	2 tbsp.	30 mL
Hard margarine (or butter), softened	2 tbsp.	30 mL
Salt	2 tsp.	10 mL
Warm milk	2 cups	500 mL
All-purpose flour	2 cups	500 mL
Whole wheat flour, approximately	2 cups	500 mL
All-purpose flour, approximately	2 cups	500 mL
Hard margarine (or butter), melted (optional)	1 tbsp.	15 mL

Stir first amount of sugar and warm water in large bowl until sugar is dissolved. Sprinkle yeast over top. Let stand for 10 minutes. Stir to dissolve yeast.

Add next 5 ingredients. Beat on low to moisten. Beat on high until smooth.

Divide batter equally between 2 medium bowls. Work whole wheat flour into 1 portion and second amount of all-purpose flour into other portion until dough forms a ball. Turn out each portion onto lightly floured surface. Knead until smooth and elastic. Place each portion in separate greased bowl, turning once to grease top. Cover with tea towels. Let stand in oven with light on and door closed for 1 to 1 1/2 hours until doubled in bulk. Punch dough down. Divide and shape dough into about 1 1/2 inch (3.8 cm) balls. Put 1 white and 1 whole wheat ball into each greased muffin cup. Cover with tea towels. Let stand in oven with light on and door closed for about 35 minutes until almost doubled in size. Bake in 400°F (205°C) oven for about 15 minutes until golden.

Brush tops with second amount of margarine. Makes 3 dozen buns.

1 bun: 93 Calories; 1.1 g Total Fat; 147 mg Sodium; 3 g Protein; 18 g Carbohydrate; 1 g Dietary Fibre

TWO-TONED BREAD TWISTS: Divide each portion into 18 pieces. Roll each piece into 8 inch (20 cm) long rope. Twist 1 all-purpose and 1 whole wheat rope together 5 or 6 times and pinch ends together tightly. Arrange about 3 inches (7.5 cm) apart on greased baking sheets. Cover with tea towels. Let stand in oven with light on and door closed for about 35 minutes until almost doubled in size. Bake in 400°F (205°C) oven for about 15 minutes until golden. Brush tops with second amount of margarine. Makes 18 bread twists.

Pictured on page 67.

Photo Legend next page:

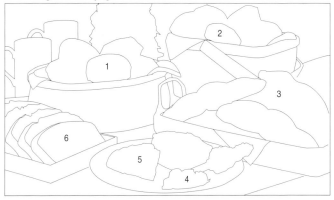

1. Sweet Potato Biscuits, this page
2. Cornmeal Muffins, page 64
3. Two-Toned Bread Twists, this page
4. Cranberry Mango Chutney, page 27
5. Cranberry Scones, page 64
6. Fruit Tea Loaf, page 64

Eggnog Candy Bread

*Butter rum and eggnog flavours make for a
wonderful aroma while this is baking and
a wonderful taste when it's being eaten.*

Cooking oil	1/3 cup	75 mL
Large eggs	2	2
Granulated sugar	2/3 cup	150 mL
Rum flavouring	2 tsp.	10 mL
Vanilla	1 tsp.	5 mL
Eggnog	1 cup	250 mL
All-purpose flour	2 1/4 cups	550 mL
Baking powder	2 tsp.	10 mL
Salt	1/2 tsp.	2 mL
Rolls of butter rum-flavoured doughnut-shaped hard candies (3/4 oz., 25 g, each)	2	2

Beat first 6 ingredients together well in large bowl.

Add flour, baking powder and salt. Stir until just moistened.

Put unwrapped hard candies into resealable plastic bag. Seal. Pound until candies are broken into small pieces. Reserve about 1/4 of candy pieces. Add remaining candy pieces to batter. Stir gently. Turn into greased 9 × 5 × 3 inch (22 × 12.5 × 7.5 cm) loaf pan. Sprinkle reserved candy pieces over top. Bake in 350°F (175°C) oven for 50 to 55 minutes until wooden pick inserted in centre comes out clean. Let stand in pan for 10 minutes before turning out onto wire rack to cool. Cuts into 18 slices.

1 slice: 168 Calories; 6.2 g Total Fat; 124 mg Sodium; 3 g Protein;
25 g Carbohydrate; 1 g Dietary Fibre

Pictured on page 69.

Mini Lemon Loaves

An attractive loaf that is very tasty.

Hard margarine (or butter), softened	6 tbsp.	100 mL
Granulated sugar	1 cup	250 mL
Large eggs	2	2
Milk	1 cup	250 mL
All-purpose flour	2 cups	500 mL
Baking powder	1 tsp.	5 mL
Baking soda	1/2 tsp.	2 mL
Salt	1/2 tsp.	2 mL
Finely grated lemon rind	2 tbsp.	30 mL
GLAZE		
Freshly squeezed lemon juice (about 1 medium)	1/3 cup	75 mL
Granulated sugar	3 tbsp.	50 mL

Left: Mini Lemon Loaves, this page

Cream margarine, sugar and 1 egg together in large bowl. Beat in second egg. Add milk. Beat until well mixed.

Add next 5 ingredients. Beat on low, or stir, until just moistened. Divide and turn into 4 greased 5 3/4 × 3 1/4 × 2 inch (14 × 8 × 5 cm) mini-loaf pans. Bake in 350°F (175°C) oven for about 30 minutes until wooden pick inserted in centre comes out clean. Poke holes all over top of hot loaves using wooden pick.

Glaze: Stir lemon juice and sugar together in small bowl. Drizzle glaze over warm loaves. Let loaves stand in pan for 10 minutes before removing to wire racks to cool. Makes 4 loaves, each cutting into 5 slices, for a total of 20 slices.

1 slice: 142 Calories; 4.2 g Total Fat; 164 mg Sodium; 2 g Protein;
24 g Carbohydrate; trace Dietary Fibre

Pictured above.

Variation: Bake in 9 × 5 × 3 inch (22 × 12.5 × 7.5 cm) loaf pan for about 1 hour until wooden pick inserted in centre comes out clean.

Centre: Cranberry Mint Loaf, below

Right: Eggnog Candy Bread, page 68

Cranberry Mint Loaf

A loaf with the traditional Christmas colours and an unusual, yet delicious, combination of flavours.

Fresh cranberries, coarsely chopped	1 cup	250 mL
Leaf-shaped spearmint gumdrops (about 20), diced (see Note)	1 cup	250 mL
All-purpose flour	1 tbsp.	15 mL
Hard margarine (or butter), softened	1/2 cup	125 mL
Granulated sugar	1 cup	250 mL
Large eggs	2	2
Mint flavouring	1/2 tsp.	2 mL
Finely grated lemon rind	2 tsp.	10 mL
All-purpose flour	2 cups	500 mL
Baking powder	1 tsp.	5 mL
Baking soda	1/2 tsp.	2 mL
Salt	1/4 tsp.	1 mL
Milk	2/3 cup	150 mL

Toss cranberries, gumdrops and first amount of flour together in small bowl until cranberries and gumdrops are coated. Set aside.

Cream margarine and sugar together in large bowl. Add eggs, 1 at a time, beating well after each addition. Beat in flavouring and lemon rind.

Combine next 4 ingredients in separate large bowl. Add to margarine mixture. Stir until just moistened. Batter will be very thick.

Stir in milk and cranberry mixture until just combined. Turn into greased 9 x 5 x 3 inch (22 x 12.5 x 7.5 cm) loaf pan. Bake in 350°F (175°C) oven for 1 to 1 1/4 hours until wooden pick inserted in centre comes out clean. Let stand in pan for 10 minutes before turning out onto wire rack to cool completely. Cuts into 18 slices.

1 slice: 205 Calories; 6.2 g Total Fat; 169 mg Sodium; 3 g Protein; 35 g Carbohydrate; 1 g Dietary Fibre

Pictured above.

Note: Gumdrops are easiest to cut with greased kitchen scissors or very sharp greased knife.

Candy Cane Bread

Such a pretty centrepiece for your brunch buffet.
Each cut slice shows off both fillings.

BREAD DOUGH

Very warm water	1 cup	250 mL
Granulated sugar	3 tbsp.	50 mL
Active dry yeast	1 1/2 tsp.	7 mL
Large egg	1	1
Hard margarine (or butter), softened	3 tbsp.	50 mL
Salt	1 tsp.	5 mL
All-purpose flour	1 cup	250 mL
All-purpose flour, approximately	2 1/3 cups	575 mL

POPPY SEED FILLING

Poppy seeds	1/4 cup	60 mL
Water	1/2 cup	125 mL
Slivered almonds	1/4 cup	60 mL
Liquid honey	2 tbsp.	30 mL
Hard margarine (or butter), melted	1 tbsp.	15 mL

ALMOND FILLING

Hard margarine (or butter), softened	1 tbsp.	15 mL
Granulated sugar	2 tbsp.	30 mL
Almond flavouring	1/4 tsp.	1 mL
Rice flour	1 tbsp.	15 mL
Salt, sprinkle		
Egg white (large)	1	1
Ground almonds	1/4 cup	60 mL
Drops of red food colouring (optional)	4 – 5	4 – 5
Green and red glazed cherries, finely chopped	1/2 cup	125 mL

Bread Dough: Stir warm water and sugar together in large bowl until sugar is dissolved. Sprinkle yeast over top. Let stand for 10 minutes. Stir to dissolve yeast.

Add next 4 ingredients. Beat on low until just moistened. Beat on medium for 2 minutes until thick and smooth.

Work in enough of second amount of flour until dough pulls away from sides of bowl. Turn out onto floured surface. Knead for 8 to 10 minutes until smooth and elastic. Place dough in large greased bowl, turning once to grease top. Cover with tea towel. Let stand in oven with light on and door closed for about 1 hour until doubled in bulk.

Poppy Seed Filling: Combine poppy seeds and water in small saucepan. Bring to a boil. Boil for 1 minute. Let stand for 30 minutes. Drain. Rinse. Drain well. Put poppy seeds into blender.

Add slivered almonds, honey and margarine. Process, scraping down sides as necessary, until poppy seeds are ground and almonds are chopped. Set aside.

Almond Filling: Beat first 6 ingredients together in small bowl until smooth.

Stir in ground almonds and food colouring until thick paste forms. Set aside.

To form bread: Punch dough down. Divide into 2 portions. Turn 1 portion out onto very lightly greased surface. Roll out to 6 x 26 inch (15 x 65 cm) rectangle about 1/4 inch (6 mm) thick. Repeat with second portion of dough.

Spread Poppy Seed Filling on 1 portion of dough to within 1/2 inch (12 mm) of edges. Spread Almond Filling on remaining portion of dough to within 1/2 inch (12 mm) of edges. Sprinkle cherries over Poppy Seed Filling. Roll up both rectangles tightly, jelly roll-style, from long sides. Dampen long edges. Pinch to seal.

Lay rolls side by side, seam-side down, on work surface. Starting in the centre and working towards one end, gently lift 1 roll over and across other roll. Lift bottom roll over and across top roll. Repeat 4 or 5 times, creating tight, twisted effect, keeping seam side down as best you can. Repeat from centre to other end.

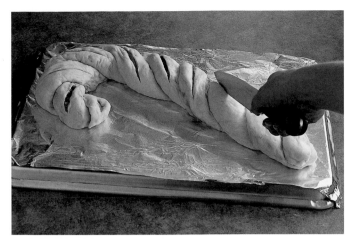

Turn 11 x 17 inch (28 x 43 cm) baking sheet upside down. Cover with sheet of greased foil. Carefully transfer dough onto foil. Curve top 1/3 of dough into hook of cane shape. Arrange remaining 2/3 of dough diagonally across baking sheet as straight and narrow as possible. Dampen ends. Pinch to seal. Tuck ends in and slightly underneath. Cover with tea towel. Let stand for 15 minutes. Cut a 2 inch (5 cm) slit into top of 1 twist of dough, following the direction of the twist, until several layers of filling are exposed. Repeat with other twists. Bake in 350°F (175°C) oven for 20 minutes until golden. Cool. Slice diagonally to serve. Cuts into about 18 slices.

1 slice: 192 Calories; 6.2 g Total Fat; 178 mg Sodium; 4 g Protein; 30 g Carbohydrate; 1 g Dietary Fibre

Variation: Pipe thin lines of Glaze, page 72, to emphasize the stripes on a candy cane.

Pictured below.

Candy Cane Bread, page 70

Old-Fashioned Bran Bread

Serve with Maple And Rye Gravlax, page 48.
Nice nutty sweet flavour.

Water	1/2 cup	125 mL
Hard margarine (or butter)	1/4 cup	60 mL
Liquid honey	1/4 cup	60 mL
Salt	1 tsp.	5 mL
Large egg	1	1
Milk	1/2 cup	125 mL
Whole wheat flour	1 1/2 cups	375 mL
Instant yeast	1 tbsp.	15 mL
Natural wheat bran	1/3 cup	75 mL
Flaxseeds, toasted (see Tip, page 100)	1 tbsp.	15 mL
Roasted sunflower seeds	1 tbsp.	15 mL
All-purpose flour, approximately	2 cups	500 mL
Hard margarine (or butter), melted (optional)	4 tsp.	20 mL

Heat water, margarine, honey and salt in small saucepan until almost boiling and margarine is melted.

Whisk egg and milk together in large bowl. Gradually add hot water mixture while whisking. Temperature should still be very warm.

Stir whole wheat flour and yeast together in small bowl. Stir into milk mixture until smooth. Add bran, flax seeds and sunflower seeds. Stir.

Work in 1 1/2 cups (375 mL) all-purpose flour, 1/2 cup (125 mL) at a time, until soft dough forms and pulls away from sides of bowl. Turn out onto well-floured surface. Knead for 5 to 10 minutes, adding more all-purpose flour as needed, until smooth and elastic but still slightly tacky. Place dough in lightly greased bowl, turning once to grease top. Cover with tea towel. Let stand in oven with light on and door closed for 30 minutes until doubled in bulk. Divide dough into 4 portions. Put into 4 greased 5 3/4 x 3 1/4 x 2 inch (14 x 8 x 5 cm) mini-loaf pans or 4 greased 19 oz. (540 mL) tins. Cover with tea towel. Let stand in oven with light on and door closed for about 45 minutes until doubled in size or at top edge of loaf pans. Bake in 350°F (175°C) oven for about 25 minutes until hollow sounding when tapped. Turn out onto wire racks to cool.

Brush warm tops with margarine. Makes 4 loaves, each cutting into 10 slices, for a total of 40 slices.

1 slice: 67 Calories; 1.7 g Total Fat; 78 mg Sodium; 2 g Protein; 11 g Carbohydrate; 1 g Dietary Fibre

Pictured on page 46.

Christmas Bread, below

Christmas Bread

Fruit and glaze add sweetness to this moist golden bread.
Use Glaze for Candy Cane Bread, page 70.

Loaf of frozen white bread dough, thawed according to package directions	1	1
Currants (or raisins)	1/4 cup	60 mL
Maraschino cherries, drained and quartered	1/4 cup	60 mL
Cut mixed peel	1 tbsp.	15 mL
Ground cinnamon	1/4 tsp.	1 mL
Hard margarine (or butter), melted (optional)	1 tsp.	5 mL
GLAZE		
Icing (confectioner's) sugar	1/3 cup	75 mL
Water	1 1/4 tsp.	6 mL
Slivered almonds, toasted (see Tip, page 100), for garnish	2 tbsp.	30 mL

Roll out bread dough on lightly floured surface into rectangle, making short side the same length as loaf pan. Scatter currants, cherries and peel over bread dough. Sprinkle cinnamon over top. Roll up, jelly roll-style, beginning at short end. Put, seam-side down, into greased 9 x 5 x 3 inch (22 x 12.5 x 7.5 cm) loaf pan. Cover with tea towel. Let stand in oven with light on and door closed until doubled in size. Bake in 375°F (190°C) oven for about 30 minutes until golden. Turn out onto wire rack to cool.

Brush warm top with margarine. Cool.

Glaze: Mix icing sugar with just enough water until desired piping consistency. Makes about 2 tbsp. (30 mL) glaze. Pipe onto loaf.

Immediately sprinkle almonds over glaze. Cuts into 16 slices.

1 slice: 100 Calories; 1 g Total Fat; 153 mg Sodium; 2 g Protein; 20 g Carbohydrate; 1 g Dietary Fibre

Pictured on front cover and above.

Brunch & Lunch

Hot Fruit Compote

*A sweet blend of fruit flavours in this easy-to-prepare dessert.
Serve over Griddle Corn Cakes, page 81.*

Can of sliced peaches, drained	14 oz.	398 mL
Fresh (or frozen) blueberries	1 cup	250 mL
Large underripe banana, sliced	1	1
Can of whole cranberry sauce	14 oz.	398 mL
Minute tapioca	1 tbsp.	15 mL
Brown sugar, packed	1/4 cup	60 mL

Toss peaches, blueberries and banana together in ungreased
1 1/2 quart (1.5 L) casserole.

Combine cranberry sauce and tapioca in small bowl until
well mixed. Spread over fruit mixture.

Sprinkle with brown sugar. Bake, uncovered, in 350°F
(175°C) oven for about 40 minutes until bubbly. Serves 8.

1 serving: 169 Calories; 0.3 g Total Fat; 22 mg Sodium; 1 g Protein;
43 g Carbohydrate; 2 g Dietary Fibre

Pictured on page 79.

Breakfast Trifle

*Bread, dairy and fruit in this delicious breakfast trifle.
Good to eat and good for you. Make the night before
to serve for breakfast Christmas morning.*

Coarsely chopped blueberry muffins (or 6 whole grain blueberry cereal bars, coarsely chopped)	4 cups	1 L
Sliced fresh strawberries	1 1/3 cups	325 mL
Fresh blueberries	1 1/3 cups	325 mL
Sliced ripe kiwifruit	1 1/3 cups	325 mL
Seedless red grapes	11	11
Strawberry-flavoured yogurt	4 cups	1 L

Put 1/2 of muffin pieces into 2 1/2 quart (2.5 L) glass bowl.
Arrange 1/2 of strawberries, blueberries and kiwi fruit in
attractive pattern over muffin pieces. Spoon 1/2 of yogurt
evenly over fruit. Cover with remaining muffin pieces.
Spoon remaining yogurt evenly over muffin pieces. Garnish
with remaining strawberries, blueberries, kiwifruit and
grapes in attractive pattern. Makes 8 cups (2 L).

1 cup (250 mL): 251 Calories; 4.5 g Total Fat; 181 mg Sodium; 7 g Protein;
46 g Carbohydrate; 2 g Dietary Fibre

Pictured on page 74.

Variation: Use your choice of muffins, fresh fruit and yogurt.

Top Left: Breakfast Trifle, page 73
Bottom Left: The Big Breakfast, page 81

Top Centre: Doctored Oatmeal Porridge, page 75
Bottom Right: Onion Cheese Pie, page 75

Onion And Potato Tart

This quiche is a very filling brunch dish.

Pastry for 2 crust pie, your own or a mix, chilled		
Medium potatoes, cut into chunks (about 2 3/4 cups, 675 mL)	3	3
Water	1 cup	250 mL
Salt	1 tsp.	5 mL
Grated Gruyère cheese	1 1/4 cups	300 mL
Dried thyme	1/2 tsp.	2 mL
Coarsely chopped onion	4 1/2 cups	1.1 L
Hard margarine (or butter)	1 1/2 tbsp.	25 mL
Seasoned salt	1 tsp.	5 mL
Ground nutmeg	1/8 tsp.	0.5 mL
Pepper, generous sprinkle		
Large eggs	5	5
Milk (homogenized is best)	1 1/2 cups	375 mL

Roll out pastry to fit 10 inch (25 cm) glass pie plate. Line pie plate, with pastry overhanging edge about 1/2 inch (12 mm). Turn overhanging edge under until level with edge of pie plate. Lightly press down against pie plate.

Make decorative edge (see Pretty Pastry, page 134). Poke bottom and sides of pie shell in several places using fork. Roll out scraps and make cut-outs with small canapé or cookie cutters. Place pie shell and cut-outs on baking sheet. Bake in 375°F (190°C) oven for 15 minutes. Remove pie crust from baking sheet. Bake cut-outs for additional 2 to 3 minutes until firm and golden.

Cook potatoes in water and salt in medium saucepan until soft. Drain. Cool. Break up potatoes with fork or pastry blender until size of large peas. Turn into crust. Do not pack down.

Sprinkle with cheese and thyme.

Sauté onion in margarine in large frying pan for about 15 minutes until soft. Reduce heat to low.

Sprinkle seasoned salt, nutmeg and pepper over onion. Cover. Cook for about 10 minutes, stirring occasionally, until onion is browned and very soft. Evenly sprinkle over cheese.

Beat eggs and milk together in small bowl using fork. Carefully pour over onion mixture. Gently shake to allow spaces to fill in. Arrange cut-outs decoratively over tart. Bake on bottom rack in oven for 55 to 60 minutes until set and crust is golden. Let stand on wire rack for 10 minutes to cool slightly. Cut into 8 wedges.

1 wedge: 412 Calories; 23.3 g Total Fat; 507 mg Sodium; 14 g Protein; 37 g Carbohydrate; 2 g Dietary Fibre

Pictured on page 76.

Doctored Oatmeal Porridge

A good change from regular oatmeal with apple and cinnamon flavours. Serve with apple slices on top.

Apple juice	1 3/4 cups	425 mL
Quick-cooking rolled oats (not instant)	1 cup	250 mL
Medium cooking apple (such as McIntosh), peeled and grated	1	1
Ground cinnamon	1/2 tsp.	2 mL
Salt	1/8 tsp.	0.5 mL

Combine all 5 ingredients in medium saucepan. Bring to a boil, stirring often. Cook for 3 to 5 minutes until porridge is thickened and apple is tender. Makes 2 1/4 cups (550 mL).

2/3 cup (150 mL): 206 Calories; 2.4 g Total Fat; 97 mg Sodium; 5 g Protein; 43 g Carbohydrate; 4 g Dietary Fibre

Pictured on page 74.

Onion Cheese Pie

A simple hearty lunch. This quiche is for cheese lovers.

Grated Swiss cheese	1 cup	250 mL
Grated Gouda cheese	1 cup	250 mL
All-purpose flour	1 tbsp.	15 mL
Unbaked 9 inch (22 cm) pie shell	1	1
Large eggs	3	3
Skim evaporated milk	1 cup	250 mL
Salt	1/2 tsp.	2 mL
Pepper	1/8 tsp.	0.5 mL
Cayenne pepper	1/8 tsp.	0.5 mL
Thinly sliced onion rings, cut into quarters	2 cups	500 mL

Toss both cheeses and flour together in medium bowl. Sprinkle over bottom of pie shell.

Beat eggs in separate medium bowl until frothy. Add evaporated milk, salt, pepper and cayenne pepper. Beat. Pour over cheese mixture.

Scatter onion over egg mixture. Bake on bottom rack in 350°F (175°C) oven for about 45 minutes until knife inserted in centre comes out clean. Let stand in pie plate for 10 minutes before cutting. Cuts into 6 wedges.

1 wedge: 351 Calories; 20.4 g Total Fat; 636 mg Sodium; 19 g Protein; 23 g Carbohydrate; 1 g Dietary Fibre

Pictured on page 74.

Egg Roll With Shrimp

A delicious brunch dish for special guests or very pretty to present on a buffet table.

Large eggs	3	3
Salt	1/2 tsp.	2 mL
Creamed horseradish	2 tsp.	10 mL
Milk	2/3 cup	150 mL
All-purpose flour	1/3 cup	75 mL
Hard margarine (or butter)	1 tbsp.	15 mL
FILLING		
Green onions, sliced	2	2
Finely diced celery	1/4 cup	60 mL
Medium roma (plum) tomatoes, seeded and diced (about 2/3 cup, 150 mL)	2	2
Salt, sprinkle		
Pepper, sprinkle		
Grated mozzarella cheese	3/4 cup	175 mL
Small frozen shrimp (about 6 oz., 170 g), thawed and blotted dry	1 cup	250 mL
Spicy cocktail sauce	2 tbsp.	30 mL
Sharp Cheddar cheese, cut into 4 strips	2 oz.	57 g

Stir first 4 ingredients together in medium bowl until smooth. Add flour. Stir until smooth.

Melt margarine in bottom of greased 9 x 13 inch (22 x 33 cm) pan in 350°F (175°C) oven for about 2 minutes until sizzling. Pour egg mixture into pan. Bake, uncovered, for 25 to 30 minutes until set and lightly browned. Loosen edges by running spatula around sides of pan. Turn out onto baking sheet.

Filling: Immediately sprinkle green onion, celery and tomato over egg mixture. Season with salt, pepper, mozzarella cheese and shrimp.

Place small dabs of cocktail sauce randomly over shrimp. Roll up, jelly roll-style, from long side. Arrange seam-side down on same baking sheet. Lay Cheddar cheese on top of roll. Bake in 350°F (175°C) oven for 8 to 10 minutes until Cheddar cheese is melted. Cuts into 8 diagonal slices. Serves 4.

1 serving: 331 Calories; 18 g Total Fat; 749 mg Sodium; 25 g Protein; 17 g Carbohydrate; 1 g Dietary Fibre

Pictured on page 76.

Spinach And Olive Braid

Wonderful Mediterranean flavours of spinach, feta and olives in this stuffed bread. Makes a good lunch served with Greek Pea Salad, page 138.

FILLING

Garlic cloves, minced (or 1/2 tsp., 2 mL, powder)	2	2
Olive (or cooking) oil	2 tsp.	10 mL
Chopped fresh spinach, packed (about 3 oz., 85 g)	1 1/2 cups	375 mL
Water	1 tbsp.	15 mL
Fine dry bread crumbs	1 tbsp.	15 mL
Sour cream	2 tbsp.	30 mL
Kalamata olives, pits removed, finely chopped	7	7
Crumbled feta cheese (about 2 1/2 oz., 70 g)	1/2 cup	125 mL
Jar of pimiento, drained, finely diced	2 oz.	57 mL
Dried whole oregano	1/4 tsp.	1 mL
Salt	1/4 tsp.	1 mL
Lemon pepper	1/4 tsp.	1 mL
Loaf of frozen white bread dough, thawed according to package directions	1	1
Large egg, fork-beaten	1	1
Sea salt (optional)	1/4 tsp.	1 mL
Poppy seeds (optional)	1/4 tsp.	1 mL

Filling: Sauté garlic in olive oil in frying pan for about 1 minute until beginning to turn golden.

Add spinach and water. Stir. Cover. Cook on medium for 2 to 3 minutes until spinach is soft and wilted. Stir. Cook, uncovered, for 2 minutes, stirring occasionally, until liquid has evaporated. Remove from heat.

Sprinkle with bread crumbs. Stir. Cool slightly.

Add next 7 ingredients. Stir. Makes 3/4 cup (175 mL) filling.

Roll out bread dough on lightly floured surface into 8 × 16 inch (20 × 40 cm) rectangle. Spread filling down centre to within 2 inches (5 cm) of edge. Cut diagonal slashes about 1 1/2 inches (3.8 cm) wide down long edges of bread dough to within 1/4 inch (6 mm) of filling. Fold bread dough strips over centre, alternating sides to form braid pattern. Carefully transfer to lightly greased baking sheet. Cover with tea towel. Let stand in oven with light on and door closed for about 40 minutes until doubled in size.

Brush with egg. Sprinkle with sea salt and poppy seeds. Bake in 375°F (190°C) oven for 17 to 20 minutes until golden brown. Cuts into 10 pieces.

1 piece: 173 Calories; 5.6 g Total Fat; 440 mg Sodium; 6 g Protein; 24 g Carbohydrate; 1 g Dietary Fibre

Pictured below.

Top Left: Onion And Potato Tart, page 74   Top Right: Egg Roll With Shrimp, page 75   Bottom Right: Spinach And Olive Braid, above

Blueberry Streusel French Toast

The perfect make-ahead brunch dish. A sure hit with maple syrup or blueberry syrup drizzled on top.

Hard margarine (or butter)	1 tbsp.	15 mL
Thick bread slices (such as Texas Toast)	12	12
Large eggs	9	9
Milk	1 1/2 cups	375 mL
Granulated sugar	1 1/2 tbsp.	25 mL
Salt	1/4 tsp.	1 mL
Vanilla	1 tbsp.	15 mL
STREUSEL		
Quick-cooking rolled oats (not instant)	1 1/4 cups	300 mL
Brown sugar, packed	1/2 cup	125 mL
All-purpose flour	1/4 cup	60 mL
Finely grated lemon zest	1/2 tsp.	2 mL
Hard margarine (or butter)	1/3 cup	75 mL
Frozen (or fresh) blueberries	1 cup	250 mL

Grease 11 x 17 inch (28 x 43 cm) baking sheet with thick coating of margarine.

Arrange bread slices close to each other on baking sheet.

Beat next 5 ingredients together in large bowl. Pour over bread slices.

Streusel: Combine rolled oats, brown sugar, flour and lemon zest in medium bowl.

Cut in margarine until mixture is crumbly. Sprinkle over bread slices.

Sprinkle blueberries over streusel. Cover. Chill overnight. Remove cover. Bake in 450°F (230°C) oven for 30 minutes until topping is crisp and golden brown around edges. Makes 12 slices.

1 slice: 364 Calories; 13.1 g Total Fat; 460 mg Sodium; 12 g Protein; 49 g Carbohydrate; 3 g Dietary Fibre

Pictured on page 79.

To keep pancakes warm and moist, but not soggy, arrange, slightly overlapping, on large platter. Loosely cover with foil. Heat in 200°F (95°C) or less oven. To keep waffles warm and crisp or to reheat, place directly on oven rack or on wire rack in oven. Do not cover. Heat for no more than 15 minutes.

Spice Coffee Cake

A delicious cake with a dark swirl.
Drizzle Butterscotch Sauce, page 98, over cake.

Spice cake mix (2 layer size)	1	1
Instant butterscotch pudding powder (4 serving size)	1	1
Large eggs	3	3
Cooking oil	1/3 cup	75 mL
Water	1 cup	250 mL
Brown sugar, packed	1/3 cup	75 mL
Cocoa, sifted if lumpy	2 tbsp.	30 mL
All-purpose flour	2 tbsp.	30 mL
Ground cinnamon	1 tsp.	5 mL
Ground nutmeg	1/4 tsp.	1 mL
Ground cloves	1/8 tsp.	0.5 mL

Empty cake mix and pudding powder into large bowl. Add eggs, cooking oil and water. Beat on low until moistened. Beat on medium for 2 minutes. Turn into greased and floured 12 cup (3 L) bundt pan.

Stir remaining 6 ingredients together in small bowl. Sprinkle over cake mix mixture. Swirl with knife to create marble effect. Bake in 350°F (175°C) oven for about 1 hour until wooden pick inserted in centre comes out clean. Let stand in pan for 20 minutes before turning out onto wire rack to cool. Cut into 16 wedges.

1 wedge: 247 Calories; 9.8 g Total Fat; 330 mg Sodium; 3 g Protein; 38 g Carbohydrate; trace Dietary Fibre

Pictured on page 78.

Photo Legend next page:

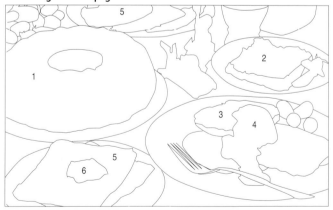

1. Spice Coffee Cake, above, with Butterscotch Sauce, page 98
2. Blueberry Streusel French Toast, this page
3. Griddle Corn Cakes, page 81
4. Hot Fruit Compote, page 73
5. Crab And Cheddar Waffles, page 81
6. Fresh Herb Sauce, page 92

Top: Seafood Focaccia Loaf, below   Bottom: Burger Strata, this page

Heat second amount of olive oil in same frying pan. Add shrimp and scallops. Stir-fry for 2 to 3 minutes until seafood is opaque and firm. Scatter over vegetable mixture.

Sprinkle olives and feta cheese over seafood mixture. Bake in 350°F (175°C) oven for 15 to 20 minutes until edges are crusty. Place top half of focaccia bread over seafood mixture. Gently press down. Serves 4 to 6.

1 serving: 406 Calories; 14 g Total Fat; 659 mg Sodium; 20 g Protein; 49 g Carbohydrate; 3 g Dietary Fibre

Pictured on this page.

Seafood Focaccia Loaf

This very appetizing dish is full of flavour.

Herb focaccia bread (about 7 1/2 – 8 inch, 19 – 20 cm, round or 6 × 9 inch, 15 × 22 cm, rectangle)	1	1
Basil pesto	1/4 cup	60 mL
Garlic clove, minced (or 1/4 tsp., 1 mL, powder)	1	1
Diced onion	1/2 cup	125 mL
Diced green pepper	1/2 cup	125 mL
Diced fresh mushrooms	1/2 cup	125 mL
Olive (or cooking) oil	1 tsp.	5 mL
Olive (or cooking) oil	1 tsp.	5 mL
Frozen medium shrimp, thawed and blotted dry	4 oz.	113 g
Frozen small scallops, thawed and blotted dry	4 oz.	113 g
Diced ripe olives (or seasoned black Italian olives)	2 tbsp.	30 mL
Crumbled feta cheese	1/2 cup	125 mL

Cut focaccia bread in half horizontally to make 2 layers. Spread each cut side with pesto. Place, cut side up, on ungreased baking sheet.

Sauté garlic, onion, green pepper and mushrooms in first amount of olive oil in frying pan for 2 to 3 minutes until onion is soft. Spread over bottom half of focaccia bread.

Burger Strata

Tastes like a cheeseburger with extra cheese. Have this ready the day before to pop in the oven for lunch the next day.

Bread slices, crusts removed, lightly toasted	8	8
Lean ground beef	1 1/2 lbs.	680 g
Finely chopped onion	1 cup	250 mL
Finely chopped celery	1/3 cup	75 mL
Salt	1/2 tsp.	2 mL
Pepper	1/4 tsp.	1 mL
Grated medium Cheddar cheese	2 cups	500 mL
Bread slices, crusts removed, lightly toasted	8	8
Large eggs	4	4
Prepared mustard	2 tbsp.	30 mL
Milk	2 cups	500 mL
Grated medium Cheddar (or mozzarella) cheese	1 cup	250 mL

Arrange first amount of bread slices in single layer in greased 9 × 13 inch (22 × 33 cm) pan.

Scramble-fry ground beef, onion and celery in frying pan until beef is no longer pink. Drain. Sprinkle with salt and pepper. Mix. Layer over bread slices.

Sprinkle first amount of cheese over beef mixture. Cover with second amount of bread slices.

Beat eggs, mustard and milk together in medium bowl until frothy. Slowly pour onto bread slices. Cover. Chill overnight. Remove cover.

Sprinkle with second amount of cheese. Bake, uncovered, in 350°F (175°C) oven for about 45 minutes until set. Serves 8.

1 serving: 507 Calories; 27.2 g Total Fat; 833 mg Sodium; 36 g Protein; 29 g Carbohydrate; 1 g Dietary Fibre

Pictured on this page.

Crab And Cheddar Waffles

Slightly sweet with nice flavour from the crab, cheese and onion. Serve with Fresh Herb Sauce, page 92.

All-purpose flour	1 1/4 cups	300 mL
Baking powder	2 tsp.	10 mL
Granulated sugar	1 1/2 tsp.	7 mL
Salt	1/2 tsp.	2 mL
Cayenne pepper (optional)	1/8 tsp.	0.5 mL
Grated sharp Cheddar cheese	1/2 cup	125 mL
Can of crabmeat, drained, cartilage removed, flaked	4 1/4 oz.	120 g
Finely sliced green onion	2 tbsp.	30 mL
Large egg, fork-beaten	1	1
Milk	1 1/4 cups	300 mL
Cooking oil	1/4 cup	60 mL

Sift first 5 ingredients into large bowl.

Add cheese, crab and green onion. Stir.

Combine egg, milk and cooking oil in small bowl. Add to flour mixture. Mix until just moistened. Do not over mix. Cook about 1/2 cup (125 mL) batter in hot waffle iron until golden. Repeat with remaining batter. Makes about 10 waffles.

1 waffle: 168 Calories; 8.9 g Total Fat; 330 mg Sodium; 7 g Protein; 15 g Carbohydrate; 1 g Dietary Fibre

Pictured on page 78/79.

The Big Breakfast

Not only big, this is no boring breakfast!

Bacon slices, diced (or Chorizo sausage, cut up or cocktail sausages)	1 lb.	454 g
Large eggs	12	12
Sliced fresh mushrooms	1 cup	250 mL
Grated sharp Cheddar cheese	3 cups	750 mL
Green onions, thinly sliced	3	3
Can of diced green chilies	4 oz.	113 g
Salt	1 tsp.	5 mL
Pepper	1/4 tsp.	1 mL
Whipping cream	1 cup	250 mL

Fry bacon in frying pan until crisp. Drain well. Cool.

Beat eggs in large bowl using fork. Stir in next 6 ingredients. Add bacon. Stir. Pour into greased 9 x 13 inch (22 x 33 cm) pan.

Slowly pour whipping cream over top. Cover and chill overnight or cook immediately. Bake, uncovered, in 350°F (175°C) oven for about 40 minutes until edges start to brown and knife inserted near centre comes out clean. Serves 10.

1 serving: 388 Calories; 32.3 g Total Fat; 750 mg Sodium; 21 g Protein; 3 g Carbohydrate; trace Dietary Fibre

Pictured on page 74.

Griddle Corn Cakes

Very nice sweet corn flavour to these filling cakes. Wonderful with Hot Fruit Compote, page 73.

All-purpose flour	1 cup	250 mL
Yellow cornmeal	1 cup	250 mL
Granulated sugar	1/4 cup	60 mL
Baking powder	4 tsp.	20 mL
Milk	1/4 cup	60 mL
Large eggs, fork-beaten	2	2
Can of cream-style corn	14 oz.	398 mL
Cooking oil	2 tbsp.	30 mL

Combine flour, cornmeal, sugar and baking powder in medium bowl.

Combine milk, eggs, corn and cooking oil in separate medium bowl. Add flour mixture to milk mixture. Stir until just moistened. Drop 1/4 cup (60 mL) batter onto hot lightly greased griddle or frying pan. Cook for 3 to 4 minutes per side until lightly browned. Makes 15 corn cakes.

1 corn cake: 131 Calories; 2.9 g Total Fat; 192 mg Sodium; 3 g Protein; 24 g Carbohydrate; 1 g Dietary Fibre

Pictured on page 79.

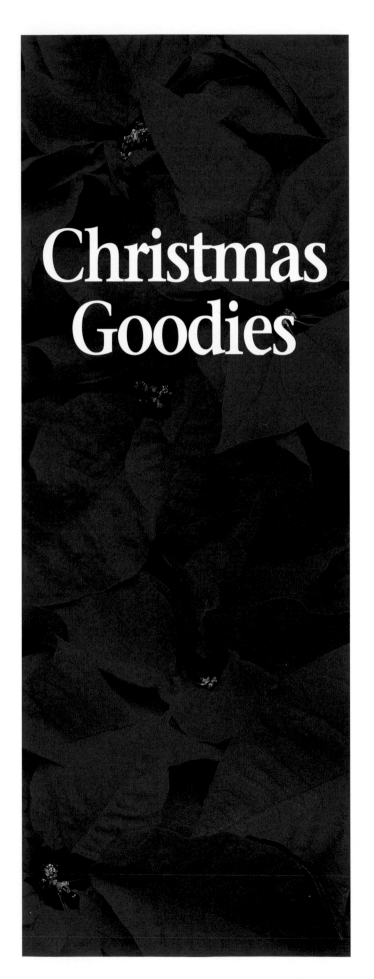

Christmas Goodies

Piña Colada Squares

Another great twist to Nanaimo bars. A nice blend of pineapple and coconut. These squares need to be kept chilled as they soften quickly.

BOTTOM LAYER		
Hard margarine (or butter), softened	1/2 cup	125 mL
Granulated sugar	1/4 cup	60 mL
Cocoa, sifted if lumpy	1/3 cup	75 mL
Large egg, fork-beaten	1	1
Milk	2 tbsp.	30 mL
Graham cracker crumbs	1 3/4 cups	425 mL
Chopped walnuts	1/2 cup	125 mL
Medium coconut	3/4 cup	175 mL
MIDDLE LAYER		
Hard margarine (or butter), softened	1/2 cup	125 mL
Icing (confectioner's) sugar	2 cups	500 mL
Crushed pineapple, very well drained	1/2 cup	125 mL
Coconut flavouring	3/4 tsp.	4 mL
TOP LAYER		
Semi-sweet chocolate chips	2/3 cup	150 mL
Hard margarine (or butter)	2 tbsp.	30 mL

Bottom Layer: Stir margarine, sugar and cocoa together in large saucepan on medium until margarine is melted. Add egg and milk. Heat and stir for a few moments until slightly thickened. Remove from heat.

Add graham crumbs, walnuts and coconut. Stir until well coated. Firmly press into ungreased 9 x 9 inch (22 x 22 cm) pan. Pan may be lined with foil for easy removal and cutting.

Middle Layer: Put all 4 ingredients into medium bowl. Mix well. Spread over first layer. Chill overnight until firm.

Top Layer: Heat and stir chocolate chips and margarine in small heavy saucepan on low until melted and smooth. Let stand until cool but still runny. Spread over second layer. Chill until ready to serve. Cuts into 36 squares.

1 square: 150 Calories; 10 g Total Fat; 100 mg Sodium; 1 g Protein; 15 g Carbohydrate; 1 g Dietary Fibre

Pictured on page 85.

White Chocolate Fudge Truffles

Fabulous! Sweet, rich and creamy truffles that are well worth the effort.

Granulated sugar	1 1/2 cups	375 mL
Evaporated milk (not skim)	1/2 cup	125 mL
White chocolate chips	1 cup	250 mL
Butter (not margarine), softened	1/3 cup	75 mL
Clear vanilla	2 tsp.	10 mL
Salt, just a pinch		
White chocolate melting wafers	1/2 cup	125 mL
Dark (or milk) chocolate melting wafers	1/2 cup	125 mL
Pink chocolate melting wafers	1/2 cup	125 mL

Combine sugar and evaporated milk in 3 quart (3 L) heavy saucepan. Heat and stir on medium for about 4 minutes until mixture comes to a rolling boil that cannot be stirred down. Reduce heat to medium-low to keep a hard boil without boiling over top of pan. Boil hard for 6 minutes, stirring occasionally. Remove from heat.

Combine chocolate chips, butter, vanilla and salt in small bowl. Add all at once to milk mixture. Beat with electric mixer in saucepan for about 8 minutes until tablespoonful will remain on surface rather than sink. Pour into greased 8 × 8 inch (20 × 20 cm) pan. Chill until cold. Drop by 1 1/2 tsp. (7 mL) onto cold waxed paper-lined baking sheet. If fudge becomes too soft to work with, chill until cold. Chill. Roll each portion into a smooth ball. Chill.

Heat melting wafers separately in small glass bowls over simmering water in small saucepan on low, stirring constantly, until smooth and melted. Remove from heat. Dip 1/3 of balls into white chocolate, allowing excess to drip back into bowl. Place on waxed paper-lined baking sheet. Repeat with remaining balls and dark and pink chocolate. Keep well chilled until completely set. Drizzle any remaining melted chocolate decoratively over truffles. Makes 47 truffles.

1 truffle: 82 Calories; 3.9 g Total Fat; 22 mg Sodium; 1 g Protein; 12 g Carbohydrate; trace Dietary Fibre

Pictured on this page.

To make truffles that are uniform in size, use a miniature ice cream scoop . If the truffles are not going to be dipped for a long period of time (i.e. until next day) cover well or place in an airtight container and chill to prevent drying out.

Top Centre: Butter Crunch, below
Centre Left, Right & Bottom: White Chocolate Fudge Truffles, this page

Butter Crunch

Thin, crunchy candy with a chocolate and nut covering. Easily breaks into pieces for gift giving.

Butter (not margarine)	1 cup	250 mL
Granulated sugar	1 cup	250 mL
Water	2 tbsp.	30 mL
Corn syrup	1 tbsp.	15 mL
Semi-sweet chocolate chips	1/2 cup	125 mL
Finely chopped pecans	1/2 cup	125 mL

Melt butter in heavy medium saucepan on medium-low. Add sugar. Stir until mixture begins to bubble.

Stir in water and corn syrup. Cook for about 35 minutes, stirring often but gently, until mixture reaches soft crack stage (270° to 290°F, 132° to 143°C) on candy thermometer or until small amount dropped in very cold water separates into hard, but pliable threads. Pour in thin layer on greased baking sheet. Let stand until cooled and hardened.

Heat chocolate chips in small heavy saucepan on lowest heat, stirring often, until just melted. Let stand until you can hold your hand on bottom of saucepan. Spread evenly over top of candy.

Sprinkle pecans over chocolate. Lightly press down with your hand. Makes about 1 lb. (454 g).

1 oz. (28 g): 212 Calories; 16.2 g Total Fat; 125 mg Sodium; 1 g Protein; 18 g Carbohydrate; 1 g Dietary Fibre

Pictured above.

Rum And Butter Balls

A delightfully decadent alternative to traditional rum balls!

Butter (or hard margarine), softened	1/4 cup	60 mL
Icing (confectioner's) sugar	1 3/4 cups	425 mL
Vanilla wafer crumbs	1 cup	250 mL
Water	2 tbsp.	30 mL
Rum flavouring	1/2 tsp.	2 mL
Butter flavouring	1/2 tsp.	2 mL
Finely chopped walnuts	1/2 cup	125 mL
Icing (confectioner's) sugar	1/3 cup	75 mL

Measure first 7 ingredients into large bowl. Mix well until stiff dough forms. Divide into 2 equal portions. Roll each portion into long rope. Cut each rope in half. Cut each half into 6 equal pieces. Roll each piece into ball.

Roll each ball in icing sugar. Makes 2 dozen balls.

1 ball: 93 Calories; 4.2 g Total Fat; 32 mg Sodium; 1 g Protein; 14 g Carbohydrate; trace Dietary Fibre

Pictured on page 3 and on page 87.

Chocolate Orange Treats

Pretty goodies that taste as good as they look.

Butterscotch chips	1 cup	250 mL
Semi-sweet chocolate chips	1 cup	250 mL
Skim evaporated milk	1/2 cup	125 mL
Graham cracker crumbs	2 cups	500 mL
Finely grated orange peel	2 tsp.	10 mL
Tiny Christmas-shaped decorating candies (optional)	1/2 cup	125 mL

Combine butterscotch and chocolate chips and milk in heavy medium saucepan. Heat on low, stirring often, until smooth.

Add graham crumbs and orange peel. Stir. Chill for at least 1 hour. Shape into 1 inch (2.5 cm) balls, using about 1 1/2 tsp. (7 mL) for each.

Roll in decorating candies. Makes 4 1/2 dozen balls.

1 ball: 46 Calories; 1.4 g Total Fat; 24 mg Sodium; 1 g Protein; 8 g Carbohydrate; trace Dietary Fibre

Pictured on page 85.

Chocolate Almond Cookies

Large soft and chewy cookies with lots of chocolate bits! Mix three kinds of chocolate for a variety of tastes. Great as a dipper in Eggnog Fondue, page 102.

Butter (not margarine), softened	1 1/2 cups	375 mL
Brown sugar, packed	2 cups	500 mL
Granulated sugar	1 cup	250 mL
Large eggs	4	4
Almond flavouring	2 tbsp.	30 mL
All-purpose flour	4 2/3 cups	1.15 L
Baking soda	2 tsp.	10 mL
Salt	2 tsp.	10 mL
Milk (or dark or white) chocolate candy bars (3 1/2 oz., 100 g, each), coarsely chopped	6	6
Slivered almonds, lightly toasted (see Tip, page 100)	1 cup	250 mL

Cream butter and both sugars together in large bowl. Beat in eggs, 1 at a time, beating well after each addition. Add almond flavouring. Beat.

Stir flour, baking soda and salt together in medium bowl. Add to butter mixture. Mix well until no dry flour remains.

Add chocolate and almonds. Stir. Drop 3 tbsp. (50 mL) batter, 3 to 4 inches (7.5 to 10 cm) apart, onto greased cookie sheet. Bake in 350°F (175°C) oven for 11 to 12 minutes until edges turn golden. Do not overbake. Cookies may still look slightly undercooked in centre. Let stand on sheet for 2 minutes before removing to wire racks to cool. Makes 3 1/2 dozen cookies.

1 cookie: 276 Calories; 13.7 g Total Fat; 268 mg Sodium; 3 g Protein; 36 g Carbohydrate; 1 g Dietary Fibre

Pictured on page 85 and on page 102.

To always have food on hand for unexpected guests, make your favourite freezable recipes and fill up your freezer. This is especially handy for casseroles, cookies, breads and squares.

Left: Piña Colada Squares, page 82   Top Centre: Chocolate Orange Treats, page 84   Right: Chocolate Almond Cookies, page 84

Ambrosia Orange Cookies

Lovely delicate orange flavour with hint of coconut.
The cookie flattens out but is still soft inside. Edible gold
glitter fancies these cookies up for any occasion.

GLAZE

Prepared orange juice	3 tbsp.	50 mL
Icing (confectioner's) sugar	1 – 2 tbsp.	15 – 30 mL
Hard margarine (or butter), softened	1/4 cup	60 mL
Granulated sugar	2/3 cup	150 mL
Large egg	1	1
Prepared orange juice	2 tbsp.	30 mL
Finely grated orange rind	2 tsp.	10 mL
All-purpose flour	1 cup	250 mL
Baking soda	1/2 tsp.	2 mL
Salt	1/4 tsp.	1 mL
Medium coconut	1/2 cup	125 mL

Edible gold glitter (or coloured
fine sugar), for garnish

Glaze: Stir first amount of orange juice and icing sugar together in small bowl until barely pourable consistency. Set aside.

Cream margarine and sugar together in large bowl. Beat in egg, second amount of orange juice and rind.

Slowly mix in flour, baking soda, salt and coconut. Drop by rounded teaspoonfuls 2 inches (5 cm) apart on greased cookie sheet. Bake in 350°F (175°C) oven for about 10 minutes until edges turn golden. Let stand for 1 minute before removing to wire racks to cool.

Brush with glaze. Sprinkle with edible gold glitter. Makes 2 dozen cookies.

1 cookie: 80 Calories; 3.6 g Total Fat; 79 mg Sodium; 1 g Protein; 11 g Carbohydrate; trace Dietary Fibre

Pictured on page 2/3 and on page 86/87.

Grasshopper Squares

A pretty green mint layer sandwiched between chocolate cake and chocolate glaze layers.

BOTTOM LAYER

Hard margarine (or butter), softened	1/2 cup	125 mL
Brown sugar, packed	1 cup	250 mL
Large eggs	2	2
Vanilla	1/2 tsp.	2 mL
All-purpose flour	1/2 cup	125 mL
Cocoa, sifted if lumpy	1/4 cup	60 mL
Baking soda	1/4 tsp.	1 mL
Salt	1/8 tsp.	0.5 mL

MIDDLE LAYER

Hard margarine (or butter), softened	2/3 cup	150 mL
Icing (confectioner's) sugar	2 cups	500 mL
Milk	1 1/2 tbsp.	25 mL
Peppermint flavouring	1 tsp.	5 mL
Drops of green food colouring	5 – 6	5 – 6

TOP LAYER

Semi-sweet chocolate chips	1 cup	250 mL
Hard margarine (or butter)	3 tbsp.	50 mL

Bottom Layer: Cream margarine and brown sugar together in medium bowl. Beat in eggs, 1 at a time, beating well after each addition. Add vanilla. Mix.

Add next 4 ingredients. Beat until moistened. Turn into greased 9 x 9 inch (22 x 22 cm) pan. Bake in 350°F (175°C) oven for 15 minutes. Do not overcook. Cool thoroughly.

Middle Layer: Beat all 5 ingredients together in separate medium bowl. Spread over bottom layer.

Top Layer: Heat and stir chocolate chips and margarine in small heavy saucepan on low until melted and smooth. Spread over mint layer. Chill overnight until set. Cuts into 36 squares.

1 square: 153 Calories; 9.1 g Total Fat; 109 mg Sodium; 1 g Protein; 18 g Carbohydrate; 1 g Dietary Fibre

Pictured on page 3 and on page 87.

Top: Peanut Butter Bites, page 88
Centre: Grasshopper Squares, above
Centre Right: Rum And Butter Balls, page 84
Bottom Left: Ambrosia Orange Cookies, page 85

Peanut Butter Bites

Always a favourite combo—soft peanut butter log encased in a chocolate shell. More like candy than a cookie.

Smooth peanut butter	1 1/2 cups	375 mL
Hard margarine (or butter), softened	1/2 cup	125 mL
Graham cracker crumbs	1 cup	250 mL
Icing (confectioner's) sugar	2 1/2 cups	625 mL
White chocolate melting wafers	2/3 cup	150 mL
Green chocolate melting wafers	2/3 cup	150 mL
Red chocolate melting wafers	2/3 cup	150 mL

Mix peanut butter and margarine in large bowl.

Add graham crumbs and icing sugar. Mix well. Let stand for 10 minutes. Press or roll out between sheets of waxed paper into 7 × 10 inch (18 × 25 cm) rectangle 1/2 inch (12 mm) thick. Chill until firm. Peel off top layer of waxed paper. Cut into 1/2 × 1 3/4 inch (1.2 × 4.5 cm) bars. Arrange close together on baking sheet. Freeze.

Heat melting wafers separately in glass bowls over simmering water in small saucepan, stirring occasionally, until just melted. Remove from heat. Dip 1/3 of frozen bars into white chocolate, allowing excess to drip back into bowl. Place on foil or waxed paper to set. Repeat with remaining frozen bars and green and red chocolate. Makes about 6 dozen bites.

1 bite: 92 Calories; 5.8 g Total Fat; 54 mg Sodium; 2 g Protein; 9 g Carbohydrate; 1 g Dietary Fibre

Pictured on page 3 and on page 87.

Butterscotch Cookies, below

Butterscotch Cookies

These no-bake cookies are golden and crunchy. Sweet with a mild peanut butter flavour!

Smooth peanut butter	3 tbsp.	50 mL
Butterscotch chips	1 cup	250 mL
Corn flakes cereal	3 cups	750 mL
Chopped pecans (or walnuts)	1/2 cup	125 mL

Heat and stir peanut butter in large saucepan on medium until hot. Add butterscotch chips. Stir until melted. Remove from heat.

Add cereal and pecans. Stir until well coated. Drop by rounded tablespoonfuls into mounds onto waxed paper. Let stand until firm. Makes about 2 1/2 dozen cookies.

1 cookie: 53 Calories; 2.4 g Total Fat; 36 mg Sodium; 1 g Protein; 8 g Carbohydrate; trace Dietary Fibre

Pictured above.

Choc-A-Nut Fudge

Smooth and creamy fudge with a nut crunch.
The best indulgence ever.

Granulated sugar	2 cups	500 mL
Cocoa, sifted if lumpy	1/3 cup	75 mL
Salt	1/8 tsp.	0.5 mL
Corn syrup	2 tbsp.	30 mL
Hard margarine (or butter)	2 tbsp.	30 mL
Milk	3/4 cup	175 mL
Smooth peanut butter	1/2 cup	125 mL
Chopped unsalted peanuts (or walnuts)	1/2 cup	125 mL

Combine first 6 ingredients in 3 quart (3 L) heavy saucepan. Heat and stir on medium until boiling. Reduce heat to medium-low. Boil gently, without stirring, for 20 to 30 minutes until mixture reaches soft ball stage (234° to 240°F, 112° to 116°C) on candy thermometer or until small amount dropped in very cold water forms a soft ball that flattens on its own accord when removed. Remove from heat. Cool, without stirring, for 10 minutes.

Stir in peanut butter and peanuts. Beat with electric mixer for about 2 minutes until thick and colour lightens. Turn into greased 8 x 8 inch (20 x 20 cm) pan. Pat smooth. Chill until firm. Makes 1 1/2 lbs. (680 g) fudge. Cuts into 36 squares.

1 square: 94 Calories; 3.8 g Total Fat; 38 mg Sodium; 2 g Protein; 15 g Carbohydrate; 1 g Dietary Fibre

Pictured below.

Ragged Chocolate Drops

Sweet, crunchy and chewy all in one.
Kids will love these no-bake confections.

Shoestring potato chips (original flavour)	2 cups	500 mL
Unsalted peanuts	1 cup	250 mL
Sultana raisins (or dried cranberries)	1/2 cup	125 mL
Miniature multi-coloured (or white) marshmallows	2 cups	500 mL
Smooth peanut butter	1/4 cup	60 mL
Milk chocolate chips	2 cups	500 mL
White chocolate chips	2 cups	500 mL

Toss first 4 ingredients together in large bowl.

Heat and stir peanut butter and both chocolate chips in small heavy saucepan on low until chocolate is almost melted. Remove from heat. Stir until smooth. Immediately pour over marshmallow mixture. Toss until well coated. Drop by rounded tablespoonfuls into mounds onto waxed paper. Let stand at room temperature until firm. Makes about 50 chocolate drops.

1 chocolate drop: 120 Calories; 7.1 g Total Fat; 24 mg Sodium; 2 g Protein; 13 g Carbohydrate; 1 g Dietary Fibre

CHUNKY FUDGE: Press warm chocolate mixture into 9 x 9 inch (22 x 22 cm) foil-lined pan, using a sheet of waxed paper to protect your hands. Chill until set, if desired. Turn out of pan and remove foil before cutting. Cuts into 54 squares.

Pictured below.

Left: Caramel Nut Squares, page 91   Bottom Centre: Choc-A-Nut Fudge, above   Right: Chunky Fudge, above

New Year's Fritters, below

New Year's Fritters

The little bits of fruit are so pretty peeking out. Many different cultures have a similar recipe—Olie Bollen in Holland and Portzelky within the Mennonite community are versions of this yummy snack.

Diced dried apricots	1/2 cup	125 mL
Dried cranberries (or other dried fruit)	1/2 cup	125 mL
Golden raisins	1/2 cup	125 mL
Boiling water	2 cups	500 mL
Chopped glazed red and/or green cherries	1/2 cup	125 mL
Large eggs, room temperature	3	3
Granulated sugar	3 tbsp.	50 mL
Salt	1/2 tsp.	2 mL
Hot milk	1 1/2 cups	375 mL
Hard margarine (or butter)	1 tbsp.	15 mL
All-purpose flour	2 cups	500 mL
Instant yeast	1 tbsp.	15 mL
All-purpose flour, approximately	2 – 2 1/2 cups	500 – 625 mL

Cooking oil, for deep-frying

Icing (confectioner's) sugar (optional)

Mix apricots, cranberries and raisins in small bowl. Add boiling water. Let stand for 5 minutes. Drain. Spread fruit on dry tea towel or paper towels. Let stand until no moisture remains. Return to bowl.

Add cherries. Stir.

Beat eggs, granulated sugar and salt together in large bowl using fork. Slowly stir in hot milk and margarine until margarine is melted. Mixture should feel very warm but not hot.

Combine first amount of flour and yeast in separate small bowl. Stir into egg mixture. Vigorously stir for 2 to 3 minutes until batter is smooth, very sticky, and yeast is dissolved. Stir in fruit mixture.

Add second amount of flour, 1/2 cup (125 mL) at a time, until soft sticky dough forms that is too soft to knead but leaves the sides of bowl while mixing. Place dough in large greased bowl, turning once to grease top. Cover with greased waxed paper and tea towel. Let stand in oven with light on and door closed for about 1 hour until doubled in bulk. Stir dough down.

Drop 4 to 5 rounded tablespoonfuls into hot (375°F, 190°C) cooking oil. Deep-fry for 4 to 4 1/2 minutes, turning to cook evenly, until deep golden colour. Remove fritters to paper towels to drain. Repeat with remaining dough.

Dust with icing sugar before serving. Makes about 5 dozen fritters.

1 fritter: 77 Calories; 2.9 g Total Fat; 29 mg Sodium; 2 g Protein; 11 g Carbohydrate; 1 g Dietary Fibre

Pictured on this page.

Fritters are best eaten the same day but can be frozen in airtight containers after cooking and cooling. To cook from frozen, do not thaw. Heat in 350°F (175°C) oven for about 10 minutes until warmed through. Or dough can also be measured out in fritter-sized portions onto lightly floured baking sheet and frozen. Once frozen solid, they can be stored in resealable freezer bags. Deep-fry, 3 at a time, in hot 360°F (182°C) cooking oil for about 5 minutes, turning to cook evenly, until deep golden colour.

Caramel Nut Squares

Sweet caramel with butter-crunch chocolate bar pieces.

All-purpose flour	1 2/3 cups	400 mL
Pecans	1/2 cup	125 mL
Brown sugar, packed	1/3 cup	75 mL
Hard margarine (or butter), chilled, cut into 8 pieces	1 cup	250 mL
Can of sweetened condensed milk	11 oz.	300 mL
Large eggs	2	2
Corn syrup	1/4 cup	60 mL
Vanilla	1 tsp.	5 mL
Chopped pecans	1 cup	250 mL
Chocolate-covered crispy toffee bars (such as Skor or Heath), 1 1/2 oz. (39 g) each, coarsely chopped	3	3

Measure flour, first amount of pecans and brown sugar into food processor. Process for a few seconds until just combined. Add margarine to flour mixture. Pulse with on/off motion several times until margarine is size of small peas. Firmly press into bottom of greased foil-lined 9 × 13 inch (22 × 33 cm) pan. Bake in 350°F (175°C) oven for 12 to 14 minutes until edges are golden. Cool for 10 minutes.

Beat condensed milk, eggs, corn syrup and vanilla together in medium bowl until blended.

Stir in second amount of pecans and chocolate bar pieces. Pour over crust. Spread evenly. Bake for 25 to 30 minutes until wooden pick inserted in centre comes out clean. Cool. Remove from pan. Remove foil. Cut into 1 1/2 inch (3.8 cm) squares. Cuts into 54 squares.

1 square: 131 Calories; 8.4 g Total Fat; 69 mg Sodium; 2 g Protein; 13 g Carbohydrate; trace Dietary Fibre

Pictured on page 89.

Toasted Popcorn Snack, below

Toasted Popcorn Snack

You get just a little nip from the Parmesan cheese and cayenne. A savoury, chunky snack that people will congregate around at your next party.

Hard margarine (or butter), melted	1/2 cup	125 mL
Grated Parmesan cheese	1/4 cup	60 mL
Worcestershire sauce	4 tsp.	20 mL
Salt	1/4 tsp.	1 mL
Garlic powder	3/4 tsp.	4 mL
Onion powder	1/2 tsp.	2 mL
Cayenne pepper	1/2 tsp.	2 mL
Popped corn (about 1/4 cup, 60 mL, unpopped)	8 cups	2 L
Rice squares cereal	3 cups	750 mL
Mini pretzels	5 cups	1.25 L

Combine first 7 ingredients in large bowl.

Add remaining 3 ingredients. Stir until coated well. Spread in large roasting pan. Bake in 300°F (150°C) oven for about 20 minutes, stirring occasionally, until lightly toasted. Makes 16 cups (4 L).

1/2 cup (125 mL): 84 Calories; 3.7 g Total Fat; 260 mg Sodium; 2 g Protein; 11 g Carbohydrate; 1 g Dietary Fibre

Pictured above.

Condiments

Honey Mustard Sauce

This sauce has a sweet flavour and a rich mustard colour.
Great with Maple And Rye Gravlax, page 48.

Grainy mustard	1/4 cup	60 mL
Brown sugar, packed	1 tbsp.	15 mL
Liquid honey	1 tbsp.	15 mL
Ground ginger	1/8 tsp.	0.5 mL

Combine all 4 ingredients in small bowl. Makes 1/3 cup (75 mL).

2 tbsp. (30 mL): 64 Calories; 1.5 g Total Fat; 311 mg Sodium; 1 g Protein; 13 g Carbohydrate; trace Dietary Fibre

Pictured on page 46.

Savoury Orange Dipping Sauce

Strong orange and mild mustard tastes in this sauce which may also be served cold. Good with Spring Rolls, page 167, meatballs, grilled chicken, chicken nuggets or pork.

Orange marmalade	1/2 cup	125 mL
Prepared horseradish	2 tsp.	10 mL
Grainy mustard	2 tsp.	10 mL

Combine all 3 ingredients in small saucepan. Heat and stir on medium until marmalade is melted. Makes 1/2 cup (125 mL).

2 tbsp. (30 mL): 103 Calories; 0.2 g Total Fat; 63 mg Sodium; trace Protein; 27 g Carbohydrate; trace Dietary Fibre

Pictured on page 164.

Fresh Herb Sauce

The perfect sauce for fish with its tarragon and thyme flavours. Good with Crab And Cheddar Waffles, page 81.

Mayonnaise (not salad dressing)	1 cup	250 mL
Milk	3 tbsp.	50 mL
Chopped fresh parsley	1 tbsp.	15 mL
Chopped fresh tarragon leaves	1 1/2 tsp.	7 mL
Fresh thyme leaves	1/2 tsp.	2 mL

Combine all 5 ingredients in small bowl. Chill until ready to serve. Makes 1 1/3 cups (325 mL).

2 tbsp. (30 mL): 155 Calories; 16.9 g Total Fat; 111 mg Sodium; trace Protein; trace Carbohydrate; trace Dietary Fibre

Pictured on page 78.

Horseradish Beet Relish

This is a delicious condiment served with turkey, beef and even egg dishes. Easy to double or even triple the recipe for hostess gifts.

Coarsely grated cooked beets	1 cup	250 mL
White vinegar	1/4 cup	60 mL
Creamed horseradish	1 tbsp.	15 mL
Granulated sugar	1 tbsp.	15 mL
Salt	1/4 tsp.	1 mL
Pepper	1/8 tsp.	0.5 mL

Combine all 6 ingredients in small bowl. Chill until ready to serve. Makes 1 1/4 cups (300 mL).

2 tbsp. (30 mL): 12 Calories; trace Total Fat; 69 mg Sodium; trace Protein; 3 g Carbohydrate; trace Dietary Fibre

Pictured on this page.

Fresh Tomato Relish

Red tomatoes and green peppers give this condiment the colours of Christmas. Delicious served with fish, chicken and roast beef or pork.

Chopped, seeded roma (plum) tomato	1 cup	250 mL
Finely chopped red onion	1/4 cup	60 mL
Finely chopped green pepper	1/4 cup	60 mL
Garlic clove, minced (or 1/4 tsp., 1 mL, powder)	1	1
Chopped fresh parsley (or cilantro), or 1 1/8 tsp. (6 mL) flakes	1 1/2 tbsp.	25 mL
Chopped fresh sweet basil (or 3/4 tsp., 4 mL, dried)	1 tbsp.	15 mL
Snipped fresh chives (or 1/4 tsp., 1 mL, dried)	1 1/2 tsp.	7 mL
Red wine vinegar	1 1/2 tsp.	7 mL
Hot pepper sauce	1/4 tsp.	1 mL
Salt	1/4 tsp.	1 mL
Freshly ground pepper, sprinkle		

Combine all 11 ingredients in medium bowl. Let stand for 2 hours at room temperature to blend flavours. Makes 1 1/3 cups (325 mL).

2 tbsp. (30 mL): 6 Calories; 0.1 g Total Fat; 58 mg Sodium; trace Protein; 1 g Carbohydrate; trace Dietary Fibre

Pictured on page 36.

Rhubarb Relish

Traditional chutney with a bit of tangy rhubarb. Serve with Handhheld Tourtières, page 166.

Chopped frozen (or fresh) rhubarb	2 cups	500 mL
Chopped onion	2 cups	500 mL
Brown sugar, packed	1 cup	250 mL
White vinegar	3/4 cup	175 mL
Ground allspice	1/2 tsp.	2 mL
Ground cinnamon	1/2 tsp.	2 mL
Ground cloves	1/2 tsp.	2 mL
Salt	1/2 tsp.	2 mL
Pepper	1/16 tsp.	0.5 mL

Combine all 9 ingredients in large saucepan. Cook, uncovered, for about 60 minutes until rhubarb is tender and liquid is thickened. Makes 1 2/3 cups (400 mL).

2 tbsp. (30 mL): 99 Calories; 0.1 g Total Fat; 117 mg Sodium; 1 g Protein; 25 g Carbohydrate; 1 g Dietary Fibre

Pictured below.

Top Left & Right: Rhubarb Relish, above
Bottom Left: Horseradish Beet Relish, this page

Desserts

Strawberry Pizza Pie

Beautiful fruit topping on a cake crust.

CRUST

Hard margarine (or butter), softened	1/4 cup	60 mL
Granulated sugar	1/4 cup	60 mL
Brown sugar, packed	1/4 cup	60 mL
Large egg	1	1
Milk	1/4 cup	60 mL
Vanilla	1/2 tsp.	2 mL
All-purpose flour	1 3/4 cups	425 mL
Cream of tartar	1 tsp.	5 mL
Baking soda	1/2 tsp.	2 mL
Salt	1/4 tsp.	1 mL

FILLING

Block of cream cheese, softened	8 oz.	250 g
Icing (confectioner's) sugar	1 1/4 cups	300 mL
Lemon juice	1 tsp.	5 mL
Frozen whipped topping, thawed	2 cups	500 mL
Sliced fresh strawberries	2 1/2 cups	625 mL
Sliced ripe kiwifruit	1 cup	250 mL
Apple jelly	1/3 cup	75 mL

Crust: Cream margarine and both sugars together in medium bowl. Add egg. Beat. Add milk and vanilla. Beat until smooth.

Mix flour, cream of tartar, baking soda and salt in small bowl. Add to margarine mixture. Mix well. Turn out and spread evenly onto greased 12 inch (30 cm) pizza pan. Bake in 375°F (190°C) oven for about 20 minutes until golden. Cool thoroughly.

Filling: Beat cream cheese, icing sugar and lemon juice together in separate medium bowl until light and fluffy. Fold in whipped topping. Spread evenly over crust.

Arrange strawberries and kiwifruit over cream cheese mixture to make attractive pattern.

Heat jelly in small saucepan on medium-low, stirring occasionally, until liquefied. Dab surface of fruit with glaze to give shine and to prevent fruit from drying out. Chill until ready to serve. Serves 10 to 12.

1 serving: 440 Calories; 18.7 g Total Fat; 277 mg Sodium; 6 g Protein; 64 g Carbohydrate; 3 g Dietary Fibre

Pictured on page 95.

Left: Strawberry Pizza Pie, page 94   Top Right: Mango Rum Fluff, page 96   Bottom Right: Peaches And Cream Cake, this page

Peaches And Cream Cake

A saucy cream forms around the peach slices.
Garnish with peach slices and whipped cream.

All-purpose flour	1 cup	250 mL
Vanilla pudding powder (not instant), 6 serving size	1	1
Baking powder	1 tsp.	5 mL
Salt	1/2 tsp.	2 mL
Hard margarine (or butter), softened	3 tbsp.	50 mL
Large egg	1	1
Milk	2/3 cup	150 mL
Can of sliced peaches, drained, juice reserved	14 oz.	398 mL
Block of cream cheese, softened	8 oz.	250 g
Granulated sugar	1/2 cup	125 mL
Reserved peach juice	3 tbsp.	50 mL
TOPPING		
Granulated sugar	2 tbsp.	30 mL
Ground cinnamon	1 tbsp.	15 mL

Measure first 7 ingredients into large bowl. Beat well until smooth. Turn into greased 8 × 8 inch (20 × 20 cm) pan.

Arrange peach slices over batter.

Beat cream cheese, sugar and peach juice together in medium bowl. Drop dabs here and there over peach slices. Spread as best you can.

Topping: Stir sugar and cinnamon together in small cup. Sprinkle over cream cheese mixture. Bake in 350°F (175°C) oven for 60 to 70 minutes until wooden pick inserted in centre comes out clean. Cuts into 16 pieces.

1 piece: 193 Calories; 8.2 g Total Fat; 252 mg Sodium; 3 g Protein; 28 g Carbohydrate; 1 g Dietary Fibre

Pictured above.

PEACHES AND COCONUT CREAM CAKE: Omit vanilla pudding powder. Use coconut cream pudding powder (not instant), 6 serving size.

Mango Rum Fluff

And a light bit of fluff it is!
A fresh taste after a heavy meal.

Envelope of unflavoured gelatin (1/4 oz., 7 g)	1	1
Cold water	1/4 cup	60 mL
Granulated sugar	1/2 cup	125 mL
Lemon juice	1 tbsp.	15 mL
Salt	1/16 tsp.	0.5 mL
Can of sliced mango in syrup, drained, puréed	14 oz.	398 mL
Amber (or dark) rum (or 1/2 tsp., 2 mL, rum flavouring)	1 tbsp.	15 mL
Almond flavouring	1/4 tsp.	1 mL
Whipping cream	1 cup	250 mL
Amber (or dark) rum (or 1/4 tsp., 1 mL, rum flavouring)	1 1/2 tsp.	7 mL
Slivered (or flaked) almonds, toasted (see Tip, page 100)	1 tbsp.	15 mL
Edible red glitter, for garnish		

Sprinkle gelatin over cold water in small saucepan. Let stand for 5 minutes until softened. Heat and stir on medium until gelatin is dissolved.

Add sugar, lemon juice and salt. Stir until sugar is dissolved. Remove from heat.

Add mango, first amount of rum and almond flavouring. Mix well. Transfer to large bowl. Chill for 50 to 60 minutes, stirring occasionally, until mixture mounds softly.

Beat whipping cream in separate large bowl until stiff peaks form. Reserve 1/2 cup (125 mL) in refrigerator. Fold remaining whipped cream into mango mixture. Chill. Makes 4 cups (1 L).

Stir second amount of rum into reserved whipped cream. Spread in centre or around rim of dessert in serving bowl. Sprinkle with almonds and edible red glitter. Serves 6.

1 serving: 259 Calories; 14.3 g Total Fat; 45 mg Sodium; 2 g Protein; 31 g Carbohydrate; trace Dietary Fibre

Pictured on page 95.

To beat whipping cream faster, chill the bowl and beaters first. To keep whipped cream from separating, add 2 tsp. (10 mL) vanilla pudding powder (not instant) per 1 cup (250 mL) whipping cream.

Chilled Chocolate Cheesecake

A good no-bake, make-ahead dessert.

VANILLA WAFER CRUST		
Hard margarine (or butter)	6 tbsp.	100 mL
Vanilla wafer crumbs	1 1/2 cups	375 mL
Cocoa, sifted if lumpy	1 tbsp.	15 mL
FILLING		
Envelopes of unflavoured gelatin (1/4 oz., 7 g, each)	2	2
Cold water	2 cups	500 mL
Semi-sweet chocolate chips	1 cup	250 mL
Block of light cream cheese, softened	12 oz.	375 g
Granulated sugar	1/2 cup	125 mL
Vanilla	1 tsp.	5 mL
Envelope of dessert topping (not prepared)	1	1
Milk	1/2 cup	125 mL
Chocolate ice cream topping	1/2 cup	125 mL

Vanilla Wafer Crust: Melt margarine in medium saucepan. Add wafer crumbs and cocoa. Stir until well mixed. Firmly press into bottom of ungreased 10 inch (25 cm) springform pan. Chill.

Filling: Sprinkle gelatin over cold water in separate medium saucepan. Let stand for 1 minute until softened. Heat and stir until gelatin is dissolved. Remove from heat.

Add chocolate chips. Stir until melted. Cool.

Beat cream cheese, sugar and vanilla together in large bowl until smooth. Beat in chocolate mixture. Chill for about 1 hour until beginning to thicken.

Beat dessert topping and milk together in medium bowl until stiff peaks form. Fold into chocolate mixture. Turn into crust. Chill for at least 6 hours or overnight.

Drizzle 2 tsp. (10 mL) ice cream topping over individual wedges. Cuts into 12 wedges.

1 wedge: 350 Calories; 20.9 g Total Fat; 332 mg Sodium; 6 g Protein; 38 g Carbohydrate; 1 g Dietary Fibre

Pictured on page 97.

Butterscotch Peanut Treat

The perfect finale to any meal.

CRUST

Hard margarine (or butter), melted	1/2 cup	125 mL
Chocolate wafer crumbs	2 cups	500 mL
Ice cream (your choice), softened	8 cups	2 L
Dry-roasted peanuts, coarsely chopped	1 cup	250 mL
Butterscotch ice cream topping	1 cup	250 mL
Chocolate ice cream topping	1 cup	250 mL
Frozen whipped topping, thawed (or whipped cream)	2 cups	500 mL

Crust: Melt margarine in medium saucepan. Add wafer crumbs. Stir until well mixed. Reserve 1/2 cup (125 mL). Firmly press remaining crumb mixture into ungreased 9 x 13 inch (22 x 33 cm) pan.

Spoon ice cream in dabs here and there over crust. Spread evenly. Sprinkle with peanuts. Drizzle both ice cream toppings over peanuts. Cover. Freeze for about 1 1/2 hours until set.

Spread whipped topping over top. Sprinkle with reserved crumb mixture. Freeze until firm. Remove from freezer about 10 minutes before cutting. Store in freezer. Serves 15 to 18.

1 serving: 510 Calories; 27.9 g Total Fat; 341 mg Sodium; 8 g Protein; 63 g Carbohydrate; 1 g Dietary Fibre

Pictured below.

Creamsicle Dessert

A cool, light dessert that's easy to make.
Good chilled or frozen.

CRUST

Hard margarine (or butter)	1/4 cup	60 mL
Graham cracker crumbs	1 cup	250 mL
Granulated sugar	1 tbsp.	15 mL
Package of orange-flavoured gelatin (jelly powder)	3 oz.	85 g
Boiling water	1 cup	250 mL
Lemon juice	1 tbsp.	15 mL
Vanilla ice cream	2 cups	500 mL

Crust: Melt margarine in medium saucepan. Add graham crumbs and sugar. Stir until well mixed. Reserve 3 tbsp. (50 mL). Firmly press remaining crumb mixture into bottom of ungreased 9 x 9 inch (22 x 22 cm) pan. Set aside.

Combine jelly powder and boiling water in medium bowl. Stir until jelly powder is dissolved.

Add lemon juice and ice cream. Stir until smooth. Pour over crust. Sprinkle with reserved crumb mixture. Chill overnight or freeze until firm. Cuts into 9 pieces.

1 piece: 194 Calories; 9.8 g Total Fat; 172 mg Sodium; 3 g Protein; 25 g Carbohydrate; trace Dietary Fibre

Pictured below.

Top Left: Chilled Chocolate Cheesecake, page 96
Top Right: Butterscotch Peanut Treat, above
Bottom Centre: Creamsicle Dessert, above

Butterscotch Sauce

An easy make-your-own sauce. Serve hot over ice cream or warm over Spice Coffee Cake, page 77.

Hard margarine (or butter)	1/2 cup	125 mL
Brown sugar, packed	1 1/3 cups	325 mL
Corn syrup	3/4 cup	175 mL
Salt	1/8 tsp.	0.5 mL
Half-and-half cream	1 cup	250 mL
Vanilla	1 tsp.	5 mL

Measure first 4 ingredients into medium saucepan. Heat and stir on medium until starting to boil and brown sugar is dissolved. Boil gently on medium-low for 5 minutes, stirring frequently. Remove from heat.

Slowly stir in cream and vanilla. Mixture may sputter a bit. Stir until well blended. Makes 2 3/4 cups (675 mL).

2 tbsp. (30 mL): 134 Calories; 5.3 g Total Fat; 86 mg Sodium; trace Protein; 22 g Carbohydrate; 0 g Dietary Fibre

Pictured on page 78 and on page 99.

Vanilla Sauce

A slightly sweet sauce, nice over puddings, pound cakes or fresh fruit. Drizzle over Fruit Pudding, page 100.

Granulated sugar	1 cup	250 mL
All-purpose flour	3 tbsp.	50 mL
Salt	1/2 tsp.	2 mL
Hot water	1 1/2 cups	375 mL
Hard margarine (or butter)	2 tbsp.	30 mL
Vanilla	1 tsp.	5 mL

Mix sugar, flour and salt in small saucepan.

Stir in hot water, margarine and vanilla. Heat and stir until boiling and thickened. Sauce will thicken as it cools. Makes 2 cups (500 mL).

2 tbsp. (30 mL): 67 Calories; 1.4 g Total Fat; 88 mg Sodium; trace Protein; 14 g Carbohydrate; trace Dietary Fibre

Pictured on page 98 and on page 99.

Top Right: Fruit Pudding, page 100, with
    Butterscotch Sauce, above
Centre Left: Honey Jewel Cake, page 101
Centre Right: Vanilla Sauce, above
Bottom Left & Right: Fruit Pudding, page 100

Fruit Pudding

Chewy, fruity and mildly spiced.
This pudding is a great gift-giving idea.
Drizzle Vanilla Sauce, page 98, over this tasty dessert.

Raisins	1 cup	250 mL
Currants	1 cup	250 mL
Chopped mixed glazed fruit	1 cup	250 mL
Chopped dates	1 cup	250 mL
Rolled oats (not instant)	2 cups	500 mL
Hard margarine (or butter), softened	1 cup	250 mL
Corn syrup	1 cup	250 mL
Large egg	1	1
All-purpose flour	1 1/2 cups	375 mL
Salt	1 1/2 tsp.	7 mL
Ground cinnamon	1 tsp.	5 mL
Baking soda	1 tsp.	5 mL
Ground cloves	1/4 tsp.	1 mL
Milk	1 cup	250 mL

Combine first 5 ingredients in large bowl. Toss well to coat fruit.

Beat margarine, corn syrup and egg together in separate large bowl until thick and smooth.

Stir next 5 ingredients together in small bowl.

Add flour mixture to margarine mixture in 3 additions, alternating with milk in 2 additions, beginning and ending with flour mixture. Stir in fruit mixture. Turn into greased 10 cup (2.5 L) pudding pan or large heatproof bowl. Cover with double layer of greased foil, domed slightly to allow for expansion. Secure foil by tying string around pan. Place pan in steamer or Dutch oven with rack (or metal jar rings). Pour boiling water into steamer until water comes 2/3 of the way up sides of pan. Cover. Simmer on low for 3 hours. Add more boiling water to keep level up as needed. Carefully remove pan from steamer. Let stand for 20 minutes before turning out onto wire rack to cool completely. Cover with plastic wrap and foil. Store in freezer for up to 2 months or in refrigerator for 2 to 3 weeks. Reheat before serving. Serves 14.

1 serving: 463 Calories; 15.7 g Total Fat; 564 mg Sodium; 6 g Protein; 80 g Carbohydrate; 5 g Dietary Fibre

Pictured on page 98 and on page 99.

Variation: Grease bottom of four 28 oz. (796 mL) cans. Line greased bottoms with circles of waxed paper. Fill each can 2/3 full with pudding batter. Top each with 1 red glazed cherry (optional). Cover each can with double layer of greased foil. Secure foil by tying string around cans. Place all 4 cans in Dutch oven with rack (or metal jar rings). Pour boiling water into Dutch oven until water comes 2/3 of the way up sides of cans. Cover. Simmer on low for 2 1/2 hours. Add more boiling water to keep level up as needed. Carefully remove cans from Dutch oven. Run knife around sides of cans to loosen pudding. Turn each out onto wire rack. Cool. Puddings may be individually covered with plastic wrap and attractively tied with ribbon to be given away as gifts. Makes 4 individual puddings.

To toast almonds, flaxseeds, pine nuts, sesame seeds and walnuts, place in single layer in ungreased shallow pan. Bake in 350°F (175°C) oven for 5 to 10 minutes, stirring or shaking often, until desired doneness

Honey Jewel Cake

A pretty, golden cake with lots of "jewels" visible once cut.
Great for dipping in Eggnog Fondue, page 102.

Sultana raisins	1 cup	250 mL
Red and/or green glazed cherries, coarsely chopped	1 cup	250 mL
Glazed pineapple, chopped	1 cup	250 mL
Golden raisins	2/3 cup	150 mL
Diced mixed peel	1/2 cup	125 mL
Sherry (or alcohol-free sherry)	1/4 cup	60 mL
Ground almonds	1/2 cup	125 mL
Butter (not margarine), softened	1 cup	250 mL
Liquid honey	1/2 cup	125 mL
Granulated sugar	1/3 cup	75 mL
Large eggs	4	4
Finely grated lemon rind	2 tsp.	10 mL
Finely grated orange rind	2 tsp.	10 mL
All-purpose flour	1 3/4 cups	425 mL
Baking powder	1/2 tsp.	2 mL
Salt	1/4 tsp.	1 mL
Slivered almonds	1 1/2 cups	375 mL
Whole blanched almonds, for garnish	1/3 cup	75 mL
Red and green glazed cherries, for garnish	1/3 cup	75 mL
Sherry (or alcohol-free sherry)	3 tbsp.	50 mL
Cheesecloth, enough to wrap cakes in double thickness		

Combine first 5 ingredients in large bowl. Sprinkle with first amount of sherry. Mix well to moisten. Cover. Let stand overnight at room temperature.

Add ground almonds. Toss well to coat. Set aside.

Cream butter, honey and sugar together in separate large bowl. Add eggs, 1 at a time, beating well after each addition. Beat in lemon and orange rind.

Combine flour, baking powder and salt in separate large bowl. Gradually beat into butter mixture.

Stir in slivered almonds. Add to fruit mixture. Stir well. Spoon batter into 2 greased parchment paper-lined 8 × 4 × 3 inch (20 × 10 × 7.5 cm) loaf pans. Bake in 300°F (150°C) oven for 40 minutes. Remove from oven.

Gently lay whole almonds and second amount of cherries in attractive pattern over surface of cakes. Bake for 1 1/2 to 2 hours until cake is firm to touch, cracks appear on surface and wooden pick inserted in centre comes out clean. Remove from oven. Cool in pan on wire rack. Turn out of pan. Peel off parchment paper.

Poke several holes into cakes using skewer. Slowly drizzle 1 tbsp. (15 mL) second amount of sherry over each cake. Soak cheesecloth in remaining sherry. Wrap cakes in cheesecloth. Wrap in waxed paper. Tightly wrap in foil. Store in cool place for at least 2 weeks. To store uncut cakes, store in cool place for up to 10 weeks. Check cakes weekly and remoisten cheesecloth with more sherry if necessary. Cut into 1/2 inch (12 mm) thick slices. Cut each slice into thirds. Makes 2 cakes, each cutting into 48 pieces, for a total of 96 pieces.

1 piece: 85 Calories; 3.9 g Total Fat; 32 mg Sodium; 1 g Protein; 12 g Carbohydrate; trace Dietary Fibre

Pictured on page 98/99 and on page 102.

Use the front cover of last year's Christmas cards as this year's gift tags. Be sure to check that there isn't any writing on the back of the cards before cutting out design.

Top Left: Chocolate Almond Cookies, page 84
Top Centre: Honey Jewel Cake, page 101
Centre Right: Eggnog Fondue, below

Eggnog Fondue

*Very good festive fondue. Great use for
eggnog and Christmas fruitcake.*

All-purpose flour	2 tbsp.	30 mL
Cornstarch	2 tbsp.	30 mL
Brown sugar, packed	1 tbsp.	15 mL
Salt, just a pinch		
Milk (not skim)	1 cup	250 mL
Eggnog	2 cups	500 mL
Large egg	1	1
Vanilla	1 tsp.	5 mL
Ground nutmeg, sprinkle		
Ground cinnamon, sprinkle		
Dark rum	2 tbsp.	30 mL

Combine first 4 ingredients in large saucepan.

Slowly stir in milk and eggnog until smooth. Cook on medium, stirring frequently, until boiling and slightly thickened. Remove from heat.

Beat egg, vanilla, nutmeg and cinnamon together in small bowl using fork. Add 2 large spoonfuls eggnog mixture to egg mixture. Mix well. Stir into hot eggnog mixture. Heat and stir on medium-low for 2 minutes. Remove from heat.

Stir in rum. Carefully pour into fondue pot to no more than 2/3 full. Place over low heat. Add more eggnog or rum as necessary to keep proper dipping consistency. Makes 3 cups (750 mL).

2 tbsp. (30 mL): 46 Calories; 1.9 g Total Fat; 20 mg Sodium; 1 g Protein; 5 g Carbohydrate; trace Dietary Fibre

Pictured on this page.

Suggested dippers: Chocolate Almond Cookies, page 84; Honey Jewel Cake pieces, page 101; angel food cake; banana; doughnut pieces; firm chocolate cake cubes; fruitcake; kiwifruit; marshmallows; mini muffin halves; soft ginger cookies; strawberries.

Peach Mousse

*A great dessert for a light finish.
Very nice served in individual glasses.*

Package of peach (or lemon) flavoured gelatin (jelly powder)	3 oz.	85 g
Boiling water	1 cup	250 mL
Cold water	1/2 cup	125 mL
Jars of strained peaches (baby food), 4 1/2 oz. (128 mL), each	3	3
Brandy flavouring (optional)	1/4 tsp.	1 mL
Frozen whipped topping, thawed	2 cups	500 mL
Sliced fresh (or frozen or canned) peaches, for garnish		

Dissolve jelly powder in boiling water in large serving bowl.

Add cold water, peaches and flavouring. Stir. Chill for about 2 hours, stirring and scraping down sides of bowl occasionally, until slightly thickened.

Fold whipped topping into peach mixture until smooth. Chill for 2 hours until softly set.

Garnish with peach slices. Serves 6.

1 serving: 182 Calories; 7.1 g Total Fat; 63 mg Sodium; 2 g Protein; 29 g Carbohydrate; 0 g Dietary Fibre

Pictured on page 103.

APRICOT MOUSSE: Omit strained peaches (baby food). Use strained apricots (baby food).

Eggnog Chantilly

This light eggnog dessert is perfect after all the turkey and heavy food! Best if chilled overnight.

Brown sugar, packed	1/4 cup	60 mL
All-purpose flour	6 tbsp.	100 mL
Ground nutmeg, sprinkle		
Ground cinnamon, sprinkle		
Eggnog	1 1/2 cups	375 mL
Milk	1 cup	250 mL
Large eggs	3	3
Unflavoured gelatin (1/2 of 1/4 oz., 7 g, envelope)	1 1/2 tsp.	7 mL
Dark rum	2 tbsp.	30 mL
Whipping cream	1 1/2 cups	375 mL
Edible gold glitter (or gold-coloured fine sugar or cinnamon sugar), for garnish		

Combine first 4 ingredients in large saucepan.

Slowly add eggnog and milk, while whisking, until smooth. Heat and whisk on medium until boiling and thickened. Remove from heat.

Beat eggs in small bowl using fork. Add 2 large spoonfuls of hot eggnog mixture to eggs. Mix well. Stir into eggnog mixture. Heat and stir for about 2 minutes until beginning to boil and thicken.

Sprinkle gelatin over rum in small dish. Let stand for 1 minute until softened. Stir into hot eggnog mixture until gelatin is dissolved. Cover with plastic wrap directly on surface to prevent skin forming. Cool to room temperature. Turn into large bowl.

Beat whipping cream in small bowl until soft peaks form. Fold 2 large spoonfuls into cooled eggnog mixture. Fold in remaining whipped cream. Cover. Chill for several hours or overnight.

Sprinkle individual servings with edible gold glitter before serving. Makes 7 cups (1.75 L).

1/2 cup (125 mL): 178 Calories; 12.1 g Total Fat; 50 mg Sodium; 4 g Protein; 12 g Carbohydrate; trace Dietary Fibre

Pictured on this page.

Top Right: Eggnog Chantilly, above
Centre Left: Peach Mousse, page 102
Bottom Right: White Chocolate
Liqueur Freeze, page 105

Pineapple Fluff Cake

A taste of the tropics. Make the day before to allow the pineapple flavour to intensify.

White cake mix (2 layer size)	1	1
Instant vanilla pudding powder (4 serving size)	1	1
Large eggs	4	4
Cooking oil	1/2 cup	125 mL
Vanilla	1 tsp.	5 mL
Pineapple juice	1 1/3 cups	325 mL
FILLING		
Block of cream cheese, softened	8 oz.	250 g
Envelope of dessert topping (prepared)	1	1
Can of crushed pineapple, drained and juice reserved	14 oz.	398 mL
ICING		
Hard margarine (or butter), softened	3/4 cup	175 mL
Icing (confectioner's) sugar	4 cups	1 L
Reserved pineapple juice	5–6 tbsp.	75–100 mL
Coconut (or vanilla) flavouring	1 tsp.	5 mL
Flake (or long thread) coconut, for garnish	2/3 cup	150 mL
Drops of yellow food colouring, for garnish	1–2	1–2

Empty cake mix into large bowl. Add pudding powder, eggs, cooking oil, vanilla and pineapple juice. Beat on low until just moistened. Beat on medium for 2 minutes until smooth. Divide between 2 greased 9 inch (22 cm) round pans. Bake in 350°F (175°C) oven for about 35 minutes until wooden pick inserted in centre comes out clean. Let stand in pans for 15 minutes before turning out onto wire racks to cool completely. Cut each layer in half horizontally to make 4 cake layers.

Filling: Beat cream cheese in medium bowl until smooth. Add dessert topping. Beat well.

Place bottom cake layer on serving plate. Spread with 1/3 of filling. Sprinkle with 1/3 of pineapple. Repeat with 2 more cake layers. Top with remaining cake layer.

Icing: Beat first 4 ingredients together in separate medium bowl until smooth and spreadable. Ice top and sides of cake.

Combine coconut and food colouring in large plastic bowl with lid. Cover. Shake for about 2 minutes until coconut is coloured. Spread on paper towel to remove excess colour. Let stand for 10 minutes to air dry. Sprinkle over icing. Chill for 24 hours. Store, covered with plastic wrap, in refrigerator. Cuts into 16 wedges.

1 wedge: 548 Calories; 27.7 g Total Fat; 482 mg Sodium; 5 g Protein; 72 g Carbohydrate; trace Dietary Fibre

Pictured on page 105.

Cherry Mix-Up Cake

A moist and colourful cake with a cream cheese icing that adds even more sweetness.

Large eggs	2	2
Water	1/2 cup	125 mL
Cooking oil	1/4 cup	60 mL
White cake mix (2 layer size)	1	1
Can of cherry pie filling	19 oz.	540 mL
CREAM CHEESE ICING		
Block of cream cheese, softened	4 oz.	125 g
Hard margarine (or butter), softened	2 tbsp.	30 mL
Icing (confectioner's) sugar	2 1/2 cups	625 mL
Vanilla	1 tsp.	5 mL
Milk	1 tbsp.	15 mL

Beat eggs, water and cooking oil together in medium bowl until frothy.

Add cake mix. Beat on low until moistened. Spread in greased 9 x 13 inch (22 x 33 cm) pan.

Spoon pie filling in dabs here and there over batter. Swirl with knife or spoon to create marble effect. Bake in 350°F (175°C) oven for about 45 minutes until wooden pick inserted in centre comes out clean. Cool.

Cream Cheese Icing: Beat all 5 ingredients together well in small bowl, adding more milk or icing sugar if necessary, until proper spreading consistency. Drizzle icing over top or ice cake. Cuts into 24 pieces.

1 piece: 228 Calories; 8.1 g Total Fat; 180 mg Sodium; 2 g Protein; 38 g Carbohydrate; trace Dietary Fibre

Pictured on page 105.

Bottom Left: Cherry Nut Crumble, below   Top Centre: Cherry Mix-Up Cake, page 104   Bottom Right: Pineapple Fluff Cake, page 104

Cherry Nut Crumble

Slight almond and nutmeg flavours with warm cherry filling.
The topping is crispy and sweet. Great with ice cream!

Can of cherry pie filling	19 oz.	540 mL
Almond flavouring	1/4 tsp.	1 mL
Ground nutmeg	1/8 – 1/4 tsp.	0.5 – 1 mL
TOPPING		
Hard margarine (or butter), softened	6 tbsp.	100 mL
Brown sugar, packed	2/3 cup	150 mL
All-purpose flour	1/2 cup	125 mL
Quick-cooking rolled oats (not instant)	1/2 cup	125 mL
Sliced (or slivered) almonds	1/2 cup	125 mL

Combine pie filling, flavouring and nutmeg in ungreased 2 quart (2 L) casserole.

Topping: Mix first 4 ingredients in medium bowl until crumbly.

Add almonds. Mix. Sprinkle over pie filling mixture. Bake, uncovered, in 350°F (175°C) oven for about 30 minutes until lightly browned. Let stand for 10 minutes before serving. Serves 6.

1 serving: 455 Calories; 18.5 g Total Fat; 156 mg Sodium; 5 g Protein; 71 g Carbohydrate; 3 g Dietary Fibre

Pictured above.

White Chocolate Liqueur Freeze

A smooth, special dessert perfect when
topped with a maraschino cherry.

Granulated sugar	3/4 cup	175 mL
Milk	2 1/2 cups	625 mL
Whipping cream	1 cup	250 mL
White chocolate baking squares (1 oz., 28 g, each), cut up	8	8
Milk	1/2 cup	125 mL
Egg whites (large), room temperature	3	3
Cherry-flavoured liqueur (such as Kirsch) or almond-flavoured liqueur (such as Amaretto)	3 tbsp.	50 mL

Combine first 3 ingredients in large bowl.

Heat and stir chocolate and second amount of milk in medium saucepan on low until smooth. Remove from heat. Add about 1 cup (250 mL) whipping cream mixture. Mix well. Add to whipping cream mixture. Stir well.

Beat egg whites in small bowl until stiff peaks form. Gently stir into whipping cream mixture. Stir in liqueur. Freeze until firm or freeze in ice-cream maker according to manufacturer's directions. Makes 6 cups (1.5 L).

1/2 cup (125 mL): 261 Calories; 13.1 g Total Fat; 70 mg Sodium; 5 g Protein; 30 g Carbohydrate; 0 g Dietary Fibre

Pictured on page 103.

Brownie Cake Dessert

Serve this dense, chewy, rich chocolate cake with ice cream for a finishing touch.

Hard margarine (or butter)	1/2 cup	125 mL
Unsweetened chocolate baking squares (1 oz., 28 g, each), cut up	2	2
Large eggs	2	2
Granulated sugar	1 cup	250 mL
Vanilla	1 tsp.	5 mL
All-purpose flour	3/4 cup	175 mL
Baking powder	3/4 tsp.	4 mL
Salt	1/4 tsp.	1 mL
Chopped walnuts (optional)	1/2 cup	125 mL
CHOCOLATE GLAZE		
Semi-sweet chocolate baking squares (1 oz., 28 g, each), cut up	1 1/2	1 1/2
Milk	2 tbsp.	30 mL

Coarsely chopped walnuts, for garnish

Melt margarine and chocolate in medium saucepan on low, stirring often, until smooth. Cool.

Beat eggs in medium bowl until frothy. Beat in sugar and vanilla. Add chocolate mixture. Mix.

Add flour, baking powder and salt. Stir until just moistened.

Add walnuts. Stir. Turn into greased 8 x 8 inch (20 x 20 cm) pan. Bake in 350°F (175°C) oven for about 30 minutes until wooden pick inserted in centre comes clean. Do not overbake.

Chocolate Glaze: Combine chocolate and milk in small saucepan. Heat and stir on low until chocolate is melted. Smooth over warm cake.

Garnish with walnuts. Cuts into 12 wedges.

1 wedge: 226 Calories; 12.6 g Total Fat; 180 mg Sodium; 3 g Protein; 28 g Carbohydrate; 1 g Dietary Fibre

Pictured on page 108.

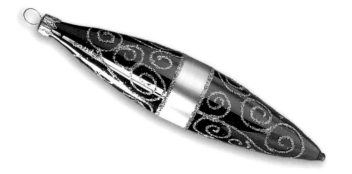

Chocolate Raspberry Biscotti

A wonderful biscotti with a hint of hazelnut.

Hard margarine (or butter), softened	1/3 cup	75 mL
Granulated sugar	1/2 cup	125 mL
Sweetened powdered raspberry-flavoured drink crystals	3 tbsp.	50 mL
Large egg	1	1
Egg yolk (large)	1	1
Cocoa, sifted if lumpy	1/4 cup	60 mL
Baking powder	1 1/2 tsp.	7 mL
Salt	1/4 tsp.	1 mL
All-purpose flour, approximately	1 1/2 cups	375 mL
Egg white (large)	1	1
Water	1 tsp.	5 mL
Flaked hazelnuts (filberts)	2 1/2 tbsp.	37 mL
White (or pink) chocolate melting wafers (optional)	1 cup	250 mL

Beat first 3 ingredients together in large bowl until thoroughly combined. Beat in egg and egg yolk until smooth.

Add cocoa, baking powder and salt. Mix well.

Gradually work in enough flour until stiff dough forms. Turn out onto lightly floured surface. Knead until smooth. Shape into log about 8 1/2 inches (21 cm) long. Flatten slightly to 1 1/2 inches (3.8 cm) high. Place on lightly greased baking sheet.

Beat egg white and water together in small dish using fork. Brush over log.

Sprinkle with hazelnuts. Bake in 375°F (190°C) oven for about 20 minutes until firm and wooden pick inserted in centre comes out clean. Remove to wire rack to cool for 1 hour. Reduce oven heat to 325°F (160°C). Cut, on slight diagonal, into 1/2 inch (12 mm) slices. Arrange, cut side down, on lightly greased baking sheet. Bake for 20 to 25 minutes, turning at halftime, until surface appears quite dry. Remove to wire rack to cool.

Heat chocolate in small glass bowl over saucepan over simmering water, stirring occasionally, until just melted. Dip biscotti halfway into chocolate, allowing excess chocolate to drip back into bowl. Place on waxed paper-lined baking sheets to dry. Makes 16 biscotti.

1 biscotti: 133 Calories; 5.7 g Total Fat; 129 mg Sodium; 3 g Protein; 19 g Carbohydrate; 1 g Dietary Fibre

Pictured on page 109.

Orange Cheesecake

A beautiful cheesecake with a decidedly orange flair.

CRUST

All-purpose flour	1 cup	250 mL
Granulated sugar	1/4 cup	60 mL
Hard margarine (or butter)	1/2 cup	125 mL

FILLING

Blocks of light cream cheese (8 oz., 250 g, each), softened	4	4
Granulated sugar	1 1/4 cups	300 mL
All-purpose flour	2 tbsp.	30 mL
Frozen concentrated orange juice, thawed	3 tbsp.	50 mL
Finely grated orange rind	2 tbsp.	30 mL
Large eggs	4	4

GLAZE

Can of mandarin orange segments, drained and juice reserved	10 oz.	284 mL
Frozen concentrated orange juice	2 tbsp.	30 mL
Water	1/4 cup	60 mL
Cornstarch	1 1/2 tbsp.	25 mL
Granulated sugar	2 tbsp.	30 mL
Whipped topping, for garnish	1/2 cup	125 mL
Chocolate curls, for garnish	24	24

Crust: Combine flour and sugar in medium bowl. Cut in margarine until crumbly. Press into ungreased 9 inch (22 cm) springform pan. Bake in 350°F (175°C) oven for 15 minutes. Cool.

Filling: Beat cream cheese, sugar, flour, concentrated orange juice and orange rind together in large bowl until smooth. Beat in eggs, 1 at a time, on low until just blended. Turn into crust. Bake on bottom rack in 350°F (175°C) oven for about 60 minutes until set. Run knife around side to allow cheesecake to settle evenly. Cool. Remove side of pan.

Glaze: Arrange orange segments in attractive pattern on top of cheesecake.

Pour reserved mandarin orange juice into medium saucepan. Add frozen orange juice and water. Stir well. Stir in cornstarch and sugar. Heat and stir on medium until clear and slightly thickened. Pour over cheesecake. Chill.

Garnish with whipped topping and chocolate curls. Cuts into 16 wedges.

1 wedge: 349 Calories; 19.5 g Total Fat; 524 mg Sodium; 9 g Protein; 36 g Carbohydrate; 1 g Dietary Fibre

Pictured on page 109.

Chocolate Oatmeal Cake

Moist, dark chocolate cake.
Top with Tropical Fruit Sauce, page 110.

Quick-cooking rolled oats (not instant)	1 cup	250 mL
Cocoa, sifted if lumpy	1/3 cup	75 mL
Boiling water	1 1/2 cups	375 mL
Hard margarine (or butter), softened	1/2 cup	125 mL
Brown sugar, packed	1 cup	250 mL
Large eggs	2	2
Vanilla	1 tsp.	5 mL
All-purpose flour	1 1/4 cups	300 mL
Baking soda	1 tsp.	5 mL
Salt	1 tsp.	5 mL
Mini semi-sweet chocolate chips	1/3 cup	75 mL

Combine rolled oats and cocoa in small bowl. Pour boiling water over top. Let stand for 15 minutes.

Cream margarine and brown sugar together in large bowl. Beat in eggs, 1 at a time, beating well after each addition. Add vanilla and rolled oat mixture. Beat until blended.

Add flour, baking soda and salt. Beat on medium for about 1 minute until well mixed.

Stir in chocolate chips. Turn into greased 9 inch (22 cm) round pan. Bake in 350°F (175°C) oven for about 55 minutes until wooden pick inserted in centre comes out clean. Cuts into 8 to 10 pieces.

1 piece: 409 Calories; 17.2 g Total Fat; 633 mg Sodium; 7 g Protein; 60 g Carbohydrate; 3 g Dietary Fibre

Pictured on page 108.

Photo Legend next page:

1. White Chocolate Cherry Cheesecake, page 110
2. Chocolate Raspberry Biscotti, page 106
3. Orange Cheesecake, this page
4. Chocolate Oatmeal Cake, above
5. Tropical Fruit Sauce, page 110
6. Brownie Cake Dessert, page 106

White Chocolate Cherry Cheesecake

So pretty when cut and the bits of cherry peek out.
A decadent dessert!

CRUST
Hard margarine (or butter)	1/2 cup	125 mL
Digestive biscuit crumbs (about 12 biscuits)	1 1/2 cups	375 mL
Cocoa, sifted if lumpy	3 tbsp.	50 mL
Ground almonds	1/2 cup	125 mL

FILLING
Blocks of cream cheese (8 oz., 250 g, each), room temperature	3	3
Sour cream	1 cup	250 mL
Granulated sugar	1/2 cup	125 mL
Cherry-flavoured liqueur (such as Kirsch) or maraschino cherry syrup	3 tbsp.	50 mL
Large eggs	4	4
White chocolate baking squares (1 oz., 28 g, each), cut up	6	6
All-purpose flour	2 tbsp.	30 mL
Quartered maraschino cherries, blotted dry	2/3 cup	150 mL
Whipping cream (or 1 envelope dessert topping, prepared)	1 cup	250 mL
Icing (confectioner's) sugar	1 tbsp.	15 mL
Maraschino cherries, for garnish		
Shaved white chocolate, for garnish		

Crust: Melt margarine in medium saucepan on low. Add biscuit crumbs, cocoa and almonds. Stir until well mixed. Firmly press into bottom and 1 inch (2.5 cm) up side of ungreased 10 inch (25 cm) springform pan.

Filling: Beat cream cheese, sour cream and granulated sugar together in large bowl until light and fluffy.

Beat in liqueur. Add eggs, 1 at a time, beating on low until just mixed.

Heat chocolate in heavy medium saucepan on lowest heat, stirring often, until just melted. Beat into cream cheese mixture on low speed.

Toss flour and cherries together in separate small bowl until cherries are coated. Stir into cream cheese mixture. Turn into crust. Bake on bottom rack in 325°F (160°C) oven for 1 1/4 to 1 1/2 hours until centre is almost set and top is golden. Run knife around side to allow cheesecake to settle evenly. Cool. Remove side of pan.

Beat whipping cream and icing sugar together until stiff peaks form. Pipe rosettes over surface of cheesecake. Garnish with cherries and chocolate. Cuts into 12 wedges.

1 wedge: 607 Calories; 48.1 g Total Fat; 396 mg Sodium; 11 g Protein; 34 g Carbohydrate; 1 g Dietary Fibre

Pictured on page 108.

Tropical Fruit Sauce

A sweet sauce with visible cherries and mangoes.
Serve over Chocolate Oatmeal Cake, page 107.

Can of cherry pie filling	19 oz.	540 mL
Can of crushed pineapple, with juice	14 oz.	398 mL
Can of sliced mango, with syrup, diced	14 oz.	398 mL
Granulated sugar	1/3 cup	75 mL
Halved maraschino cherries	1/2 cup	125 mL
Coconut (or almond) flavouring	1 tsp.	5 mL

Heat first 5 ingredients in medium saucepan, stirring occasionally, until boiling.

Stir in flavouring. Store in airtight container in refrigerator for up to 4 weeks or freeze for up to 4 months. To serve, thaw at room temperature. Makes 6 1/2 cups (1.6 L).

2 tbsp. (30 mL): 28 Calories; trace Total Fat; 1 mg Sodium; trace Protein; 7 g Carbohydrate; trace Dietary Fibre

Pictured on page 108.

BANANA FRUIT SAUCE: Stir 1/2 cup (125 mL) broken up banana chips into sauce with flavouring. Banana chips will soften in sauce.

COCONUT FRUIT SAUCE: Stir 1/2 cup (125 mL) flake (or fancy) coconut into sauce with flavouring.

Main Dishes

Cajun Chicken

This slow cooker recipe is tops in flavour!
The tender chicken falls off the bones. Serve with
a hearty rye or pumpernickel bread.

Large onion, chopped	1	1
Garlic cloves, minced (or 1 tsp., 5 mL, powder)	4	4
Large red pepper, chopped	1	1
Large celery rib, chopped	1	1
Cooking oil	2 tbsp.	30 mL
All-purpose flour	2 tbsp.	30 mL
Green onions, sliced	4	4
Lean kielbasa (or ham) sausage ring, cut into 6 pieces, each piece halved lengthwise	10 oz.	300 g
Chicken thighs (about 10 pieces), skin removed	2 lbs.	900 g
Bay leaf	1	1
Can of condensed chicken broth	10 oz.	284 mL
Chili powder	1 1/2 tsp.	7 mL
Dried sweet basil	1/2 tsp.	2 mL
Dried whole oregano	1/2 tsp.	2 mL
Ground thyme	1/4 tsp.	1 mL
Pepper	1/4 tsp.	1 mL
Chili sauce	1/2 cup	125 mL

Sauté onion, garlic, red pepper and celery in cooking oil in large frying pan for 3 to 4 minutes until onion is soft.

Sprinkle flour over vegetable mixture. Stir well. Turn into 4 quart (4 L) slow cooker.

Layer green onion, sausage and chicken over vegetable mixture. Drop in bay leaf.

Combine remaining 7 ingredients in same frying pan. Heat and stir for 5 minutes, scraping up any brown bits from frying pan, until heated through. Pour over chicken. Cover. Cook on Low for 7 to 8 hours or on High for 3 1/2 to 4 hours. Serves 6 to 8.

1 serving: 341 Calories; 16.5 g Total Fat; 1103 mg Sodium; 32 g Protein; 16 g Carbohydrate; 3 g Dietary Fibre

Pictured on page 112.

Top Left: Cajun Chicken, page 111　　　　Bottom Centre: Beef Bourguignon, below　　　　Top Right: Slow-Cooker Lamb Curry, page 113

Beef Bourguignon

A wonderful, rich and hearty stew that can be made ahead for a crowd. Serve over egg noodles or mashed potatoes.

Boneless sirloin tip roast, cut into 1 1/4 inch (3 cm) cubes	5 lbs.	2.3 kg
Hard margarine (or butter)	1 tbsp.	15 mL
Dried rosemary, crushed	1 tsp.	5 mL
Dried thyme, crushed	1 tsp.	5 mL
Dried whole oregano	1 tsp.	5 mL
Medium onions, cut lengthwise in 8 wedges	5	5
Brown (cremini) mushrooms, halved if large	6 cups	1.5 L
Garlic cloves, minced (or 1 tsp., 5 mL, powder)	4	4
Sliced carrot, cut 1/4 inch (6 mm) thick	3 1/2 cups	875 mL
Can of condensed beef broth	10 oz.	284 mL
Dry red (or alcohol-free) wine	2 cups	500 mL
Water	1 cup	250 mL
Can of tomato paste	5 1/2 oz.	156 mL
Parsley flakes	1 tbsp.	15 mL
Salt	1 tsp.	5 mL
Granulated sugar	1/2 tsp.	2 mL
Coarsely ground pepper	1/2 tsp.	2 mL
Water	1 1/2 cups	375 mL
All-purpose flour	3/4 cup	175 mL

Brown beef, in 3 batches, in margarine in large frying pan on medium-high, adding more margarine as needed. Transfer to large roasting pan.

Add rosemary, thyme and oregano. Stir.

Sauté onion, mushrooms and garlic in same frying pan for about 5 minutes, scraping up any browned bits from frying pan, until onion is clear and soft. Add to beef mixture.

Add carrot.

Combine next 8 ingredients in same frying pan. Reduce heat to medium. Heat and stir for about 5 minutes until boiling. Add to beef mixture. Stir. Cover. Cook in 325°F (160°C) oven for 1 1/2 hours until beef is tender.

Stir water into flour in small bowl until smooth. Stir into beef mixture. Cover. Cook in oven for 30 minutes until boiling and thickened. Makes twenty 3 oz. (84 g) servings.

1 serving: 240 Calories; 6.9 g Total Fat; 312 mg Sodium; 28 g Protein; 12 g Carbohydrate; 2 g Dietary Fibre

Pictured above.

Slow-Cooker Lamb Curry

Lots of mild curry sauce, with a subtle coconut flavour, to serve over rice or potatoes.

All-purpose flour	2 tbsp.	30 mL
Seasoned salt	1 tsp.	5 mL
Cayenne pepper	1/4 tsp.	1 mL
Lean lamb stew meat, trimmed of fat and cut into 1 inch (2.5 cm) pieces	1 lb.	454 g
Cooking oil	2 tbsp.	30 mL
Sliced carrot	1 1/2 cups	375 mL
Cauliflower florets	1 cup	250 mL
Coarsely chopped green pepper	1 cup	250 mL
Medium onion, coarsely chopped	1	1
Garlic cloves, minced (or 1/2 tsp., 2 mL, powder)	2	2
Mild curry paste	2 tbsp.	30 mL
Can of condensed chicken broth	10 oz.	284 mL
Reserved pineapple juice	1/4 cup	60 mL
Can of pineapple chunks, drained and juice reserved	14 oz.	398 mL
Grated solid coconut cream (1/2 of 7 1/2 oz., 200 g, package)	2/3 cup	150 mL
All-purpose flour	2 tbsp.	30 mL
Plain yogurt	1/2 cup	125 mL
Chopped fresh cilantro (or mint), optional	2 tbsp.	30 mL

Combine first amount of flour, seasoned salt and cayenne pepper in large resealable plastic bag. Add lamb. Shake until completely coated.

Brown lamb in cooking oil in large frying pan. Turn into 3 quart (3 L) slow cooker.

Add carrot, cauliflower and green pepper. Stir.

Sauté onion, garlic and curry paste in same frying pan for 2 minutes.

Slowly add chicken broth and reserved pineapple juice. Heat and stir for about 5 minutes, scraping up any browned bits from pan, until boiling. Add to lamb mixture. Stir. Cover. Cook on Low for 6 hours or on High for 3 hours.

Stir in pineapple and coconut cream into lamb mixture.

Stir second amount of flour into yogurt in small bowl until smooth. Stir into lamb mixture with heat on high. Cover. Cook for about 1 hour until sauce is thickened.

Sprinkle with cilantro. Makes 7 cups (1.75 L).

1 cup (250 mL): 297 Calories; 14.7 g Total Fat; 521 mg Sodium; 18 g Protein; 24 g Carbohydrate; 4 g Dietary Fibre

Pictured on page 112.

Tangy Beef Rolls

Mild horseradish and rich tomato flavours in these rolls. Serve with rice or noodles.

Cream cheese, softened	2 oz.	62.5 g
Prepared horseradish	2 tsp.	10 mL
Minute steaks (about 1 lb., 454 g, in total)	4	4
Cooking oil	1 tsp.	5 mL
Chopped fresh mushrooms	1 cup	250 mL
Hard margarine (or butter)	1/2 tsp.	2 mL
Can of tomato sauce	7 1/2 oz.	213 mL
Dried marjoram, crushed	1/2 tsp.	2 mL
Salt	1/2 tsp.	2 mL
Pepper	1/4 tsp.	1 mL

Combine cream cheese and horseradish in small bowl. Spread over 1 side of each steak. Roll up. Secure with wooden picks. Brown rolls in cooking oil in non-stick frying pan. Remove rolls to plate. Keep warm.

Sauté mushrooms in margarine in same frying pan for 2 minutes.

Stir in tomato sauce, marjoram, salt and pepper. Add rolls. Bring to a boil. Reduce heat. Cover. Simmer for 10 minutes. Serves 4.

1 serving: 258 Calories; 13.6 g Total Fat; 752 mg Sodium; 28 g Protein; 6 g Carbohydrate; 1 g Dietary Fibre

Pictured on page 115.

Don't remove the lid on your slow cooker unless instructed to do so in the recipe. Each time the cover is removed, quite a lot of heat is lost, lengthening the cooking time.

Roast Duck

Succulent duck with a different, yet scrumptious, dressing.
Serve with applesauce, chutney or relish.

SAGE STUFFING		
Medium onions, chopped	2	2
Hard margarine (or butter)	1 tbsp.	15 mL
Coarse dry bread crumbs	4 cups	1 L
Parsley flakes	2 tsp.	10 mL
Dried sage	2 tsp.	10 mL
Salt	1 tsp.	5 mL
Pepper	1/4 tsp.	1 mL
Prepared orange juice, approximately	1 cup	250 mL
Domestic duck	6 lbs.	2.7 kg
GRAVY		
Fat drippings	1/4 cup	60 mL
All-purpose flour	1/4 cup	60 mL
Salt	1/2 tsp.	2 mL
Pepper	1/8 tsp.	0.5 mL
Drippings without fat (if any), plus water to make	2 cups	500 mL

Sage Stuffing: Sauté onion in margarine in frying pan until soft.

Combine next 5 ingredients in medium bowl. Add onion. Stir.

Add enough orange juice until stuffing is moist and holds together when squeezed.

Stuff duck with stuffing. Fasten with skewer. Tie wings to body with string. Tie legs to tail. Pierce skin all over with tip of paring knife to allow fat to run out. Put into roasting pan. Cover. Roast in 350°F (175°C) oven for about 2 1/2 hours until duck is tender, skin is crisp and meat thermometer registers 180°F (82°C). Remove cover. Roast for about 15 minutes until browned. Remove duck to serving platter. Tent with foil. Let stand for 10 minutes before carving.

Gravy: Pour off all but 1/4 cup (60 mL) drippings in roaster. Mix in flour, salt and pepper until smooth.

Stir in drippings and water. Heat and stir until boiling and thickened. Taste for salt and pepper, adding more as needed. Makes 2 cups (500 mL). Serves 8.

1 serving: 779 Calories; 48.3 g Total Fat; 1032 mg Sodium; 33 g Protein; 51 g Carbohydrate; 3 g Dietary Fibre

Pictured on page 115.

Stuffed Chicken Rolls

The seasoned sauce and Swiss cheese are just the right things for this delicious chicken cooked in the slow cooker.

Boneless, skinless chicken breast halves (about 1 1/2 lbs., 680 g)	6	6
Thin deli ham slices, cut to fit chicken	6	6
Hot water	1/2 cup	125 mL
Chicken bouillon powder	2 tsp.	10 mL
White (or alcohol-free) wine (or apple juice)	1/2 cup	125 mL
Liquid gravy browner (optional)	1 tsp.	5 mL
Dried marjoram	1/2 tsp.	2 mL
Salt	1/2 tsp.	2 mL
Pepper	1/4 tsp.	1 mL
Grated Swiss cheese	1 cup	250 mL
Water	2 1/2 tbsp.	37 mL
Cornstarch	1 tbsp.	15 mL

Place chicken breasts between sheets of plastic wrap. Pound with meat mallet or rolling pin until very thin. Lay 1 ham slice on each chicken breast. Roll up. Secure with wooden picks. Arrange in 3 1/2 quart (3.5 L) slow cooker.

Measure next 7 ingredients into small bowl. Stir. Pour over chicken rolls. Cover. Cook on Low for 8 to 9 hours or on High for 4 to 4 1/2 hours.

Remove chicken rolls to serving dish using slotted spoon. Scatter cheese over chicken rolls to melt. Keep warm.

Stir water into cornstarch in separate small bowl until smooth. Stir into liquid in slow cooker with heat on High. Cover. Cook for 15 minutes, stirring occasionally, until slightly thickened. Makes about 1 1/3 cups (325 mL) sauce. Serves 6.

1 serving: 284 Calories; 11.1 g Total Fat; 932 mg Sodium; 37 g Protein; 3 g Carbohydrate; trace Dietary Fibre

Pictured on page 115.

Top Left: Greek Pea Salad, page 138
Top Right: Roast Duck, this page
Centre Left: Tangy Beef Rolls, page 113
Bottom Right: Stuffed Chicken Rolls, above

Portobello Penne

Rich mushroom, walnut and cheese flavours make this pasta dish very satisfying. Serve with a green salad.

Penne pasta (about 10 oz., 285 g)	3 1/3 cups	825 mL
Boiling water	12 cups	3 L
Salt	1 tbsp.	15 mL
Garlic clove, minced (or 1/4 tsp., 1 mL, powder)	1	1
Medium portobello mushrooms, black "gills" cut off and discarded, coarsely chopped	3	3
Olive (or cooking) oil	2 tsp.	10 mL
Dry white (or alcohol-free) wine	1/4 cup	60 mL
Can of evaporated milk	13 1/2 oz.	385 mL
Milk	1/3 cup	75 mL
Dijon mustard	2 tsp.	10 mL
Salt	1/2 tsp.	2 mL
Diced Havarti cheese (about 1/3 lb., 150 g)	1 cup	250 mL
Coarsely chopped walnuts, toasted (see Tip, page 100)	1/4 cup	60 mL

Cook pasta in boiling water and salt in large uncovered pot or Dutch oven for 12 to 15 minutes until tender but firm. Drain. Transfer to large bowl. Keep warm.

Sauté garlic and mushrooms in olive oil in large frying pan for about 5 minutes until mushrooms are barely tender.

Add wine. Boil, uncovered, until liquid reduces by half.

Centre Left: Portobello Penne, above
Bottom Right: Chicken Raspberry, this page

Add next 4 ingredients. Bring to a boil. Reduce heat. Simmer, uncovered, for about 10 minutes, stirring occasionally, until sauce reduces slightly. The sauce will still be quite thin but will thicken when combined with pasta. Add to pasta.

Add cheese and walnuts. Toss gently until cheese begins to melt and some sauce is absorbed into pasta. Makes 6 cups (1.5 L).

1 cup (250 mL): 429 Calories; 17.7 g Total Fat; 497 mg Sodium; 20 g Protein; 47 g Carbohydrate; 2 g Dietary Fibre

Pictured on this page.

Chicken Raspberry

Nicely browned, tender chicken enhanced by raspberry vinegar and rosemary.

Hard margarine (or butter)	1 tbsp.	15 mL
Cooking oil	1 tbsp.	15 mL
Boneless, skinless chicken breast halves (about 1 1/2 lbs., 680 g)	6	6
Salt, sprinkle		
Pepper, sprinkle		
Ground rosemary	1/4 tsp.	1 mL
Finely chopped onion	1/4 cup	60 mL
Raspberry vinegar	1/3 cup	75 mL
Water	1/2 cup	125 mL
Chicken bouillon powder	1 tsp.	5 mL
Dried chives	1 tsp.	5 mL

Heat margarine and cooking oil in frying pan. Add chicken. Brown both sides, sprinkling with salt, pepper and rosemary. Transfer to plate. Keep warm.

Sauté onion in same frying pan, scraping up any browned bits from pan, until golden.

Add vinegar, water and bouillon powder. Boil for 5 minutes until slightly reduced. Makes 1/3 cup (75 mL) sauce.

Add chives. Stir. Add chicken. Bring to a boil. Reduce heat. Cover. Simmer for about 5 minutes to blend flavours. Serves 6.

1 serving: 173 Calories; 6.3 g Total Fat; 132 mg Sodium; 26 g Protein; 2 g Carbohydrate; trace Dietary Fibre

Pictured on this page.

Left: Creamy Onion Sauce, page 118   Top Centre: Shrimp Marinara Sauce, page 118   Bottom Right: Creamy Seafood Sauce, this page

Creamy Seafood Sauce

A rich sauce you won't believe is low in fat! A lot of great colour in this delicious sauce. Serve over pasta.

Raw medium shrimp (about 15), peeled and deveined (or frozen, thawed)	1/2 lb.	225 g
Fresh (or frozen, thawed) small scallops	1/2 lb.	225 g
Water	1/2 cup	125 mL
White (or alcohol-free) wine (or sherry)	1/4 cup	60 mL
Seafood (or chicken) bouillon powder	1 tsp.	5 mL
Garlic clove, minced (or 1/4 tsp., 1 mL, powder)	1	1
Small zucchini, diced	1	1
Small broccoli florets	2 cups	500 mL
Sliced fresh mushrooms	1 cup	250 mL
Diced red pepper	1/2 cup	125 mL
Green onions, sliced	2	2
Ripe medium roma (plum) tomato, diced	1	1
Basil pesto	2 tbsp.	30 mL
Can of skim evaporated milk	13 1/2 oz.	385 mL
All-purpose flour	3 tbsp.	50 mL

Combine first 5 ingredients in medium saucepan on medium-high. Bring to a boil. Reduce heat to medium. Simmer, uncovered, for 3 minutes until shrimp is pink. Do not drain. Remove seafood to small bowl using slotted spoon. Cover. Keep warm.

Add garlic, zucchini, broccoli and mushrooms to liquid in saucepan. Bring to a boil. Reduce heat to medium. Cover. Simmer for 3 minutes.

Add red pepper, green onion, tomato and pesto. Bring to a boil. Reduce heat. Cover. Simmer for 3 minutes.

Stir evaporated milk into flour in small bowl until smooth. Stir into vegetable mixture until boiling and thickened. Gently stir in shrimp and scallops until heated through. Makes 7 cups (1.75 L).

3/4 cup (175 mL): 125 Calories; 2.4 g Total Fat; 204 mg Sodium; 14 g Protein; 11 g Carbohydrate; 1 g Dietary Fibre

Pictured above.

Creamy Onion Sauce

A thin, sweet, versatile sauce with a hint of nutmeg. Serve over pasta or as an accompaniment to beef, chicken or fish.

Medium Spanish (or white) onions, coarsely chopped	2	2
Hard margarine (or butter)	2 tbsp.	30 mL
Brown sugar, packed	1 tsp.	5 mL
Water	1 cup	250 mL
Vegetable (or chicken) bouillon powder	2 tsp.	10 mL
Can of evaporated milk	13 1/2 oz.	385 mL
Cornstarch	2 tsp.	10 mL

Salt, sprinkle
Pepper, sprinkle
Ground nutmeg, sprinkle

Fresh sprigs of parsley, for garnish

Sauté onion in margarine in large frying pan until soft. Reduce heat to low.

Stir in brown sugar. Cover. Cook for about 15 minutes, stirring occasionally, until onion is very soft and beginning to turn golden.

Add water and bouillon powder. Stir well. Bring to a boil. Reduce heat. Cover. Simmer for 30 minutes. Cool slightly.

Combine onion mixture and 1/2 of evaporated milk in blender. Process until very smooth. Return to frying pan.

Stir remaining evaporated milk into cornstarch in small bowl until smooth. Stir into onion mixture.

Add salt, pepper and nutmeg. Heat and stir until boiling and slightly thickened.

Garnish with parsley. Makes 3 cups (750 mL).

1/4 cup (60 mL): 76 Calories; 4.7 g Total Fat; 168 mg Sodium; 3 g Protein; 6 g Carbohydrate; trace Dietary Fibre

Pictured on page 117.

To warm your plates just before using, place them in the oven on lowest heat for 2 minutes. Turn heat off.

Shrimp Marinara Sauce

The sweet tang of vinegar and herbs is nicely balanced with shrimp. Thin, tomato-coloured broth with chunky pieces. Serve over your favourite pasta. Garnish with finely grated Parmesan cheese.

Garlic cloves, minced (or 1/2 tsp., 2 mL, powder)	2	2
Chopped onion	1/2 cup	125 mL
Olive (or cooking) oil	2 tbsp.	30 mL
Can of diced tomatoes, with juice	28 oz.	796 mL
Dried whole oregano	1 1/2 tsp.	7 mL
Dried sweet basil	1 1/2 tsp.	7 mL
Red wine vinegar	1 tbsp.	15 mL
Granulated sugar	1 1/2 tbsp.	25 mL
Salt	1/2 tsp.	2 mL
Pepper	1/2 tsp.	2 mL
Cooked salad shrimp	8 oz.	225 g

Sauté garlic and onion in olive oil in large frying pan until onion is soft.

Add next 7 ingredients. Stir. Bring to a boil. Reduce heat. Simmer, uncovered, for 30 minutes.

Stir in shrimp. Cook for 3 to 4 minutes until heated through. Makes 3 2/3 cups (900 mL).

3/4 cup (175 mL): 148 Calories; 6.3 g Total Fat; 586 mg Sodium; 11 g Protein; 13 g Carbohydrate; 2 g Dietary Fibre

Pictured on page 117.

Paprika Stew With Zucchini Biscuits

A hearty, chunky stew with puffy golden biscuit topping and very tender beef.

Beef stew meat, cut into 1 1/2 inch (3.8 cm) pieces	2 lbs.	900 g
Cooking oil	2 tbsp.	30 mL
Medium onions, cut into 6 wedges each	4	4
Garlic clove, minced (or 1/4 tsp., 1 mL, powder)	1	1
Paprika	4 tsp.	20 mL
Hot water	1 cup	250 mL
Cans of diced tomatoes (14 oz., 398 mL, each), with liquid	2	2
Can of tomato paste	5 1/2 oz.	156 mL
Seasoned salt	1 tsp.	5 mL
Pepper	1/4 tsp.	1 mL
Medium carrots, sliced into 1/2 inch (12 mm) pieces	5	5
Celery ribs, cut into 1 1/2 inch (3.8 cm) pieces	4	4
Red (or alcohol-free) wine	1/3 cup	75 mL
ZUCCHINI BISCUITS		
Biscuit mix	2 1/2 cups	625 mL
Grated zucchini, with peel	2/3 cup	150 mL
Sour cream	1/2 cup	125 mL

Brown beef, in 2 batches, in cooking oil in large frying pan. Remove to ungreased 4 quart (4 L) casserole using slotted spoon.

Add onion, garlic and paprika to same frying pan. Sauté for 3 to 4 minutes, scraping up any browned bits from pan, until onion is soft.

Stir in hot water. Bring to a boil. Pour over beef.

Add next 7 ingredients to beef mixture. Stir. Cover. Bake in 325°F (160°C) oven for 2 1/2 hours. Increase heat to 425°F (220°C).

Zucchini Biscuits: Combine biscuit mix, zucchini and sour cream in medium bowl until just moistened. Turn out onto lightly floured surface. Knead 5 or 6 times until dough holds together. Pat out to same diameter as casserole surface. Cut into wedges or pieces. Assemble on top of beef mixture. Bake, uncovered, for about 15 minutes until biscuits are golden. Serves 8.

1 serving: 500 Calories; 20.5 g Total Fat; 945 mg Sodium; 32 g Protein; 46 g Carbohydrate; 5 g Dietary Fibre

Pictured on page 120.

Saucy Chicken

Good homemade flavour with a little bite and lots of excellent sauce to serve over fettuccine noodles or rice.

Chicken parts, skin and visible fat removed	4 lbs.	1.8 kg
Envelope of dry onion soup mix	1 1/2 oz.	42 g
Can of whole cranberry sauce	14 oz.	398 mL
French dressing	1 cup	250 mL

Arrange chicken in roasting pan.

Combine soup mix, cranberry sauce and dressing in medium bowl. Spoon over chicken, being sure to get some on every piece. Cover tightly with lid or foil. Bake in 350°F (175°C) oven for 1 hour. Remove cover. Baste chicken with sauce. Cover. Bake for 30 minutes until chicken is tender. Serves 6 to 8.

1 serving: 488 Calories; 22.5 g Total Fat; 1464 mg Sodium; 32 g Protein; 40 g Carbohydrate; 1 g Dietary Fibre

Pictured on page 120.

Gypsy Stew

Comfort food with very Old World flavour.
Serve over buttered noodles or mashed potatoes.

Bacon slices, chopped	6	6
Lean pork stew meat	2 1/4 lbs.	1 kg
Large onions, halved lengthwise and thinly sliced	2	2
Garlic cloves, minced (or 3/4 tsp., 4 mL, powder)	3	3
Paprika	4 tsp.	20 mL
Caraway seed	1 tsp.	5 mL
Water	2 cups	500 mL
Jar of sauerkraut, rinsed and drained	17 1/2 oz.	500 mL
Chicken bouillon powder	1 tsp.	5 mL
All-purpose flour	2 tbsp.	30 mL
Sour cream	1 cup	250 mL
Salt, sprinkle		
Pepper, sprinkle		
Bacon slice, cooked crisp and crumbled, for garnish	1	1

Fry first amount of bacon in large uncovered pot or Dutch oven until browned. Drain all but 1 tbsp. (15 mL) drippings.

Add pork, onion, garlic, paprika and caraway seed to bacon. Sauté for about 10 minutes, stirring frequently, until onion is soft.

Stir in water. Bring to a boil. Reduce heat. Cover. Simmer for 1 hour.

Stir in sauerkraut and bouillon powder. Bring to a boil. Reduce heat. Cover. Simmer for 45 to 60 minutes until pork is tender.

Stir flour into sour cream in small bowl until smooth. Stir into pork mixture for about 10 minutes on low until boiling and slightly thickened.

Add salt and pepper. Stir.

Sprinkle second amount of bacon over individual servings. Makes 8 cups (2 L).

1 cup (250 mL): 307 Calories; 16.5 g Total Fat; 565 mg Sodium; 29 g Protein; 10 g Carbohydrate; 2 g Dietary Fibre

Pictured below.

Top Left: Paprika Stew With Zucchini Biscuits, page 119
Top Right: Saucy Chicken, page 119
Bottom Centre: Gypsy Stew, above

Stuffed Turkey Breast

The cranberry stuffing imparts a tart but subtle sweetness.
A very impressive presentation. This may look complicated
and fussy, but is really very easy. The drippings can be used
for making gravy. Leftover turkey can be used to
make Meaty Turkey Rice Soup, page 157.

SPICED CRANBERRY STUFFING

Chopped onion	1/2 cup	125 mL
Chopped celery	1/2 cup	125 mL
Garlic cloves, minced (or 1/2 tsp., 2 mL, powder), optional	2	2
Hard margarine (or butter)	1/4 cup	60 mL
Chopped cranberries	2/3 cup	150 mL
Grated peeled tart cooking apple (such as Granny Smith)	1/2 cup	125 mL
Fine dry bread crumbs	1/2 cup	125 mL
Brown sugar, packed	1 tbsp.	15 mL
Ground cinnamon	1/4 tsp.	1 mL
Ground nutmeg	1/8 tsp.	0.5 mL
Ground allspice	1/8 tsp.	0.5 mL
Cayenne pepper	1/8 tsp.	0.5 mL
Salt	1/2 tsp.	2 mL
Pepper	1/8 tsp.	0.5 mL
Apple juice (or water), approximately	1 tbsp.	15 mL
Whole bone-in turkey breast (see Note)	6 lbs.	2.7 kg
Margarine (or butter), melted	2 tbsp.	30 mL
Seasoned salt	1/2 tsp.	2 mL
Pepper, sprinkle		

Spiced Cranberry Stuffing: Sauté onion, celery and garlic in margarine in large frying pan for about 4 minutes until onion is soft. Remove from heat.

Add next 10 ingredients. Mix well.

Add enough apple juice until stuffing is moist and holds together when squeezed.

Cut turkey crosswise into 1 inch (2.5 cm) thick slices right to the bone on both sides. You should be able to cut about 6 slices on each side. Use very sharp knife to keep skin intact. Divide stuffing among "pockets" cut into turkey. Tie butcher's string horizontally around turkey once or twice to hold slices with stuffing together. Place turkey, cut side up, in medium roasting pan.

Drizzle second amount of margarine over turkey. Sprinkle seasoned salt and second amount of pepper over top. Cover. Roast in 325°F (160°C) oven for 1 3/4 to 2 hours, basting turkey several times with juices from bottom of roasting pan, until meat thermometer registers 180°F (82°C). Increase heat to 400°F (205°C). Remove cover. Roast for about 15 minutes until skin is browned. Serves 10 to 12.

1 serving: 404 Calories; 13.9 g Total Fat; 433 mg Sodium; 58 g Protein; 9 g Carbohydrate; 1 g Dietary Fibre

Pictured on page 122.

Note: A 14 to 15 lb. (6.4 to 6.8 kg) turkey will yield a 6 lb. (2.7 kg) turkey breast.

Plan your Christmas meals ahead of time, being realistic and time conscious. Planning ahead will save you the headache of last minute rushes or forgotten items. Check our Menu Suggestions section starting on page 38.

Photo Legend next page:

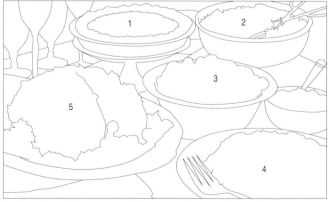

1. Pumpkin Chiffon Pie, page 130
2. Slaw Special, page 137
3. Sautéed Sprouts, page 146
4. Cherry Walnut Cutlets, page 124
5. Stuffed Turkey Breast, this page

Cherry Walnut Cutlets

Feed a bunch with this hearty main dish.

All-purpose flour	1/2 cup	125 mL
Walnuts	1/2 cup	125 mL
Lemon pepper	2 tsp.	10 mL
Seasoned salt	2 tsp.	10 mL
Chicken breast cutlets (about 5 oz., 140 g, each)	12	12
Hard margarine (or butter)	4 tsp.	20 mL
CHERRY SAUCE		
Chopped onion	1 cup	250 mL
Garlic clove, minced (or 1/4 tsp., 1 mL, powder)	1	1
Chopped celery	1/2 cup	125 mL
Grated carrot	1 cup	250 mL
Hard margarine (or butter)	3 tbsp.	50 mL
All-purpose flour	1/4 cup	60 mL
Chicken (or vegetable) bouillon powder	2 tsp.	10 mL
Salt	1/2 tsp.	2 mL
Pepper	1/4 tsp.	1 mL
Ground cloves, just a pinch		
Water	1 cup	250 mL
Red (or alcohol-free) wine	1/2 cup	125 mL
Can of pitted Bing cherries, with juice, halved	14 oz.	398 mL
Chopped walnuts	1/4 cup	60 mL

Measure first 4 ingredients into blender. Process until walnuts are finely chopped. Transfer to shallow dish or onto waxed paper.

Press cutlets in flour mixture on both sides to coat completely. Heat 2 tsp. (10 mL) margarine in large frying pan on medium-high until hot. Brown cutlets, in batches, for about 1 minute per side. Add remaining margarine as needed. Put cutlets into small roasting pan.

Cherry Sauce: Sauté onion, garlic, celery and carrot in margarine in same frying pan until onion is soft.

Add flour, bouillon powder, salt, pepper and cloves. Stir. Stir in water and wine until boiling and thickened.

Add cherries and juice. Bring to a boil. Pour over cutlets. Cover. Bake in 350°F (175°C) oven for 40 minutes until cutlets are no longer pink in centre.

Arrange cutlets on serving platter. Sprinkle walnuts over cutlets. Serves 12.

1 serving: 318 Calories; 12.8 g Total Fat; 572 mg Sodium; 33 g Protein; 15 g Carbohydrate; 1 g Dietary Fibre

Pictured on page 123.

Beef Melt

A different kind of hot beef sandwich with an interesting mix of flavours. A great way to use leftover roast beef.

Whole wheat bread slices (buttered, optional), see Note	4	4
Cooked (or deli) roast beef slices (about 4 oz., 113 g)	4	4
Chili sauce	3 tbsp.	50 mL
Prepared horseradish	1 tsp.	5 mL
Grated Swiss (or medium Cheddar or Monterey Jack) cheese	1/2 cup	125 mL
Pepper, sprinkle (optional)		

Arrange bread slices, buttered side up, on ungreased baking sheet. Top with beef slices.

Combine chili sauce and horseradish in small cup. Spread over beef.

Sprinkle with cheese and pepper. Broil about 8 inches (20 cm) from heat until cheese is melted and lightly browned. Makes 4 melts.

1 melt: 196 Calories; 7.6 g Total Fat; 378 mg Sodium; 16 g Protein; 17 g Carbohydrate; 3 g Dietary Fibre

Pictured on page 125.

Note: Toast 1 side of bread first, if desired. Layer ingredients on untoasted side and broil as directed.

Bottom Left: Beef Melt, page 124

Top Right: Beef Curry Hotpot, this page

Beef Curry Hotpot

The mild curry flavour is complemented by the raisins, apricots and very tender beef. Serve over rice.

Inside round steak, trimmed of fat and cubed	2 lbs.	900 g
Cooking oil	1 tbsp.	15 mL
Medium onions, sliced	2	2
Medium cooking apples (such as McIntosh), peeled, cored and chopped	3	3
Chopped tomato	2 cups	500 mL
Mild (or hot) curry paste	1 tbsp.	15 mL
Water	1 cup	250 mL
Can of condensed beef broth	10 oz.	284 mL
Dark raisins	1/3 cup	75 mL
Chopped dried apricots	1/2 cup	125 mL
Brown sugar, packed	1 tbsp.	15 mL
All-purpose flour	1 tbsp.	15 mL
Pepper, sprinkle		

Brown beef in cooking oil in large frying pan. Transfer to ungreased 4 quart (4 L) casserole.

Sauté onion and apple in same frying pan. Add to beef.

Sauté tomato and curry paste in same frying pan, stirring up any browned bits from pan, until hot and fragrant. Add to beef mixture.

Add water, broth, raisins and apricots to beef mixture. Stir. Cover. Bake in 325°F (160°C) oven for 2 hours until beef is tender.

Combine brown sugar, flour and pepper in small dish. Stir into beef mixture. Cover. Bake for 10 to 15 minutes until boiling and thickened. Makes 8 cups (2 L).

1 cup (250 mL): 261 Calories; 5.9 g Total Fat; 305 mg Sodium; 28 g Protein; 25 g Carbohydrate; 3 g Dietary Fibre

Pictured above.

Slow Cooker Method: Put browned beef mixture into 4 1/2 quart (4.5 L) slow cooker. Cook on Low for 6 to 8 hours or on High for 3 to 4 hours until beef is tender. Stir brown sugar mixture into beef mixture with heat on High. Cover. Cook for 15 minutes until thickened.

Seafood And Shell Stew

A shrimp and fish stew with shell pasta.
Serve with plenty of crusty bread to soak up the broth.

Medium shell pasta	1 cup	250 mL
Boiling water	4 cups	1 L
Salt	1 tsp.	5 mL
AÏOLI SAUCE		
Mayonnaise (not salad dressing)	1/2 cup	125 mL
Garlic clove, minced (or 1/8 tsp., 0.5 mL, powder)	1/2	1/2
Chopped fresh parsley (or 1/4 tsp., 1 mL, flakes)	1 tsp.	5 mL
Medium leeks (white and tender parts only), thinly sliced	2	2
Garlic cloves, minced (or 1/2 tsp., 2 mL, powder)	2	2
Small red pepper, diced	1	1
Fennel seed, crushed	1/4 tsp.	1 mL
Olive (or cooking) oil	1 tbsp.	15 mL
Clam tomato beverage	1 cup	250 mL
Can of stewed tomatoes, with juice, chopped	14 oz.	398 mL
White (or alcohol-free) wine	1/2 cup	125 mL
Water	1 cup	250 mL
Finely grated lemon peel	1/2 tsp.	2 mL
Dried thyme, crushed	1/8 tsp.	0.5 mL
Saffron threads (or turmeric), just a pinch		
Raw medium shrimp (about 30), peeled and deveined (or frozen, thawed)	1 lb.	454 g
Halibut fillets, cut into 1 inch (2.5 cm) chunks	8 oz.	225 g
Cod fillets, cut into 1 inch (2.5 cm) chunks	8 oz.	225 g
Chopped fresh cilantro (optional)	1 tbsp.	15 mL
Chopped fresh parsley (or 3/4 tsp., 4 mL, flakes), optional	1 tbsp.	15 mL
Hot pepper sauce (optional)	1/4 – 1/2 tsp.	1 – 2 mL

Cook pasta in boiling water and salt in medium saucepan for 6 minutes until partially cooked. Drain. Rinse under cold water. Drain. Set aside.

Aïoli Sauce: Combine mayonnaise, garlic and parsley in small bowl. Chill for 30 minutes to blend flavours.

Sauté next 4 ingredients in olive oil in large uncovered pot or Dutch oven for about 5 minutes until leeks are soft.

Add next 7 ingredients. Stir. Cover. Bring to a simmer. Simmer for 15 minutes.

Add remaining 6 ingredients and pasta. Stir. Bring to a boil. Reduce heat. Cover. Simmer for about 10 minutes until fish flakes easily when tested with fork and pasta is tender but firm. Serve with Aïoli Sauce. Makes 8 cups (2 L).

1 cup (250 mL): 353 Calories; 15.7 g Total Fat; 462 mg Sodium; 26 g Protein; 24 g Carbohydrate; 2 g Dietary Fibre

Pictured on page 127.

Stuffed Ham Casserole

Lots of bite-sized ham cubes with a pineapple bread stuffing.

Boneless ham, cut into 1/2 inch (12 mm) pieces (about 5 cups, 1.25 L)	2 lbs.	900 g
PINEAPPLE STUFFING		
Chopped onion	1/2 cup	125 mL
Chopped celery	1/2 cup	125 mL
Hard margarine (or butter)	2 tsp.	10 mL
Can of crushed pineapple, drained, juice reserved	14 oz.	398 mL
Dry coarse bread crumbs	2 cups	500 mL
Poultry seasoning	1 tsp.	5 mL
Parsley flakes	1/2 tsp.	2 mL
Salt (optional)	1/8 tsp.	0.5 mL
Pepper	1/8 tsp.	0.5 mL
Reserved pineapple juice	2 tbsp.	30 mL
SAUCE		
White vinegar	1 tbsp.	15 mL
Cornstarch	1 1/2 tbsp.	25 mL
Brown sugar, packed	1/4 cup	60 mL
Reserved pineapple juice, plus water to make	3/4 cup	175 mL

Scatter 1/2 of ham in greased 3 quart (3 L) casserole.

Pineapple Stuffing: Sauté onion and celery in margarine in non-stick frying pan until soft.

Add next 6 ingredients to onion mixture. Stir.

Drizzle reserved pineapple juice over pineapple mixture. Stir well until stuffing is moist and holds together when squeezed. Lightly pack stuffing over ham. Scatter remaining ham over stuffing.

Sauce: Mix all 4 ingredients in small saucepan. Heat and stir on medium until boiling and thickened. Drizzle over ham. Cover. Bake in 350°F (175°C) oven for 30 minutes. Serves 8.

1 serving: 352 Calories; 10.9 g Total Fat; 1530 mg Sodium; 22 g Protein; 41 g Carbohydrate; 2 g Dietary Fibre

Pictured on page 127.

Bottom Left: Rich Chicken Stew, below   Top Centre: Stuffed Ham Casserole, page 126   Bottom Right: Seafood And Shell Stew, page 126

Rich Chicken Stew

Very tender and flavourful chicken in a creamy sauce made in a slow cooker. Serve over potatoes or pasta.

Bacon slices, diced	2	2
Medium onion, sliced	1	1
Chopped fresh mushrooms	1 cup	250 mL
All-purpose flour	2 tbsp.	30 mL
Diced carrot	1 1/2 cups	375 mL
Diced celery with leaves	1 1/2 cups	375 mL
Chicken parts, skin removed	3 lbs.	1.4 kg
Can of condensed chicken broth	10 oz.	284 mL
Parsley flakes	1 tbsp.	15 mL
Dried sage	1/2 tsp.	2 mL
Dried thyme	1/2 tsp.	2 mL
Salt	1/4 tsp.	1 mL
Pepper	1/4 tsp.	1 mL
Sour cream	2/3 cup	150 mL
All-purpose flour	2 tbsp.	30 mL

Fry bacon in large frying pan on medium-high until crispy. Do not drain.

Add onion and mushrooms. Sauté for 3 to 4 minutes until onion is beginning to brown and is soft.

Sprinkle first amount of flour over mushroom mixture. Stir well. Turn into 4 1/2 quart (4.5 L) slow cooker.

Layer carrot, celery and chicken over mushroom mixture.

Combine next 6 ingredients in same frying pan. Heat and stir for 5 minutes, scraping up any browned bits from pan, until heated through. Pour over chicken. Cover. Cook on Low for 7 to 8 hours or on High for 3 1/2 to 4 hours. Remove chicken to serving dish using slotted spoon. Keep warm.

Stir sour cream into second amount of flour in small bowl until smooth. Stir into carrot mixture with heat on High. Cover. Cook for about 5 minutes until slightly thickened. Pour sauce over chicken to serve. Serves 6.

1 serving: 274 Calories; 11.4 g Total Fat; 600 mg Sodium; 29 g Protein; 13 g Carbohydrate; 2 g Dietary Fibre

Pictured above.

Pies

Arctic Freeze

This pie changes every time you use a different ice cream.

VANILLA WAFER CRUST

Hard margarine (or butter)	1/3 cup	75 mL
Vanilla wafer crumbs	1 1/4 cups	300 mL
Brown (or granulated) sugar, packed	2 tbsp.	30 mL

FILLING

Hot fudge ice cream topping	1 cup	250 mL
Ice cream (your choice), softened	4 cups	1 L
Frozen whipped topping, thawed (or whipped cream)	2 cups	500 mL
Apricot-flavoured liqueur (such as Crème d'abricots) or peach schnapps (optional), see Note	1 tbsp.	15 mL

TOPPING

Hard margarine (or butter)	1 1/2 tsp.	7 mL
Sliced almonds	1/4 cup	60 mL
Granulated sugar	2 tsp.	10 mL
Ground cinnamon	1/4 tsp.	1 mL

Vanilla Wafer Crust: Melt margarine in medium saucepan. Add wafer crumbs and brown sugar. Stir until mixed well. Press firmly into bottom and up side of 9 inch (22 cm) pie plate. Bake in 350°F (175°C) oven for 10 minutes. Cool.

Filling: Spread ice cream topping over crust. Freeze until firm.

Spread ice cream over ice cream topping. Freeze until firm.

Fold whipped topping and liqueur together in medium bowl. Smooth over ice cream. Freeze until firm.

Topping: Melt margarine in medium saucepan on medium-low. Add almonds, granulated sugar and cinnamon. Heat and stir until almonds are toasted. Cool. Sprinkle over whipped topping. Freeze. Cuts into 8 wedges.

1 wedge: 533 Calories; 31.3 g Total Fat; 265 mg Sodium; 6 g Protein; 62 g Carbohydrate; trace Dietary Fibre

Pictured on page 131.

Note: Choose a liqueur that complements your choice of ice cream. For example, coffee-flavoured liqueur (such as Kahlúa) with mocha ice cream. Or mint-flavoured liqueur (such as Créme de Menthe) with mint chocolate chip ice cream.

Orange Chocolate Pie

Dark chocolate crust complements orange filling so nicely.
A splendid dessert.

CHOCOLATE CRUST

Hard margarine (or butter)	6 tbsp.	100 mL
Chocolate wafer crumbs	1 1/2 cups	375 mL
Icing (confectioner's) sugar	2 tbsp.	30 mL

FILLING

Cream cheese, softened	12 oz.	375 g
Granulated sugar	1/2 cup	125 mL
Hard margarine (or butter), softened	2 tbsp.	30 mL
Water	2 tbsp.	30 mL
Skim milk powder	1/2 cup	125 mL
Frozen concentrated orange juice, thawed	1/2 cup	125 mL
Finely grated orange peel	2 tsp.	10 mL
Frozen whipped topping, thawed	2 cups	500 mL

Candied orange slices, for garnish

Chocolate Crust: Melt margarine in medium saucepan. Add wafer crumbs and icing sugar. Stir until well mixed. Reserve 1 tbsp. (15 mL). Firmly press remaining crumb mixture into bottom and up side of 10 inch (25 cm) pie plate. Bake in 350°F (175°C) oven for 10 minutes. Cool.

Filling: Beat cream cheese and granulated sugar together in large bowl until smooth. Add margarine, water and milk powder. Beat well. Add concentrated orange juice and orange peel. Beat until mixed well.

Fold in whipped topping. Turn into crust. Sprinkle with reserved crumb mixture. Chill.

Garnish with orange slices. Cuts into 10 wedges.

1 wedge: 435 Calories; 29 g Total Fat; 361 mg Sodium; 7 g Protein; 39 g Carbohydrate; trace Dietary Fibre

Pictured on page 131.

Peach Blueberry Pie

Moist juicy blueberries contrasted by golden peach slices.
A delicious combination.

Pastry for a 2 crust (9 inch, 22 cm) pie, your own or a mix		
Minute tapioca	1 tbsp.	15 mL

Peach Blueberry Pie, this page

Frozen blueberries	1 1/2 cups	375 mL
Cans of sliced peaches (14 oz., 398 mL, each), drained	3	3
Granulated sugar	1/2 cup	125 mL
Minute tapioca	1 tbsp.	15 mL
Salt	1/4 tsp.	1 mL
Granulated sugar	1/2 tsp.	2 mL

Roll out large 1/2 of pastry. Line pie plate. Sprinkle first amount of tapioca over bottom. Roll out top crust slightly larger than top surface of pie plate using remaining pastry. If desired, cut out shapes with cookie cutter.

Toss next 5 ingredients together in large bowl. Turn into pie shell. Dampen pastry edge with water. Cover pie with top crust. Tuck edge under bottom crust. Press lightly to seal. Trim and crimp (see Pretty Pastry, page 134). Cut small vents in top crust if not doing cutouts.

Sprinkle second amount of sugar over crust. Bake on bottom rack in 400°F (205°C) oven for about 45 minutes until crust is golden. Cuts into 8 wedges.

1 wedge: 275 Calories; 10.7 g Total Fat; 284 mg Sodium; 2 g Protein; 44 g Carbohydrate; 3 g Dietary Fibre

Pictured on front cover and above.

Pear And Ginger Pie

An excellent pie with mild pear flavour
and the occasional burst of ginger.

Brown sugar, packed	1/2 cup	125 mL
All-purpose flour	3 tbsp.	50 mL
Ground cardamom	1/4 tsp.	1 mL
Ground cinnamon	1/4 tsp.	1 mL
Salt	1/4 tsp.	1 mL
Minced candied ginger	1 tbsp.	15 mL
Large egg	1	1
Lemon juice	1 tbsp.	15 mL
Vanilla	1 1/2 tsp.	7 mL
Large firm pears, peeled, cored and thinly sliced (about 2 lbs., 900 g)	5	5
Pastry for a 2 crust (9 inch, 22 cm) pie, your own or a mix		
Hard margarine (or butter), cut into small pieces	1 tbsp.	15 mL
Milk	1 tbsp.	15 mL
Granulated sugar	1 tsp.	5 mL

Combine first 6 ingredients in large bowl.

Beat egg, lemon juice and vanilla together in small bowl using fork. Stir into brown sugar mixture.

Fold pears into brown sugar mixture until well coated.

Roll out large 1/2 of pastry. Line pie plate. Turn pear mixture into pie shell. Drop margarine pieces here and there over pear mixture. Dampen pastry edge with water. Roll out top crust slightly larger than top surface of pie plate using remaining pastry. Cover pie with top crust. Tuck edge under bottom crust. Press lightly to seal. Trim and crimp edge (see Pretty Pastry, page 135). Cut small vents in top crust.

Brush milk over top crust. Sprinkle granulated sugar over top. Bake on bottom rack in 450°F (230°C) oven for 10 minutes. Reduce heat to 350°F (175°C). Bake for about 40 minutes until starting to bubble and crust is golden. Cuts into 8 wedges.

1 wedge: 291 Calories; 12.5 g Total Fat; 313 mg Sodium; 3 g Protein; 42 g Carbohydrate; 2 g Dietary Fibre

Pictured on page 131.

Pumpkin Chiffon Pie

Lighter in texture than the typical pumpkin pie.

Egg yolks (large)	3	3
Can of pure pumpkin (not filling)	14 oz.	398 mL
Granulated sugar	3/4 cup	175 mL
Ground cinnamon	3/4 tsp.	4 mL
Ground nutmeg	1/2 tsp.	2 mL
Ground ginger	1/2 tsp.	2 mL
Ground cloves	1/8 tsp.	0.5 mL
Salt	1/4 tsp.	1 mL
Sour cream	1 cup	250 mL
Egg whites (large), room temperature	3	3
Unbaked 9 inch (22 cm) pie shell	1	1
Whipped cream, for garnish	1/2 cup	125 mL

Beat egg yolks well in large bowl. Add next 7 ingredients. Beat.

Add sour cream. Beat.

Beat egg whites with clean beaters in medium bowl until stiff peaks form. Fold into pumpkin mixture.

Turn into pie shell. Bake on bottom rack in 450°F (230°C) oven for 10 minutes. Reduce heat to 350°F (175°C). Bake for 40 minutes until set and knife inserted in centre comes out clean. Cool.

Decorate with whipped cream. Cuts into 8 wedges.

1 wedge: 252 Calories; 11.5 g Total Fat; 216 mg Sodium; 5 g Protein; 34 g Carbohydrate; 1 g Dietary Fibre

Pictured on page 122/123.

Top: Orange Chocolate Pie, page 129
Centre: Pear And Ginger Pie, this page
Bottom: Arctic Freeze, page 128

Pineapple Cheese Pie

A light and fluffy pie with bits of pineapple.
A very delicious dessert.

GRAHAM CRUST

Hard margarine (or butter)	1/3 cup	75 mL
Graham cracker crumbs	1 1/3 cups	325 mL
Granulated sugar	2 tbsp.	30 mL
Block of cream cheese, softened	8 oz.	250 g
Granulated sugar	1 cup	250 mL
Can of crushed pineapple, drained	8 oz.	227 mL
Lemon juice	1/2 tsp.	2 mL
Salt, just a pinch		
Frozen whipped topping, thawed	2 cups	500 mL

Graham Crust: Melt margarine in small saucepan. Add graham crumbs and first amount of sugar. Stir until well mixed. Reserve 2 tbsp. (30 mL). Firmly press remaining crumb mixture into bottom and up side of 9 inch (22 cm) pie plate. Bake in 350°F (175°C) oven for 10 minutes. Cool.

Beat cream cheese and second amount of sugar together in medium bowl until smooth.

Add pineapple, lemon juice and salt. Stir. Fold in whipped topping. Turn into crust. Sprinkle with reserved crumb mixture. Chill. Cuts into 8 wedges.

1 wedge: 430 Calories; 25.4 g Total Fat; 281 mg Sodium; 4 g Protein; 49 g Carbohydrate; 1 g Dietary Fibre

Pictured on page 133.

Pineapple Pie

A takeoff from the traditional Southern chess pie
that tastes mildly of pineapple.

Large eggs	3	3
Granulated sugar	1 1/2 cups	375 mL
All-purpose flour	6 tbsp.	100 mL
Hard margarine (or butter), softened	6 tbsp.	100 mL
Can of crushed pineapple, drained	14 oz.	398 mL
Milk	6 tbsp.	100 mL
Vanilla	1 1/2 tsp.	7 mL
Salt	1/2 tsp.	2 mL
Unbaked 9 inch (22 cm) pie shell	1	1

Beat eggs in medium bowl until frothy. Add sugar, flour and margarine. Beat until smooth.

Add pineapple, milk, vanilla and salt. Stir.

Turn into pie shell. Bake on bottom rack in 350°F (175°C) oven for about 60 minutes until set and golden. Cool. Cuts into 8 wedges.

1 wedge: 385 Calories; 16 g Total Fat; 383 mg Sodium; 4 g Protein; 57 g Carbohydrate; 1 g Dietary Fibre

Pictured on page 136.

Forgotten Apple Pie

A golden brown crumb topping and a creamy white filling
with bits of pale yellow apple. The tartness of the apple is
a nice contrast to the sweet topping. Serve with ice cream.

Large egg	1	1
All-purpose flour	2 tbsp.	30 mL
Salt	1/4 tsp.	1 mL
Sour cream	1 cup	250 mL
Granulated sugar	2/3 cup	150 mL
Vanilla	1/2 tsp.	2 mL
Peeled and chopped cooking apple (such as McIntosh)	3 1/2 cups	875 mL
Unbaked 9 inch (22 cm) pie shell	1	1

TOPPING

Brown sugar, packed	1/3 cup	75 mL
All-purpose flour	1/3 cup	75 mL
Hard margarine (or butter), softened	1/4 cup	60 mL

Beat egg, flour and salt together in medium bowl until smooth. Beat in sour cream, granulated sugar and vanilla until sugar is dissolved.

Add apple. Stir. Turn into pie shell. Bake on bottom rack in 400°F (205°C) oven for 10 minutes. Reduce heat to 350°F (175°C). Bake for 20 minutes.

Topping: Mix brown sugar, flour and margarine until crumbly. Sprinkle over pie. Bake for about 40 minutes until apple is tender. Cuts into 8 wedges.

1 wedge: 352 Calories; 16.4 g Total Fat; 273 mg Sodium; 3 g Protein; 50 g Carbohydrate; 1 g Dietary Fibre

Pictured on page 136.

Top Left: Rocky Road Pie, below

Bottom Left & Right: Pineapple Cheese Pie, page 132

Rocky Road Pie

*A favourite among big and little kids with
the chocolate and marshmallows.*

CHOCOLATE CRUST

Hard margarine (or butter)	1/3 cup	75 mL
Chocolate wafer crumbs	1 cup	250 mL
Graham cracker crumbs	1/4 cup	60 mL
Finely chopped almonds	1/4 cup	60 mL
Granulated sugar	1 tbsp.	15 mL

FILLING

Miniature marshmallows	1 2/3 cups	400 mL
Semi-sweet chocolate baking squares (1 oz., 28 g, each), cut up	3	3
Milk	6 tbsp.	100 mL
Salt	1/8 tsp.	0.5 mL
Block of cream cheese, softened and cut up	8 oz.	250 g
Frozen whipped topping, thawed	2 cups	500 mL
Miniature marshmallows	1 cup	250 mL
Milk chocolate candy bar, coarsely chopped	3 1/2 oz.	100 g

Chocolate Crust: Melt margarine in medium saucepan. Add wafer and graham crumbs, almonds and sugar. Stir until well mixed. Reserve 2 tbsp. (30 mL). Firmly press remaining crumb mixture into bottom and up side of 9 inch (22 cm) pie plate. Bake in 350°F (175°C) oven for 10 minutes. Cool.

Filling: Put first 4 ingredients into large saucepan. Heat and stir on medium-low until melted and smooth.

Add cream cheese. Stir until melted. Whisk to blend well. Chill for 20 minutes, stirring occasionally, until slightly thickened.

Fold in whipped topping. Fold in second amounts of marshmallows and chocolate. Turn into crust. Sprinkle with reserved crumb mixture. Chill. Cuts into 8 wedges.

1 wedge: 521 Calories; 35.7 g Total Fat; 358 mg Sodium; 7 g Protein; 48 g Carbohydrate; 1 g Dietary Fibre

Pictured above.

Pretty Pastry

When you learn how to make these pretty pastry edges, you will want to bring your pie and plates to the table for serving to hear the exclamations of delight from your guests. Whether a single or double-crust pie, your filling will be presented in a pretty frame of pastry.

Make your favourite single-crust pie pastry. Roll out pastry to line 9 inch (22 cm) pie plate. Trim pastry, leaving a 1 inch (2.5 cm) overhang. Fold edge under to width of pie plate. Gently press down to flatten. Choose one of the methods shown below, or on page 135, and follow the instructions.

FLUTED EDGE

Squeeze pastry edge between thumb and forefinger at an angle. Continue around pastry edge.

PINCHED EDGE

Have thumb and forefinger of one hand pointing outward towards edge of pastry, and have forefinger of other hand pointing inward towards edge of pastry, in between fingers. Push towards each other at the same time, crimping the edge. Continue around pastry edge.

FORKED EDGE

Press underside of fork tines along pastry edge at a straight angle. Next, press down at a 45° angle to first mark. Repeat pattern around pastry edge.

PINWHEEL EDGE

Make 45° cuts at alternating angles to form triangles around entire pastry edge. Remove cut triangles from edge, leaving attached triangles. Fold back every other triangle to stand up.

DECORATIVE EDGE

Gather up and roll out leftover pastry. Cut out desired shapes. Dampen bottom of shapes with water using fingertips. Arrange shapes on pastry edge and gently press down.

CUT-OUTS

Make enough pastry for a double-crust pie. Roll out large 1/2 of pastry to line pie plate. Fill as desired. Roll out remaining pastry slightly larger than top surface of pie. Cut out desired shapes from centre of pastry. Dampen bottom of shapes with water using fingertips. Place shapes on pastry and gently press down. Carefully lift and lay pastry over filling. Dampen around bottom pastry edge. Pinch flute edge (see page 134).

LATTICE TOP

Make enough pastry for a double-crust pie. Roll out large 1/2 of pastry to line pie plate. Fill as desired. Roll out remaining pastry. Using fluted pastry cutter, cut into eight 1 inch (2.5 cm) strips about 6 inches (15 cm) in length.

Dampen 1 end of 1 strip with water using fingertips. Twist strip. Place dampened end on pastry edge and lay other end in centre on filling. Repeat at equal intervals around pastry edge with remaining 7 strips. Gather and pinch ends together in centre, using a bit more water.

Berry Blend Pie

Such a festive colour and lots of fruity berries in this pie.

Granulated sugar	1 cup	250 mL
Cornstarch	3 tbsp.	50 mL
Reserved mixed berries juice (plus water to make)	1 cup	250 mL
Package of raspberry-flavoured gelatin (jelly powder)	3 oz.	85 g
Bag of frozen mixed berries, thawed, drained and liquid reserved	21 oz.	600 g
Baked 9 inch (22 cm) pie shells, cooled	2	2
TOPPING		
Envelope of dessert topping (prepared), optional	1	1

Fresh blueberries (or raspberries or strawberries), for garnish

Stir sugar, cornstarch and reserved juice together in large saucepan until smooth. Heat and stir until boiling and thickened. Remove from heat.

Add jelly powder. Stir until dissolved. Chill, stirring and scraping down sides often, until beginning to gel.

Fold mixed berries into jelly mixture. Divide between pie shells.

Topping: Pipe or place dollops of dessert topping over pies.

Garnish with blueberries. Chill until ready to serve. Makes 2 pies, each cutting into 8 wedges, for a total of 16 wedges.

1 wedge: 182 Calories; 5.3 g Total Fat; 117 mg Sodium; 1 g Protein; 33 g Carbohydrate; 1 g Dietary Fibre

Pictured below.

Bottom Left: Berry Blend Pie, above   Top Centre: Pineapple Pie, page 132   Bottom Right: Forgotten Apple Pie, page 132

Salads

Slaw Special

A brightly coloured and crunchy salad
with a hint of Thai flavours.

DRESSING
White vinegar	1/4 cup	60 mL
Cooking oil	3 tbsp.	50 mL
Dark sesame (or cooking) oil	1 tbsp.	15 mL
Granulated sugar	1/4 cup	60 mL
Minced onion flakes	1 tbsp.	15 mL
Reserved seasoning packet from instant noodles		
Shredded savoy (or green) cabbage, packed	2 cups	500 mL
Bag of broccoli coleslaw (about 4 cups, 1 L) or broccoli stems and carrots, cut julienne	12 oz.	340 g
Green onions, chopped	5	5
Fresh sugar snap peas, sliced diagonally (about 5 oz., 140 g)	1 1/2 cups	375 mL
Dry (or honey) roasted peanuts, chopped	1/2 cup	125 mL
Package of instant noodles with beef- flavoured packet, broken up and seasoning packet reserved	3 oz.	85 g

Dressing: Stir first 6 ingredients together in small bowl until sugar is dissolved. Can be prepared 1 to 2 days ahead and chilled.

Toss next 5 ingredients together in large bowl. Can be prepared 1 to 2 days ahead and chilled.

To serve, add noodles and dressing to salad. Toss well. Makes about 11 cups (2.75 L).

3/4 cup (175 mL): 120 Calories; 6.6 g Total Fat; 56 mg Sodium; 3 g Protein; 13 g Carbohydrate; 2 g Dietary Fibre

Pictured on page 123.

HOT SLAW STIR-FRY: Heat non-stick wok or frying pan on medium-high. Add leftover Slaw Special. Stir-fry for 3 to 5 minutes until heated through.

Blackened Chicken Caesar Salad, this page

Greek Pea Salad

A creamy salad with a nice pea and feta cheese combination. Great with Spinach And Olive Braid, page 76.

Frozen peas	2 cups	500 mL
Water		
Crumbled feta cheese	1 cup	250 mL
Hard-boiled egg, chopped	1	1
Deli ham slice (about 1 oz., 28 g), cut into short narrow strips	1	1
Sliced ripe olives	1/4 cup	60 mL
Green onions, sliced	3	3
Small red pepper, diced	1	1

DRESSING

Salad dressing (or mayonnaise)	1/4 cup	60 mL
Red wine vinegar	1 tsp.	5 mL
Greek seasoning	2 tsp.	10 mL

Cook peas in water in medium saucepan for about 3 minutes until tender. Drain. Rinse with cold water. Drain well. Transfer to medium bowl.

Add next 6 ingredients. Stir.

Dressing: Mix all 3 ingredients in small bowl. Makes 1/4 cup (60 mL) dressing. Drizzle over salad. Stir to coat. Chill for at least 1 hour to blend flavours. Makes 3 cups (750 mL) salad.

1/2 cup (125 mL): 201 Calories; 13.1 g Total Fat; 626 mg Sodium; 9 g Protein; 12 g Carbohydrate; 3 g Dietary Fibre

Pictured on page 115.

Blackened Chicken Caesar Salad

A full-meal salad with a bit of bite from the chicken.

Large heads of romaine lettuce, cut up or torn	2	2
Croutons	1 cup	250 mL
Finely grated Parmesan cheese	1/4 cup	60 mL

DRESSING

Cooking oil	3 tbsp.	50 mL
Sour cream	3 tbsp.	50 mL
White wine vinegar	1 tbsp.	15 mL
Lemon juice	1 tsp.	5 mL
Worcestershire sauce	1 tsp.	5 mL
Garlic salt	1/2 tsp.	2 mL
Pepper	1/4 tsp.	1 mL
Finely grated Parmesan cheese	1/2 cup	125 mL

BLACKENED CHICKEN

Cooking oil	1 tbsp.	15 mL
Boneless, skinless chicken breast halves, cut into 3/4 inch (2 cm) pieces	2 lbs.	900 g
Ketchup	2 tbsp.	30 mL
Paprika	1 tbsp.	15 mL
Salt	2 tsp.	10 mL
Pepper	1/2 tsp.	2 mL
Onion powder	1/2 tsp.	2 mL
Ground thyme	1/2 tsp.	2 mL
Chili powder	1/2 tsp.	2 mL
Cayenne pepper	1/2 tsp.	2 mL

Finely grated Parmesan cheese, to taste

Toss lettuce, croutons and Parmesan cheese together in large bowl. Chill.

Dressing: Mix all 8 ingredients in small bowl. Let stand for 10 minutes to blend flavours.

Blackened Chicken: Heat wok or frying pan until hot. Add cooking oil. Add chicken. Stir-fry for 6 to 7 minutes until partially cooked.

Add next 8 ingredients. Stir-fry until chicken juices run clear. Add dressing to salad. Toss. Divide among 8 large plates. Divide chicken over individual salads.

Sprinkle Parmesan cheese over individual salads. Serves 8.

1 serving: 284 Calories; 13.2 g Total Fat; 947 mg Sodium; 32 g Protein; 9 g Carbohydrate; 3 g Dietary Fibre

Pictured on this page.

Elegant Eggnog Mold

So practical—this salad can stand out for up to 3 hours.

Reserved mandarin orange juice (plus water to make)	1/2 cup	125 mL
Envelopes of unflavoured gelatin (1/4 oz., 7 g, each)	2	2
Granulated sugar	1/4 cup	60 mL
Eggnog	2 cups	500 mL
Orange-flavoured liqueur (such as Grand Marnier), optional	1/4 cup	60 mL
Cranberry cocktail	1 cup	250 mL
Package of cranberry (or raspberry) flavoured gelatin (jelly powder)	3 oz.	85 g
Large ice cubes	3	3
Whipping cream	1 cup	250 mL
Can of mandarin orange segments, drained and juice reserved	10 oz.	284 mL

Fresh mint leaves, for garnish
Fresh raspberries, for garnish

Measure mandarin orange juice into small saucepan. Sprinkle unflavoured gelatin over top. Let stand for 5 minutes until softened. Stir. Add sugar. Heat and stir on medium until gelatin and sugar are dissolved. Remove from heat. Let stand at room temperature for about 10 minutes, stirring several times, until lukewarm but still liquid. If beginning to set, heat on low or microwave on medium (50%) for about 30 seconds until liquefied. Transfer to large bowl.

Add eggnog and liqueur. Chill for about 20 minutes, stirring several times, until slightly thickened and beginning to curdle slightly. Stir vigorously. Keep at room temperature to prevent further thickening, stirring several times to keep soft.

Heat cranberry cocktail in separate small saucepan on medium-high until boiling. Remove from heat. Stir in cranberry-flavoured gelatin until dissolved. Stir in ice cubes until melted. Chill, stirring several times, until syrupy.

Beat whipping cream in medium bowl until stiff peaks form. Add 2 large spoonfuls eggnog mixture to whipped cream. Stir. Add to eggnog mixture. Fold in orange segments. Pour into lightly greased 6 1/2 to 7 cup (1.6 to 1.75 L) mold or bundt pan. Mixture should stay softly mounded when 1 spoonful is placed on top of another. Chill for 10 minutes. Pour cranberry mixture over eggnog mixture. Poke soft spatula deeply into eggnog mixture 8 to 10 times, particularly around sides of mold, allowing cranberry mixture to fill spaces. Chill for at least 4 hours or overnight until firmly set. Invert onto dampened serving plate. Dampness makes it easier to centre mold. To loosen salad in mould, place hot tea towel over top. Let stand until tea towel is cool. Repeat 6 to 8 times. Shake mold slightly. Chill until firm.

Garnish with mint and raspberries. Serves 14.

1 serving: 166 Calories; 8.7 g Total Fat; 47 mg Sodium; 3 g Protein; 20 g Carbohydrate; trace Dietary Fibre

Pictured on page 140.

Vegetable Salad

A brightly coloured salad.

Can of kernel corn, drained	12 oz.	341 mL
Can of peas, drained	14 oz.	398 mL
Can of cut green beans, drained	14 oz.	398 mL
Thinly sliced celery	1 cup	250 mL
Medium onion, finely chopped	1	1
Diced red pepper	1/2 cup	125 mL
Diced green pepper	1/2 cup	125 mL
DRESSING		
Granulated sugar	1 cup	250 mL
White vinegar	3/4 cup	175 mL
Water	1/3 cup	75 mL
Cooking oil	2 tbsp.	30 mL
Salt	1/2 tsp.	2 mL

Combine first 7 ingredients together in large bowl. Transfer to airtight container.

Dressing: Stir all 5 ingredients together in small bowl until sugar is dissolved. Pour over salad. Stir until coated. Cover. Chill for 24 hours to blend flavours. Store in refrigerator for up to 4 weeks. Makes 8 cups (2 L).

1/2 cup (125 mL): 101 Calories; 1.9 g Total Fat; 190 mg Sodium; 1 g Protein; 21 g Carbohydrate; 2 g Dietary Fibre

Pictured on page 140.

Top Left: Elegant Eggnog Mold, page 139   Bottom Centre: Potato And Bean Salad, below   Top Right: Vegetable Salad, page 139

Potato And Bean Salad

A creamy and tangy dressing over crunchy red radishes and bright green peas. The potato salad for Christmas.

Whole medium potatoes, with peel (about 2 lbs., 900 g)	5	5
Water	2 cups	500 mL
Salt	1 tsp.	5 mL
Can of garbanzo beans (chick peas), drained	19 oz.	540 mL
Frozen peas, thawed (or fresh, barely cooked)	1 cup	250 mL
Thinly sliced radish	1/2 cup	125 mL
Green onions, thinly sliced	3	3
GARLIC MUSTARD DRESSING		
Buttermilk (or reconstituted from powder)	1/2 cup	125 mL
Plain yogurt	1/2 cup	125 mL
Mayonnaise (not salad dressing)	1/4 cup	60 mL
Garlic cloves, minced (or 1/2 tsp., 2 mL, powder)	2	2
Dijon mustard	1 1/2 tbsp.	25 mL
White vinegar	2 tsp.	10 mL
Salt	1 1/2 tsp.	7 mL
Granulated sugar	1/2 tsp.	2 mL
Pepper	1/8 tsp.	0.5 mL

Thinly sliced radish, for garnish
Fresh sugar snap peas, for garnish

Simmer potatoes in water and salt in large covered saucepan for about 35 minutes until tender. Drain. Cool. Peel. Dice into 3/4 inch (2 cm) pieces. Put into large bowl.

Add beans, peas, radish and green onion. Stir gently.

Garlic Mustard Dressing: Stir first 9 ingredients together in small bowl until smooth. Add to potatoes. Stir until coated. Cover. Chill for at least 2 hours to blend flavours.

Garnish with radish and peas. Makes 9 1/2 cups (2.4 L).

1 cup (250 mL): 181 Calories; 6.3 g Total Fat; 547 mg Sodium; 6 g Protein; 26 g Carbohydrate; 3 g Dietary Fibre

Pictured above.

For an attractive way to catch dripping wax from lighted candles, and to protect delicate wood surfaces, place large plant leaves, such as magnolia or lemon, under the candle. To make candles last longer, freeze before burning.

Side Dishes

Barley And Rice Pilaf

A chewy side dish that makes a nice substitution for plain rice or mashed potatoes.

Chopped onion	1 cup	250 mL
Chopped celery	1 cup	250 mL
Garlic cloves, minced (or 1/2 tsp., 2 mL, powder)	2	2
Olive (or cooking) oil	1 tbsp.	15 mL
Olive (or cooking) oil	1 tbsp.	15 mL
Long grain brown rice, uncooked	1 cup	250 mL
Pearl barley	1 1/4 cups	300 mL
Julienned carrots	1 cup	250 mL
Chicken (or vegetable) bouillon powder	3 tbsp.	50 mL
Parsley flakes	1 tbsp.	15 mL
Dried crushed chilies (optional)	1/4 – 1/2 tsp.	1 – 2 mL
Boiling water	6 cups	1.5 L

Sauté onion, celery and garlic in first amount of olive oil in large frying pan until onion is soft. Turn into ungreased 3 quart (3 L) casserole.

Add second amount of olive oil to same frying pan. Sauté rice and barley for about 5 minutes until starting to turn golden. Add to onion mixture.

Stir in remaining 5 ingredients. Cover. Bake in 350°F (175°C) oven for 1 1/2 to 1 3/4 hours until liquid is absorbed and barley is tender. Stir to distribute vegetables. Makes 9 1/2 cups (2.4 L).

1/2 cup (125 mL): 112 Calories; 2.2 g Total Fat; 319 mg Sodium; 3 g Protein; 21 g Carbohydrate; 2 g Dietary Fibre

Pictured on page 143.

For best results when cooking rice, choose a saucepan with a tight-fitting lid to prevent steam escaping. Avoid lifting the lid or stirring the rice while cooking. Better yet, put an automatic rice cooker on your Christmas wish list. It cooks rice perfectly every time.

Corn And Bean-Stuffed Peppers

Beautiful stuffed peppers that are made in the slow cooker.

Large red peppers	6	6
Long grain white (or brown) rice, uncooked	1/4 cup	60 mL
Lean ground chicken	11 oz.	310 g
Sliced green onion	1/4 cup	60 mL
Garlic clove, minced (or 1/4 tsp., 1 mL, powder), optional	1	1
Frozen kernel corn	1 cup	250 mL
Can of black beans (19 oz., 540 mL, size), drained (see Note)	1/2	1/2
Seasoned salt	1/2 tsp.	2 mL
Dried sweet basil	1/4 tsp.	1 mL
Dried whole oregano	1/4 tsp.	1 mL
Pepper	1/4 tsp.	1 mL
Can of diced tomatoes, with juice	14 oz.	398 mL
Couscous, approximately	2/3 cup	150 mL
Chopped fresh parsley (or cilantro), for garnish		

Slice tops off red peppers. Discard core, seeds and ribs. If necessary, cut small slice from bottom of each pepper, without making a hole, to allow peppers to stand upright. Sprinkle 2 tsp. (10 mL) rice into each pepper shell. Stand in 6 quart (6 L) slow cooker.

Combine next 9 ingredients in medium bowl. Evenly divide and spoon into each pepper shell.

Pour tomatoes with juice over and around stuffed peppers. Cook on low for 5 hours or on high for 2 1/2 hours. Remove stuffed peppers to serving dish. Keep warm.

Pour liquid from slow cooker into 2 cup (500 mL) liquid measure. Add same amount of couscous to liquid. Let stand for 5 minutes until liquid is absorbed. Spoon couscous onto stuffed peppers.

Sprinkle with parsley. Serves 6.

1 serving: 289 Calories; 8 g Total Fat; 299 mg Sodium; 16 g Protein; 41 g Carbohydrate; 5 g Dietary Fibre

Pictured on page 143.

Note: Freeze remaining beans to use another time.

Broccoli With Lemon Cheese Sauce

A very delicious change from Cheddar cheese sauce and broccoli. Serve in Hot Carrot Ring, page 146.

Fresh broccoli	1 1/2 lbs.	680 g
Boiling water		
Salt	1/2 tsp.	2 mL
LEMON CHEESE SAUCE		
Milk	1/2 cup	125 mL
Block of cream cheese, cut into chunks	4 oz.	125 g
Finely grated lemon peel	1/2 tsp.	2 mL
Lemon juice	1 tsp.	5 mL
Ground ginger	1/4 tsp.	1 mL
Salt, sprinkle		

Cut broccoli into bite-size florets. Peel stalks. Cut into thin slices or julienne. Cook in boiling water and salt in large covered pot or Dutch oven for about 5 minutes until bright green and tender-crisp. Drain well. Keep warm.

Lemon Cheese Sauce: Heat milk in small saucepan until hot.

Add cream cheese. Stir on low until cream cheese is melted and smooth.

Stir in lemon peel, lemon juice, ginger and salt. Makes 3/4 cup (175 mL) sauce. Pour over broccoli. Makes 6 cups (1.5 L).

1/2 cup (125 mL): 57 Calories; 4 g Total Fat; 51 mg Sodium; 3 g Protein; 4 g Carbohydrate; 1 g Dietary Fibre

Pictured on page 143.

Centre Left: Corn And Bean-Stuffed Peppers, this page
Top Right: Barley And Rice Pilaf, page 141
Bottom Right: Hot Carrot Ring, page 146, with Broccoli With Lemon Cheese Sauce, above

Potato Ruffles In Mushroom Sauce

*Potato rolled in pasta and covered
in a mushroom and pepper sauce.*

Lasagna noodles	7	7
Spinach lasagna noodles	7	7
Boiling water	16 cups	4 L
Salt	4 tsp.	20 mL

MUSHROOM SAUCE

Sliced brown (cremini) mushrooms	3 cups	750 mL
Hard margarine (or butter)	2 tbsp.	30 mL
All-purpose flour	1/2 cup	125 mL
Water	2 1/2 cups	625 mL
Can of skim evaporated milk (or half-and-half cream)	13 1/2 oz.	385 mL
Beef bouillon powder	1 tbsp.	15 mL
Granulated sugar	1 tsp.	5 mL
Dill weed	3/4 tsp.	4 mL
Salt	1/2 tsp.	2 mL
Pepper	1/4 tsp.	1 mL

FILLING

Medium potatoes (about 1 1/2 lbs., 680 g), cut into chunks	4	4
Coarsely chopped onion	1 cup	250 mL
Water	2 cups	500 mL
Salt	1 tsp.	5 mL
Dry curd cottage cheese	1 cup	250 mL
Salt	1 tsp.	5 mL
Pepper	1/4 tsp.	1 mL
Grated white Cheddar (or mozzarella) cheese	3/4 cup	175 mL

Fresh dill sprigs, for garnish

Cook both noodles in boiling water and salt in large uncovered pot or Dutch oven for 10 to 12 minutes until tender but firm. Drain. Rinse in cold water. Drain well. Cover noodles with plastic wrap. Set aside.

Mushroom Sauce: Sauté mushrooms in margarine in large frying pan until liquid from mushrooms has evaporated.

Sprinkle flour over mushroom mixture. Stir well on medium-low for 2 to 3 minutes until flour mixture begins to brown.

Gradually stir in water and evaporated milk. Add next 5 ingredients. Heat and stir until mixture is boiling and slightly thickened. Makes 4 cups (1 L) sauce. Keep warm.

Filling: Cook potato and onion in water and first amount of salt in medium saucepan for about 15 minutes until potato is soft. Drain. Return to saucepan. Mash until no lumps remain.

Add cottage cheese, second amount of salt and pepper. Mash well. Makes about 3 3/4 cups (925 mL) filling. Spoon 4 to 5 tbsp. (60 to 75 mL) filling at 1 end of each noodle. Roll up, jelly roll-style, pressing down slightly halfway through rolling to force potato mixture to fill noodle more evenly. Spoon 1/3 of sauce into greased deep casserole. Place potato ruffles, in single layer, ruffled edges up, on sauce. Spoon remaining sauce over and around potato ruffles. Cover casserole with greased foil. Bake in 350°F (175°C) oven for 40 minutes. Remove foil. Spoon sauce in casserole over potato ruffles.

Sprinkle with Cheddar cheese. Bake, uncovered, for 12 to 15 minutes until cheese is melted and sauce is bubbly.

Garnish with dill. Makes 14 potato ruffles.

1 potato ruffle: 212 Calories; 4.6 g Total Fat; 484 mg Sodium; 10 g Protein; 32 g Carbohydrate; 2 g Dietary Fibre

Pictured on page 147.

Cabbage Rolls

A regular at the holiday table of
many families with Ukrainian roots.

Large head of cabbage (thin-leafed cabbage works best), about 5 lbs. (2.3 kg), see Note	1	1
Boiling water		
FILLING		
Short grain white (or pearl) rice, rinsed	1 1/2 cups	375 mL
Water	2 1/4 cups	550 mL
Salt	1 1/2 tsp.	7 mL
Pepper	1/2 tsp.	2 mL
Bacon slices, diced	6	6
Finely chopped onion	2 cups	500 mL
Tomato juice	1 cup	250 mL
Water	1/3 cup	75 mL
Hard margarine (or butter)	1 tbsp.	15 mL
Water	1/4 – 1/2 cup	60 – 125 mL

Remove core from cabbage and about 1/2 inch (12 mm) of surrounding leaf stems. Put cabbage, core side down, into Dutch oven. Cover with boiling water. Cover. Simmer for about 30 minutes until leaves begin to soften and loosen. Peel leaves, layer by layer, using tongs. Place on tea towel to drain. If leaves are too soft, run under cold water to stop cooking process. Place leaves on cutting board. Remove hard centre ribs by cutting long, narrow "V" from larger leaves. Cut larger leaves into 3 equal pieces and smaller leaves into 2 equal pieces, keeping size of pieces uniform. You should end up with 4 to 4 1/2 inch (10 to 11 cm) pieces. Stack leaves on plate. Line bottom of greased medium roasting pan with some of very small and torn leaves.

Filling: Combine rice, water and 1 tsp. (5 mL) salt in medium saucepan. Bring to a boil. Reduce heat to medium-low. Cover. Simmer for 10 minutes until water is absorbed and rice is very firm. Remove cover. Cool. Fluff with fork several times while cooling to break up any clumps. Turn into large bowl. Sprinkle remaining salt and pepper over rice. Mix.

Fry bacon in large frying pan on medium for about 10 minutes until beginning to brown. Do not drain.

Cabbage Rolls, this page

Add onion. Sauté for about 10 minutes until very soft. Add to rice. Mix well. Place 1 to 1 1/2 tbsp. (15 to 25 mL) filling in centre of each leaf. Fold 1 end over filling. Fold sides in. Roll up to enclose filling. Arrange cabbage rolls close together, in layers if necessary, in roasting pan.

Heat tomato juice, first amount of water and margarine in small saucepan until almost boiling. Pour over cabbage rolls. Place any extra cabbage leaves over cabbage rolls. Cover. Cook in 350°F (175°C) oven for 1 hour. Tip pan to check amount of liquid. If dry, add second amount of water. Cover. Bake for 30 to 45 minutes until all liquid is absorbed and cabbage rolls are golden. Makes 7 to 8 dozen cabbage rolls.

1 cabbage roll: 29 Calories; 1 g Total Fat; 69 mg Sodium; 1 g Protein; 5 g Carbohydrate; trace Dietary Fibre

Pictured above.

Note: If cabbage leaves are especially white and seem tough, arrange in layers on baking sheet after steaming. Cover. Freeze overnight. Thaw completely before using.

To remove cabbage rolls easily from pan, let stand for 15 minutes after baking. Gently shake pan from side to side to loosen cabbage rolls. They should separate without breaking. Tip pan and use soft spatula to help direct cabbage rolls into serving bowl.

Hot Carrot Ring

Dress up your table with a soft, moist ring of carrots.
Fill the centre with Broccoli With Lemon Cheese Sauce,
page 142, or Sautéed Sprouts, this page, if desired.

Medium carrots, cut up (about 3 cups, 750 mL, cooked and mashed)	2 lbs.	900 g
Water		
Salt	1/2 tsp.	2 mL
Milk	1/2 cup	125 mL
Fine dry bread crumbs	1 cup	250 mL
Grated medium Cheddar cheese	1 1/2 cups	375 mL
Parsley flakes	2 tsp.	10 mL
Seasoned salt	1 tsp.	5 mL
Large eggs, fork-beaten	3	3
Pepper	1/4 tsp.	1 mL

Cook carrots in water and salt until tender. Drain. Mash until no lumps remain. Transfer to large bowl.

Add remaining 7 ingredients. Mix well. Turn into well-greased ring-shaped pan. Bake in 350°F (175°C) oven for 45 to 50 minutes until knife inserted in centre comes out clean. Let stand in pan for 10 minutes before turning out onto serving plate. Serves 10 to 12.

1 serving: 184 Calories; 8.4 g Total Fat; 385 mg Sodium; 9 g Protein; 19 g Carbohydrate; 3 g Dietary Fibre

Pictured on page 143.

Ginger Honey-Glazed Beans

Tangy, yet sweet, bean with a nice ginger taste.

Hard margarine (or butter)	3 tbsp.	50 mL
Soy sauce	2 tsp.	10 mL
Finely grated gingerroot (or 1/2 tsp., 2 mL, ground ginger)	2 tsp.	10 mL
Frozen (whole or cut) green beans (about 6 cups, 1.5 L)	1 lb.	454 g
Water	1 tbsp.	15 mL
Cornstarch	2 tsp.	10 mL
Liquid honey	3 tbsp.	50 mL
Roasted peanuts, coarsely chopped	2 tbsp.	30 mL

Melt margarine in large frying pan on medium. Stir in soy sauce and ginger until bubbling. Add green beans. Stir to coat. Cover. Cook for 10 to 11 minutes until beans are tender-crisp.

Stir water into cornstarch in small cup until smooth. Stir into beans.

Add honey. Heat and stir until sauce is boiling and thickened. Turn into serving dish.

Sprinkle peanuts over top. Makes about 3 1/2 cups (875 mL).

1/2 cup (125 mL): 113 Calories; 6.4 g Total Fat; 160 mg Sodium; 2 g Protein; 14 g Carbohydrate; trace Dietary Fibre

Pictured on page 147.

Sautéed Sprouts

Grapes and almonds give a uniqueness to ordinary sprouts.
Serve in Hot Carrot Ring, this page, if desired.

Fresh (or frozen) Brussels sprouts, trimmed	1 lb.	454 g
Boiling water		
Salt	1 tsp.	5 mL
Hard margarine (or butter)	2 tbsp.	30 mL
Seedless red (or green) grapes	1 cup	250 mL
Slivered almonds	2 tbsp.	30 mL
Salt, sprinkle		
Pepper, sprinkle		

Cook Brussels sprouts in boiling water and salt in medium saucepan for about 10 minutes until tender. Drain. Quickly cool in cold water. Drain.

Melt margarine in large frying pan until sizzling. Add brussels sprouts, grapes and almonds. Gently stir for 3 to 4 minutes until heated through.

Sprinkle with salt and pepper. Makes 4 cups (1 L).

1/2 cup (125 mL): 77 Calories; 4.3 g Total Fat; 49 mg Sodium; 3 g Protein; 9 g Carbohydrate; 3 g Dietary Fibre

Pictured on front cover and on page 123.

Top Left: Potato Ruffles In Mushroom Sauce, page 144   Bottom Left: Ginger Honey-Glazed Beans, page 146   Bottom Right: Chutney-Glazed Squash, this page

Chutney-Glazed Squash

Sweet, buttery squash rings that are
soft and tender and have a slight tang.

Hard margarine (or butter)	1/2 tsp.	2 mL
Acorn squash, with peel, cut into 3/4 inch (2 cm) slices, seeds removed	3	3
Seasoned salt	1/2 tsp.	2 mL
Hard margarine (or butter)	3 tbsp.	50 mL
Mango chutney, large pieces finely chopped	1/2 cup	125 mL
Orange (or apple) juice (or water)	2 tbsp.	30 mL
Ground cinnamon	1/4 tsp.	1 mL
Ground nutmeg	1/8 tsp.	0.5 mL
Chopped pecans	1/4 cup	60 mL

Line large baking sheet with foil. Grease with first amount of margarine.

Arrange squash in single layer on foil. Sprinkle with seasoned salt. Cover with foil, sealing sides. Bake in 350°F (175°C) oven for about 30 minutes until slightly firm.

Melt second amount of margarine in small saucepan on medium. Heat and stir in next 4 ingredients until hot. Brush over both sides of squash. Bake, uncovered, for about 20 minutes until squash is tender.

Sprinkle pecans over squash. Makes about 13 squash slices.

1 squash slice: 87 Calories; 4.5 g Total Fat; 81 mg Sodium; 1 g Protein; 12 g Carbohydrate; 1 g Dietary Fibre

Pictured above.

Scalloped Tomatoes And Corn

*This very good side dish is a
nice addition to any dinner buffet!*

Cans of stewed tomatoes, with juice (14 oz., 398 mL, each)	3	3
Garlic clove, minced (or 1/4 tsp., 1 mL, powder)	1	1
Finely diced celery	1/3 cup	75 mL
Finely diced onion	1/3 cup	75 mL
Finely diced green pepper	1/3 cup	75 mL
All-purpose flour	3 tbsp.	50 mL
Granulated sugar	2 tsp.	10 mL
Dried marjoram	1/2 tsp.	2 mL
Dried thyme	1/4 tsp.	1 mL
Salt	1 tsp.	5 mL
Pepper	1/4 tsp.	1 mL
Whipping cream	1/2 cup	125 mL
Frozen kernel corn	1 cup	250 mL
White bread slices, toasted and buttered, cut into small cubes	4	4
French-fried onions (from can)	3/4 cup	175 mL
Grated Swiss cheese	1 cup	250 mL

Heat first 5 ingredients in large saucepan on medium-high until boiling. Reduce heat to medium-low. Cover. Simmer for about 15 minutes until onion is soft.

Combine next 6 ingredients in small bowl. Slowly stir in whipping cream until smooth. Stir into tomato mixture.

Add corn. Heat and stir until boiling and thickened.

Stir toast cubes into tomato mixture. Turn into greased 2 1/2 quart (2.5 L) casserole.

Crumble french-fried onions into small bowl. Add cheese. Toss. Sprinkle over tomato mixture. Cover. Bake in 350°F (175°C) oven for 30 minutes. Remove cover. Cook for 10 minutes until browned. Let stand for 5 minutes before serving. Serves 8 to 10.

1 serving: 268 Calories; 12.8 g Total Fat; 902 mg Sodium; 9 g Protein; 33 g Carbohydrate; 3 g Dietary Fibre

Pictured on page 149.

Sweet Apple And Turnip

Pretty to serve and even better to eat.

Medium yellow turnip (about 1 3/4 lbs., 790 g), cut into 1/4 inch (6 mm) slices	1	1
Water		
Medium cooking apples (such as McIntosh), with peel	2 – 3	2 – 3
Liquid honey	1/4 cup	60 mL
Lemon juice	2 tbsp.	30 mL
Ground cinnamon	1/16 tsp.	0.5 mL
Salt	1/4 tsp.	1 mL
Pepper, sprinkle		
Hard margarine (or butter)	1 tbsp.	15 mL
Coarsely chopped pecans	1/4 cup	60 mL

Place turnip slices on rack over simmering water in large saucepan. Cover. Steam for 20 minutes until barely tender. Cool.

Core apples, leaving whole. Cut apples into 1/2 inch (12 mm) thick rings. You should have same amount of apple slices as turnip slices.

Combine next 5 ingredients in small cup. Pour into small pie plate. Coat turnip and apple on both sides. Arrange overlapping, alternating turnip and apple in rows, in greased shallow 2 1/2 quart (2.5 L) casserole.

Melt margarine in small frying pan. Stir in pecans. Heat and stir on medium until bubbly and pecans are lightly browned. Sprinkle over turnip and apple. Drizzle any remaining margarine over top. Cover. Bake in 350°F (175°C) oven for 30 minutes until turnip is soft. Serves 8 to 10.

1 serving: 131 Calories; 4.4 g Total Fat; 109 mg Sodium; 1 g Protein; 24 g Carbohydrate; 3 g Dietary Fibre

Pictured on page 149.

To Make Ahead: Turnip can be prepared 2 to 3 days ahead of time, stored covered in refrigerator and assembled with apple rings when needed.

Spicy Sausage And Bread Stuffing

A large recipe that can be served from the slow cooker.
Has a nice kick from the jalapeño peppers.

Package of frozen sausage meat, thawed	13 oz.	375 g
Finely chopped pickled jalapeño pepper	2 tbsp.	30 mL
Herb (or garlic) seasoned croutons	10 cups	2.5 L
Chopped onion	2 cups	500 mL
Chopped celery, with leaves	2 cups	500 mL
Hard margarine (or butter)	1/2 cup	125 mL
Chopped fresh parsley (or 2 tbsp., 30 mL, flakes)	1/2 cup	125 mL
Dried sage	2 tsp.	10 mL
Dried thyme	1 tsp.	5 mL
Dried whole oregano	1 tsp.	5 mL
Pepper, sprinkle		
Can of condensed chicken broth	10 oz.	284 mL
Hot water, approximately	1/2 cup	125 mL
Hard margarine (or butter)	1 tbsp.	15 mL

Scramble-fry sausage in large frying pan until browned. Drain. Turn into large bowl.

Add jalapeño pepper and croutons. Stir.

Sauté onion and celery in first amount of margarine in same frying pan for about 10 minutes until soft.

Add next 5 ingredients. Stir. Add to sausage mixture. Stir.

Drizzle with chicken broth and enough hot water until stuffing is moist and holds together when squeezed. Mixture should not be mushy.

Grease inside liner of 3 1/2 to 4 quart (3.5 to 4 L) slow cooker with second amount of margarine. Lightly pack stuffing into liner. Cover. Cook on Low for about 2 hours until heated through and flavours are blended. Makes 7 3/4 cups (1.9 L).

1/2 cup (125 mL): 253 Calories; 16.4 g Total Fat; 648 mg Sodium; 6 g Protein; 21 g Carbohydrate; 2 g Dietary Fibre

Pictured below.

Top Left: Sweet Apple And Turnip, page 148
Top Right: Spicy Sausage And Bread Stuffing, this page
Bottom Right: Scalloped Tomatoes And Corn, page 148

Spiced Cauliflower

Nutty and aromatic with identifiable East Indian influence.
A great make ahead.

Large head of cauliflower (about 2 lbs., 900 g), large green leaves removed	1	1
Water	1 cup	250 mL
Hard margarine (or butter)	3 tbsp.	50 mL
Garlic cloves, minced (or 1/2 tsp., 2 mL, powder)	2	2
Grated gingerroot (or 1/4 tsp., 1 mL, ground ginger)	1 tsp.	5 mL
Salt	1/2 tsp.	2 mL
Ground coriander	1/2 tsp.	2 mL
Ground cumin	1/4 tsp.	1 mL
Dried crushed chilies	1/4 tsp.	1 mL
Plain yogurt	1/4 cup	60 mL
Hot water	1/4 cup	60 mL
Granulated sugar	1/2 tsp.	2 mL
Garam masala (optional)	1/2 tsp.	2 mL
Shelled and chopped pistachios (or almonds)	2 tbsp.	30 mL

Place cauliflower, root end down, on rack in large pot or Dutch oven. Add water. Bring to a boil. Cover. Reduce heat to medium-low. Cook for about 15 minutes until cauliflower is tender-crisp. Cool under cold running water until able to handle. Drain well. Cut away and discard very thick core. Cut cauliflower into serving-size pieces.

Heat margarine in large saucepan on medium. Stir in next 6 ingredients.

Add yogurt and hot water. Stir in cauliflower until coated. Cover. Cook on medium-low for about 15 minutes, stirring occasionally, until soft. Remove cover.

Sprinkle with sugar and garam masala. Heat and stir until most of liquid is absorbed and sauce is thickened. Turn into serving bowl.

Sprinkle pistachios over cauliflower mixture. Makes about 5 1/2 cups (1.4 L).

1/2 cup (125 mL): 51 Calories; 4.1 g Total Fat; 171 mg Sodium; 1 g Protein; 3 g Carbohydrate; 1 g Dietary Fibre

Pictured on page 151.

Orange Couscous With Sultanas

The perfect side dish to serve with poultry, pork or fish.

Diced onion	1/2 cup	125 mL
Diced celery	1/2 cup	125 mL
Garlic clove, minced (or 1/4 tsp., 1 mL, powder)	1	1
Hard margarine (or butter)	2 tbsp.	30 mL
Can of condensed vegetable broth	10 oz.	284 mL
Prepared orange juice	1 cup	250 mL
Water	2/3 cup	150 mL
Dried crushed chilies	1/4 tsp.	1 mL
Sultana raisins	1/2 cup	125 mL
Chopped fresh parsley (or 1 1/2 tsp., 7 mL, flakes)	2 tbsp.	30 mL
Finely grated orange zest	1 tsp.	5 mL
Couscous	2 cups	500 mL
Mandarin orange segments, for garnish	2	2
Strips of orange peel, for garnish	2	2

Sauté onion, celery and garlic in margarine in large saucepan until soft.

Stir in next 6 ingredients. Bring to a boil.

Stir in orange zest and couscous. Cover. Let stand for 10 minutes.

Garnish with orange segments and orange peel. Makes 6 cups (1.5 L).

1/2 cup (125 mL): 189 Calories; 2.6 g Total Fat; 195 mg Sodium; 5 g Protein; 36 g Carbohydrate; 2 g Dietary Fibre

Pictured on page 151.

To reheat food in the microwave, always use some form of cover. To prevent moisture loss when cooking, cover food loosely with plastic wrap and make air vents. If moisture loss is not a concern, cover food with a paper towel.

Top & Bottom: Spiced Cauliflower, page 150   Centre: Orange Couscous With Sultanas, page 150   Left & Right: Green Beans With Bacon, this page

Green Beans With Bacon

Try this yummy way to get fussy eaters to eat their vegetables. Recipe is easily doubled or tripled to serve more.

Frozen cut green beans	2 cups	500 mL
Water		
Bacon slices, diced	2	2
Chopped onion	1/4 cup	60 mL
Soy sauce	2 tsp.	10 mL
Granulated sugar	1/2 tsp.	2 mL
Salt	1/4 tsp.	1 mL
Pepper	1/16 tsp.	0.5 mL

Cook beans in small amount of water in medium saucepan for about 5 minutes until tender. Drain.

Sauté bacon and onion in medium frying pan until browned. Drain.

Add remaining 4 ingredients. Stir. Add beans. Toss to coat with sauce. Cook until heated through. Makes 2 1/4 cups (550 mL). Serves 4.

1 serving: 46 Calories; 1.7 g Total Fat; 380 mg Sodium; 2 g Protein; 6 g Carbohydrate; 2 g Dietary Fibre

Pictured above.

Maple Yams

Creamy smooth yam sprinkled with dark specks of cinnamon. Has a light maple syrup flavour.

Fresh yams, peeled and cubed	3 lbs.	1.4 kg
Water		
Maple syrup	1/4 cup	60 mL
Hard margarine (or butter)	2 tbsp.	30 mL
Salt	1/4 tsp.	1 mL
Ground cinnamon	1/2 tsp.	2 mL
Fresh parsley, for garnish		

Cook yams in water in large saucepan until tender. Drain. Mash until no lumps remain.

Add next 4 ingredients to yams. Stir.

Garnish with parsley. Makes 5 1/4 cups (1.3 L).

1/4 cup (60 mL): 69 Calories; 1.3 g Total Fat; 48 mg Sodium; 1 g Protein; 14 g Carbohydrate; 1 g Dietary Fibre

Pictured on page 172/173.

Soups

Cheese-Topped Soup

Chunks of carrots and mushrooms are nicely complemented by the melting cheese in this hearty soup.

Chopped onion	2 cups	500 mL
Diced potato	3 1/2 cups	875 mL
Sliced carrots	1 cup	250 mL
Chopped celery	1 cup	250 mL
Diced fresh mushrooms	1 cup	250 mL
Water	6 cups	1.5 L
Beef bouillon powder	1 tbsp.	15 mL
Chicken bouillon powder	1 tsp.	5 mL
Hard margarine (or butter)	1/3 cup	75 mL
All-purpose flour	1/3 cup	75 mL
Salt	1 tsp.	5 mL
Pepper	1/4 tsp.	1 mL
Grated medium Cheddar (or your favourite) cheese	1 1/2 cups	375 mL

Combine first 8 ingredients in large pot or Dutch oven. Bring to a boil. Reduce heat. Cover. Simmer for about 35 minutes until vegetables are tender.

Melt margarine in small saucepan. Mix in flour, salt and pepper until smooth. Heat and stir until golden. Stir into vegetable mixture until boiling and thickened.

Sprinkle individual servings with cheese. Makes 10 cups (2.5 L).

1 cup (250 mL): 215 Calories; 12.7 g Total Fat; 687 mg Sodium; 7 g Protein; 19 g Carbohydrate; 2 g Dietary Fibre

Pictured on page 153.

If you saved your poinsettias from last Christmas, October is the time to start getting them ready for this Christmas. Keep the plants in complete darkness during the night and leave them in a spot with lots of natural sunshine during the day.

Top Left: Barley Vegetable Soup, below

Bottom Right: Cheese-Topped Soup, page 152

Barley Vegetable Soup

Lots of colourful vegetable chunks with
plump barley in this pot of comfort food.

Can of condensed tomato soup	10 oz.	284 mL
Water	6 cups	1.5 L
Pearl barley	1/2 cup	125 mL
Frozen mixed vegetables, chop before measuring	2 cups	500 mL
Shredded cabbage	2 cups	500 mL
Sliced carrot	2 cups	500 mL
Beef bouillon powder	2 tbsp.	30 mL
Granulated sugar	2 tbsp.	30 mL
Salt	1/2 tsp.	2 mL
Pepper	1/2 tsp.	2 mL
Dried sweet basil	1/2 tsp.	2 mL
Dried whole oregano	1/4 tsp.	1 mL

Combine all 12 ingredients in large pot or Dutch oven. Bring to a boil. Reduce heat. Cover. Simmer for about 1 1/4 hours until vegetables are tender. Makes 9 cups (2.25 L).

1 cup (250 mL): 126 Calories; 1.2 g Total Fat; 796 mg Sodium; 4 g Protein; 27 g Carbohydrate; 3 g Dietary Fibre

Pictured above.

Smoky Lentil Chowder

A very good chowder for those cold days.

Medium onion, chopped	1	1
Small green pepper, chopped	1	1
Hard margarine (or butter)	1 1/2 tbsp.	25 mL
Water	6 cups	1.5 L
Cans of tomatoes, with juice (14 oz., 398 mL, each), broken up	2	2
Hickory smoke barbecue sauce	1/2 cup	125 mL
Green lentils	2 cups	500 mL
Salt	1 tsp.	5 mL
Pepper	1/4 tsp.	1 mL
Smoked pork hock (or meaty ham bone), about 1 1/3 lbs. (600 g), optional	1	1

Sauté onion and green pepper in margarine in large uncovered pot or Dutch oven until onion is soft.

Add remaining 7 ingredients. Stir. Bring to a boil. Reduce heat. Cover. Simmer for about 40 minutes until lentils and vegetables are tender. Remove pork hock. Cut off meat. Discard skin, fat and bone. Dice meat. Return meat to soup. Makes 12 cups (3 L).

1 cup (250 mL): 156 Calories; 2.2 g Total Fat; 418 mg Sodium; 11 g Protein; 25 g Carbohydrate; 5 g Dietary Fibre

Pictured on page 154.

Scotch Broth

Tender lamb in a broth with a hint of thyme.

Lamb (or beef) stew meat, diced	1 lb.	454 g
Yellow split peas	1/4 cup	60 mL
Dried green peas	1/4 cup	60 mL
Pearl barley	1/4 cup	60 mL
Water	10 cups	2.5 L
Medium carrots, diced	2	2
Diced yellow turnip	1/2 cup	125 mL
Medium onions, chopped	2	2
Medium leeks (white and tender parts only), chopped	2	2
Chopped cabbage	1/2 cup	125 mL
Salt	2 tsp.	10 mL
Pepper	1/2 tsp.	2 mL
Ground thyme	1/4 tsp.	1 mL

Place first 5 ingredients in large pot or Dutch oven. Bring to a boil. Reduce heat. Cover. Simmer for 1 hour, stirring occasionally.

Add remaining 8 ingredients. Bring to a boil. Reduce heat. Cover. Simmer for 30 to 45 minutes until vegetables are tender. Makes 13 cups (3.25 L).

1 cup (250 mL): 115 Calories; 2.1 g Total Fat; 402 mg Sodium; 10 g Protein; 14 g Carbohydrate; 2 g Dietary Fibre

Pictured on page 154/155.

Top Left: Smoky Lentil Chowder, page 153
Top Right: Cream Of Mushroom Soup, page 156
Bottom Left: Scotch Broth, above
Bottom Right: Wonton Soup, page 156

Cream Of Mushroom Soup

A creamy, smooth soup with lots of mushroom flavour and a good tang from the sour cream and vinegar.

Mayonnaise (not salad dressing)	1/2 cup	125 mL
Water	2 1/2 cups	625 mL
Beef bouillon powder	1 tbsp.	15 mL
Fresh mushrooms, large ones cut smaller	1 lb.	454 g
Sour cream	1 1/2 cups	375 mL
White vinegar	4 tsp.	20 mL
Salt	1/2 tsp.	2 mL
Pepper	1/4 tsp.	1 mL

Freshly ground pepper, for garnish
Sliced fresh mushrooms, for garnish

Process first 4 ingredients, in 2 batches, in blender until smooth. Pour into large saucepan. Bring to a boil. Reduce heat to medium-low. Cook, uncovered, for 2 minutes.

Add sour cream, vinegar, salt and pepper. Stir. Heat for about 5 minutes, stirring often, until hot.

Garnish with pepper and mushroom slices. Makes 6 cups (1.5 L).

1 cup (250 mL): 258 Calories; 24.6 g Total Fat; 625 mg Sodium; 4 g Protein; 7 g Carbohydrate; 1 g Dietary Fibre

Pictured on page 155.

Wonton Soup

A distinctive soup with a hint of orange. You'll want to make extra to freeze. Delicious!

Lean ground pork	1/4 lb.	113 g
Water chestnuts, chopped	4	4
Chopped fresh mushrooms	3/4 cup	175 mL
Grated orange peel	1/4 tsp.	1 mL
Large egg, fork-beaten	1	1
Cornstarch	1 tbsp.	15 mL
Soy sauce	1 tbsp.	15 mL
Pepper, sprinkle		
Wonton wrappers	18	18
Large egg	1	1
Water	1 tbsp.	15 mL
Chicken broth	6 cups	1.5 L
Chopped bok choy	1/2 cup	125 mL
Sliced celery	1/4 cup	60 mL
Chopped broccoli	1/4 cup	60 mL
Raw medium shrimp, peeled and deveined (about 5)	3 oz.	85 g

Scramble-fry ground pork in medium frying pan until no pink remains. Remove from heat. Drain.

Add next 7 ingredients. Mix well.

Place scant 1 tbsp. (15 mL) filling on each wrapper.

Beat second egg with water in small bowl using fork. Dampen 3 sides of each wonton wrapper with egg mixture. Roll up, tucking in sides. Pinch to seal.

Combine chicken broth, bok choy, celery and broccoli in large saucepan. Bring to a boil. Boil for 1 minute. Add wontons. Bring to a boil.

Stir in shrimp. Cook for 3 to 4 minutes until shrimp are pink. Makes 7 1/2 cups (1.9 L).

1 cup (250 mL): 174 Calories; 6.3 g Total Fat; 956 mg Sodium; 13 g Protein; 15 g Carbohydrate; trace Dietary Fibre

Pictured on page 155.

To make the most of the holiday season, make a difference in your community. Call a local charity and ask what they need, then plan a party to provide it—whether it's serving meals, carolling or decorating a tree. Or find out what items are needed (blankets, toys, canned food), and have a party to assemble these donations as well as to celebrate the holidays.

Meaty Turkey Rice Soup, below

Meaty Turkey Rice Soup

Uses remaining turkey from Stuffed Turkey Breast, page 121.
Count on two days to do this soup: one day to boil, strain and chill
the broth, and the next day to make the soup. A lot of flavour.

DAY 1

Water	12 cups	3 L
Turkey parts, with skin	6 lbs.	2.7 kg
Whole celery heart (see Note)	1	1
Medium onions, halved	2	2
Large carrot, halved	1	1
Bay leaves	2	2
Peppercorns	10	10
Fresh parsley sprigs	2	2
Salt	1 tbsp.	15 mL

DAY 2

Water		
Chopped onion	1 cup	250 mL
Chopped celery	1 cup	250 mL
Diced carrot	1 cup	250 mL
Reserved diced cooked turkey	4 cups	1 L
Cooked long grain white rice	1 1/2 cups	375 mL
Frozen peas	1 cup	250 mL
Chopped fresh parsley (or 1 tbsp., 15 mL, flakes)	1/4 cup	60 mL
Salt, to taste		
Pepper, to taste		

Day 1: Combine water and turkey parts in at least 6 quart (6 L) Dutch oven or stockpot. Bring to a boil. Boil, uncovered, for 5 minutes. Remove from heat. Carefully spoon off and discard foam from surface. Bring to a boil.

Add next 7 ingredients. Reduce heat. Simmer, partially covered, for about 3 hours until meat is almost falling off bones. Pour through sieve over large liquid measure. Remove meat from turkey bones as soon as cool enough to handle. Dice meat. Reserve 4 cups (1 L). Cover. Chill. Discard skin, turkey bones and strained solids. Chill broth overnight until fat comes to surface and solidifies.

Day 2: Carefully spoon off and discard fat from surface of broth. Add water, if necessary, to make 10 cups (2.5 L). Pour into Dutch oven or stockpot. Bring to a boil. Add onion, celery and carrot. Reduce heat. Simmer, partially covered, for 1 hour.

Add remaining 6 ingredients. Cook gently for 10 minutes until heated through. Makes about 10 1/2 cups (2.6 L) soup.

1 cup (250 mL): 289 Calories; 6.9 g Total Fat; 431 mg Sodium; 40 g Protein; 14 g Carbohydrate; 2 g Dietary Fibre

Pictured above.

Note: The celery heart is the very centre of a celery bunch, including the small white-coloured stalks with leaves. Celery hearts are available in ready-to-use packages from the produce section in grocery stores.

Boxing Day— Help Yourself!

Now it's time to relax and settle down for a true
day of rest during the holidays. Here are some
simple-to-make recipes and menu suggestions
that will keep everyone, including the cook,
satisfied without a lot of work.

Making It Easy

Ribbons and wrappings, boxes and bows—another hectic but memorable Christmas Day has come and gone! But not so your guests! Grandma and Grandpa will be with you for a few more days and the kids won't be going back to school until the new year.

There's been baking goodies since November, wrapping gifts since mid-December and your house has been given a complete Christmas makeover. Everyone's worked hard to be ready and it was all worth it! But now it's Boxing Day— a day to take it easy. Children want to play with their new toys and games or head outdoors to try the new toboggan. Teens want to sleep in and have a lazy day. Some people want to curl up and start reading the book that was in their stocking. No one wants to make any hard and fast plans. Friends or relatives may drop in, or may even come for dinner. Regardless of what your household might do on Boxing Day, it will no doubt be casual, casual, casual.

Plan for a day of "grazing," that is, serve the food so that it can be eaten at will. Everyone simply roams around, nibbling and eating when they feel like it. In the morning, pull Gingerbread Muffins, page 63, and Cranberry Scones, page 64, from the freezer and place them in a basket lined with a Christmas napkin. Lay another napkin over top to keep them from drying out. Place some butter and jams beside them, along with a stack of plates. Set a platter of fresh fruit and cheeses, covered loosely with plastic wrap, on the counter or table beside the basket. Arrange knives, rolled individually in paper napkins, in a pretty Christmas container to complete this oh-so-simple early to late morning fare.

Around midday, bring out the leftover turkey and all the fixings for Turkey Salad Wraps, page 37, or Turkey Cristo Sandwich, page 161, and let people make their own when they're ready. Replace the muffins and cheese with a tray of Christmas cookies and squares.

At the same time, or even earlier in the morning when the household is still quiet, assemble Cajun Chicken, page 111, in your slow cooker. Set it on Low to cook all day. When it's ready, serve with a simple lettuce and tomato salad, some buns and refill the Christmas goodies tray. Supper is on the table!

There are numerous ways to mix and match the recipes found in this book to accommodate the kind of Boxing Day that your family would enjoy. Following are a few menu suggestions to get you started.

Come-And-Go Boxing Day

Ricotta and Jalapeño Tarts, page 44

Hot Mushroom Dip, page 51 (with crackers)

Holiday Whirls, page 50

Peanut Butter Dip, page 54 (with fresh fruit)

Turkey Mixed Bean Soup, page 161 (with buns)

Tray of Christmas goodies, pages 82 to 91

Leftovers Party

Turkey Salad Wraps, page 37

Christmas Bread, page 72

Feta Spinach Mushroom Caps, page 43

Chocolate Almond Cookies, page 84

Travellers' Take-Away Lunch

Turkey Cristo Sandwich, page 161

(with carrot and cucumber sticks, and pickles)

Ragged Chocolate Drops, page 89

Boxing Day Buffet

Cranberry Cheese, page 55 (with crackers)

Honey Mustard Turkey Salad, page 34

Sweet Potato Biscuits, page 65

Beef Bourguignon, page 112

Peaches And Cream Cake, page 95

Boxing Day Trivia

When is Boxing Day?

In some countries, Boxing Day is celebrated on December 26, the day after Christmas Day. But in other countries, it falls on the first weekday following Christmas Day.

Who celebrates Boxing Day?

For many people, the day after Christmas Day is a holiday from work and generally schools are closed, but they have no idea there is a name, let alone a reason, for the day. Commonwealth countries such as Australia, Canada and New Zealand, along with Britain, are widely known to celebrate Boxing Day.

What is the origin of Boxing Day?

There are differing stories and folklore attached to this aprés Christmas holiday, but there are a few basic facts that almost everyone agrees upon when discussing the origin of Boxing Day: This annual holiday began in Britain in the 19th century under Queen Victoria and it has to do with giving presents such as money or household goods to the less fortunate. Beyond that, the details grow hazy.

The following are the more popular of the Boxing Day stories:

* Churches used to open their alms boxes that contained money from people making special holiday donations. The clergy would distribute the contents to the poor the following day.

* English servants were required to work on Christmas Day to help their masters' celebrations run smoothly. They were, therefore, given leave the next day to visit their own families. Typically, their employers would give each servant a box containing gifts and bonuses to take home.

* Masters gave their servants an allotment of practical goods at Christmas, the amount and value being determined by the status of the workers and the size of their family. Spun cloth, durable food supplies, tools and leather goods were packed into one box per family for easy travelling. These gifts were not voluntary but more of an obligation by masters because often servants were completely dependant on their masters for food and clothing.

* British servants used to take boxes to their masters in which the masters would place coins as a special year-end gift. Or the servants would smash open small earthenware boxes filled with money given specifically to them by their masters.

* The poor would carry empty boxes door to door the day after Christmas and people would fill these boxes with clothing, goods, sweets and money.

* Centuries ago, the merchant class gave boxes of food and fruit to the tradespeople and servants the day after Christmas as a form of a tip for service done. In the same way, nowadays, we might give the piano teacher or paper boy a little something extra at Christmas to show our gratitude—only now it's in an envelope rather than a box!

The common theme in all of these stories is that the rich (landowners, employers, royalty) gave gifts to the poor (servants, tradespeople, the general poor), sometimes out of obligation and sometimes out of simple generosity. It should be noted that the poor never gave a gift back to the rich as this would have been seen as a presumptuous act of claiming equality with the rich.

What does Boxing Day mean today?

It would seem that Boxing Day has nothing to do with the empty boxes piled in the corner by the Christmas tree. The origin of the name seems to have something to do with boxes, but the true meaning has been lost over time. Boxing Day in the 21st century is a day to be together with family, celebrating the holidays with food, fun and love. Many people use this day to go shopping to exchange gifts or to purchase sale-priced items. Many churches and organizations follow the original tradition of donating special money and goods collected to assist families who are in need.

Turkey Cristo Sandwich, below

Turkey Cristo Sandwich

An excellent and easy-to-make sandwich.
A very filling meal for one person or perfect for
two people, along with a leafy green side salad.

Cooked turkey slices (1 oz., 28 g), to cover	2	2
Salt, sprinkle		
Pepper, sprinkle		
Process Swiss cheese slice	1	1
Whole wheat (or white) bread slice (buttered, optional)	1	1
Cooked ham slice (about 3/4 oz., 21 g)	1	1
Process Swiss cheese slice	1	1
White bread slices (buttered, optional)	2	2
Large egg	1	1
Water	1 tbsp.	15 mL
Hard margarine (or butter)	2 tsp.	10 mL

Layer first 7 ingredients, in order given, on white bread slice. Top with remaining white bread slice.

Beat egg and water together in shallow bowl using fork. Dip sandwich on both sides to soak up all of egg mixture.

Heat margarine in frying pan on medium until sizzling. Place sandwich in frying pan. Cook for 3 to 4 minutes per side until golden and cheese is melted. Serves 1 or 2.

1 serving: 580 Calories; 30.1 g Total Fat; 974 mg Sodium; 36 g Protein; 41 g Carbohydrate; 3 g Dietary Fibre

Pictured above and on page 36.

Turkey Mixed Bean Soup

A great way to use up leftover holiday turkey.
Serve with Two-Toned Buns, page 65.

Turkey carcass	1	1
Water	12 cups	3 L
Bay leaves	2	2
Large onion, chopped	1	1
Celery ribs, with leaves, chopped	2	2
Medium carrots, chopped	3	3
Can of mixed beans, with liquid	19 oz.	540 mL
Can of diced tomatoes, with juice	14 oz.	398 mL
Chicken bouillon powder	1 tbsp.	15 mL
Dried whole oregano	1 tsp.	5 mL
Salt	1 tsp.	5 mL
Pepper	1/4 tsp.	1 mL

Bring turkey carcass, water and bay leaves to a boil in large pot or Dutch oven. Skim off and discard foam that forms on top. Reduce heat. Cover. Simmer for 1 1/2 hours. Remove turkey carcass. Remove meat from bones. Dice meat. Discard bones. Pour stock through sieve over large saucepan. Discard solids. Add meat to soup.

Add remaining 9 ingredients. Bring to a boil on medium. Reduce heat to medium-low. Simmer, uncovered, for 30 to 45 minutes, stirring occasionally, until vegetables are tender. Makes about 19 cups (4.75 L).

1 cup (250 mL): 188 Calories; 4.5 g Total Fat; 399 mg Sodium; 27 g Protein; 9 g Carbohydrate; 1 g Dietary Fibre

Pictured on page 35.

Turkey Mixed Bean Soup, above

International Buffet

Import a new tradition into your arrary of holiday menus
with this collection of recipes with influences from
around the world. There's a mosiac of flavours to match
our country's diverse cultural background.

Slow-Cooker Dolmades

Pronounced dohl-MAH-dehs. The name of this Greek dish comes from the Arabic word for "something stuffed." Makes a big batch. Serve garnished with fresh lemon slices. Delicious with Greek tzatziki dip or plain yogurt.

Medium-large grapevine leaves (see Note)	4 cups	1 L
Cold water, several changes		
Long grain white rice, uncooked	1 3/4 cups	425 mL
Water	2 1/2 cups	625 mL
Salt	1 tsp.	5 mL
Diced onion	1 1/2 cups	375 mL
Olive (or cooking) oil	1 tbsp.	15 mL
Garlic cloves, minced (or 3/4 tsp., 4 mL, powder)	3	3
Lean ground lamb	1 lb.	454 g
Raisins, chopped (optional)	1/2 cup	125 mL
Dried mint leaves	1 tsp.	5 mL
Parsley flakes	1 tsp.	5 mL
Dried whole oregano	1 tsp.	5 mL
Salt	1 tsp.	5 mL
Pepper	1/4 tsp.	1 mL
Boiling water	4 1/3 cups	1.1 L
Olive (or cooking) oil	3 tbsp.	50 mL
Lemon juice	1/2 cup	125 mL
Garlic cloves, cut in half (or 1/4 tsp., 1 mL, powder)	4	4
Granulated sugar	1/2 tsp.	2 mL

Carefully unroll grapevine leaves. Put into large bowl. Cover with cold water. Let stand for 10 minutes. Drain and repeat twice more with cold water until brine is rinsed from grapevine leaves. Set aside.

Combine rice, water and first amount of salt in medium saucepan. Bring to a boil. Stir. Reduce heat. Cover. Simmer for about 12 minutes until liquid is absorbed and rice is firm. Remove cover. Cool. Fluff with fork several times while cooling to break up any clumps.

Sauté onion in first amount of olive oil in large frying pan for about 5 minutes until soft.

Add first amount of garlic and ground lamb. Scramble-fry for about 5 minutes, breaking up large pieces, until lamb is no longer pink. Drain. Turn into large bowl.

Add rice and next 6 ingredients. Stir well. Carefully separate grapevine leaves, reserving any torn or small leaves to separate layers. Trim off and discard any hard stems. Line bottom of 5 quart (5 L) slow cooker with few torn or small grapevine leaves. Place 1 to 2 tbsp. (15 to 30 mL) filling (depending on size of leaves) in centre of each grapevine leaf on rough side. Roll up, from stem end, tucking in sides to enclose filling. Do not roll too tightly as rice will expand. Arrange rolls close together, seam-side down, in layers in slow cooker. Separate layers with torn or small grapevine leaves. Place any remaining grapevine leaves over top layer of dolmades.

Stir remaining 5 ingredients together in medium bowl. Slowly pour enough water mixture over dolmades, allowing all air spaces to fill, until almost covered and water mixture is just visible on sides. Reserve any remaining water mixture. Cook on Low for 3 1/2 to 4 hours, checking after 2 1/2 hours to see if more water mixture is needed. Turn off slow cooker. Do not uncover. Let stand in slow cooker for at least 30 minutes to set rolls. Drain off and discard liquid. Carefully remove dolmades to serving plate or airtight containers for freezing. Serve at room temperature. Large rolls can be cut in half diagonally. Makes about 6 dozen dolmades.

1 dolmade: 46 Calories; 2.3 g Total Fat; 111 mg Sodium; 2 g Protein; 5 g Carbohydrate; trace Dietary Fibre

Pictured on page 165.

Note: Grapevine leaves can be purchased fresh or in various sized jars. Some jars have a lot of very small leaves that are unusable for rolling in this type of recipe, so you may need 1 to 2 jars, or possibly more, if all the leaves in one jar are small.

Photo Legend next page:

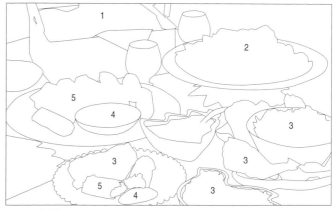

1. Handheld Tourtières, page 166
2. Slow-Cooker Dolmades, this page
3. Shrimp Salad Rolls, page 166
4. Savoury Orange Dipping Sauce, page 92
5. Spring Rolls, page 167

Shrimp Salad Rolls

*The interesting contrast of ingredients provides
excellent colour to this Asian appetizer.*

CHILI MAYONNAISE

Mayonnaise (not salad dressing)	1/3 cup	75 mL
Plain yogurt	1/4 cup	60 mL
Seafood cocktail sauce	2 tbsp.	30 mL
Sambal oelek (chili paste)	2 tsp.	10 mL
Finely chopped green onion	1 tbsp.	15 mL

SAUCE

Water	2 tbsp.	30 mL
Chili sauce	1 tbsp.	15 mL
Sherry (or alcohol-free sherry)	1 tbsp.	15 mL
Hoisin sauce	1 tbsp.	15 mL
Dark sesame (or cooking) oil	1 tsp.	5 mL
Granulated sugar	1 tsp.	5 mL
Cornstarch	2 tsp.	10 mL

FILLING

Garlic clove, minced (or 1/4 tsp., 1 mL, powder)	1	1
Finely grated gingerroot (or 1/4 tsp., 1 mL, ground ginger)	1 tsp.	5 mL
Finely chopped broccoli, with stems	1 cup	250 mL
Grated carrot	1/4 cup	60 mL
Cooking oil	2 tbsp.	30 mL
Raw medium shrimp (about 15), peeled, deveined and chopped (about 2 cups, 500 mL)	1/2 lb.	225 g
Green onions, sliced	2	2
Salt	1/2 tsp.	2 mL
Cellophane (mung bean) noodles	2 oz.	57 g
Cold water, to cover		
Large butter (or iceberg) lettuce leaves	24	24
Chopped roasted peanuts, for garnish		

Chili Mayonnaise: Combine all 5 ingredients in small bowl. Cover. Chill. Makes 2/3 cup (150 mL) chili mayonnaise.

Sauce: Stir all 7 ingredients together in separate small bowl. Set aside.

Filling: Sauté garlic, ginger, broccoli and carrot in cooking oil in wok or large frying pan on medium-high for 1 minute.

Add shrimp and green onion. Stir-fry for 2 to 3 minutes until shrimp is pink. Add salt. Stir. Stir sauce. Add to shrimp mixture. Stir-fry for 1 to 2 minutes until sauce is thickened. Transfer to large bowl.

Soak noodles in cold water for 5 minutes. Drain well. Snip noodles with scissors to make more manageable for serving. Add to shrimp mixture. Toss. Makes about 3 cups (750 mL) filling.

Place lettuce leaves in stacks around filling. Individuals serve themselves by placing about 2 tbsp. (30 mL) filling on each lettuce leaf. Serve with peanuts and Chili Mayonnaise. Serves 6 to 8.

1 serving: 259 Calories; 16.9 g Total Fat; 508 mg Sodium; 10 g Protein; 17 g Carbohydrate; 1 g Dietary Fibre

Pictured on page 164 and on page 165.

Handheld Tourtières

*Meat-filled French-Canadian pastries.
Serve with Rhubarb Relish, page 93.*

Lean ground beef	1 lb.	454 g
Lean ground pork	1/2 lb.	225 g
Diced onion	1 cup	250 mL
Seasoned salt	1 1/2 tsp.	7 mL
Beef bouillon powder	1 tsp.	5 mL
Pepper	1 tsp.	5 mL
Poultry seasoning	1 tsp.	5 mL
Water	1 1/2 cups	375 mL
Instant potato flakes, approximately	1 cup	250 mL
Pastry for three 2 crust pies, your own or a mix		

Put first 8 ingredients into large saucepan. Bring to a boil on medium. Boil slowly, uncovered, for 30 minutes. Remove from heat.

Add enough instant potato flakes, 1/4 cup (60 mL) at a time, until liquid is absorbed. Mixture should be thick enough to hold its shape. Cool. Makes 5 cups (1.25 L) filling.

Roll out 1/3 of pastry into 16 x 16 inch (40 x 40 cm) square on lightly floured surface. Cut into 16 squares. Place about 1 1/2 to 2 tbsp. (25 to 30 mL) filling in centre of each square. Dampen edges with water. Fold diagonally. Seal edges using fork. Cut small slits in top using tip of sharp knife. Arrange on ungreased baking sheet. Repeat with remaining pastry and filling. Bake in 375°F (190°C) oven for about 25 minutes until golden. Makes 4 dozen tourtières.

1 tourtière: 119 Calories; 7.6 g Total Fat; 162 mg Sodium; 3 g Protein; 9 g Carbohydrate; trace Dietary Fibre

Pictured on page 164.

Spring Rolls

Traditionally these Asian appetizers are deep-fried but are also very good baked. Serve with Savoury Orange Dipping Sauce, page 92.

Cooking oil	1 tbsp.	15 mL
Boneless, skinless chicken breast halves (about 2), finely chopped	1/2 lb.	225 g
Medium carrot, grated	1	1
Finely grated gingerroot (or 1/4 tsp., 1 mL, ground ginger)	1 1/2 tsp.	7 mL
Garlic clove, minced (or 1/4 tsp., 1 mL, powder)	1	1
Grated cabbage, lightly packed	2 cups	500 mL
Fresh bean sprouts	2 cups	500 mL
Chopped green onion	1/3 cup	75 mL
Soy sauce	1 1/2 tbsp.	25 mL
Salt	1 tsp.	5 mL
Pepper	1/8 tsp.	0.5 mL
Spring roll wrappers (6 inch, 15 cm, size)	24	24
Cooking oil, for deep-frying	5 cups	1.25 L

Heat cooking oil in wok or large frying pan on medium. Add chicken, carrot, ginger and garlic. Stir-fry for 5 minutes.

Add cabbage and bean sprouts. Stir-fry for 2 minutes. Add green onion. Stir-fry for 2 minutes. Remove from heat.

Stir in soy sauce, salt and pepper. Makes 3 cups (750 mL) filling.

Place 1 spring roll wrapper on work surface with 1 point towards you. Spread about 2 tbsp. (30 mL) filling in between point and centre (see Figure 1). Fold point over filling (see Figure 2). Moisten open edges with water. Fold each side point toward centre (see Figure 3). Roll up. Seal. Repeat with remaining spring roll wrappers and filling, stirring filling occasionally to keep moisture evenly distributed.

Deep-fry, in batches, in hot (375°F, 190°C) cooking oil for about 5 minutes, turning at halftime, until golden. Remove to paper towels to drain. Makes 24 spring rolls.

1 spring roll: 136 Calories; 3.6 g Total Fat; 350 mg Sodium; 6 g Protein; 20 g Carbohydrate; trace Dietary Fibre

Pictured on page 164.

BAKED SPRING ROLLS: Arrange, seam-side down, on greased baking sheet. Bake in 375°F (190°C) oven for about 18 minutes until golden.

Sauerkraut Salad

This German salad is very good and very colourful with red and green bits showing. Must be made the day before serving.

Can of sauerkraut, rinsed, drained and squeezed dry	28 oz.	796 mL
Chopped onion	1 cup	250 mL
Chopped celery	1 cup	250 mL
Green pepper, chopped	1	1
Jars of pimiento (2 oz., 57 mL, each), chopped	2	2
Large tart cooking apple (such as Granny Smith), peeled and grated	1	1
Granulated sugar	3/4 cup	175 mL

Combine all 7 ingredients in large bowl. Chill for 24 hours to blend flavours. Stir. Store in airtight container in refrigerator for about 1 month. Makes about 4 cups (1 L).

1/2 cup (125 mL): 124 Calories; 0.3 g Total Fat; 673 mg Sodium; 2 g Protein; 31 g Carbohydrate; 4 g Dietary Fibre

Pictured on page 168.

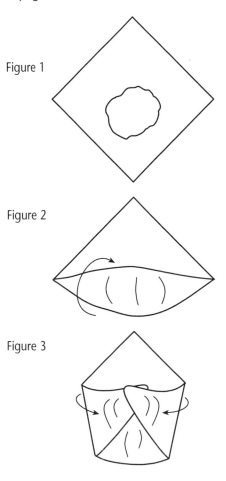

Figure 1

Figure 2

Figure 3

Bottom Left: Mexican Christmas Salad, below

Top Right: Sauerkraut Salad, page 167

Mexican Christmas Salad

A beautiful, colourful, crunchy salad using crunchy jicama, fresh and canned fruit and beets.

BALSAMIC DRESSING

Cooking oil	1 tbsp.	15 mL
All-purpose flour	1 tbsp.	15 mL
Reserved pineapple juice	1/3 cup	75 mL
Balsamic vinegar	2 tbsp.	30 mL
Brown sugar, packed	2 tbsp.	30 mL
Medium navel oranges (or other seedless oranges), peel and outside membrane removed, cut in half and cut crosswise into 1/4 inch (6 mm) slices	4	4
Medium red grapefruit, peeled, sectioned, membrane and seeds discarded, cut bite size	1	1
Can of pineapple tidbits, juice drained and reserved	14 oz.	398 mL
Ripe kiwifruit, peeled and diced	2	2
Peeled and julienned jicama	1 cup	250 mL
Can of sliced beets, rinsed, drained and cut julienne	14 oz.	398 mL

Crisp romaine lettuce and/or Belgian endive leaves	8	8
Roasted unsalted peanuts, chopped	2 tbsp.	30 mL
Shelled, roasted sunflower seeds	1 tbsp.	15 mL

Balsamic Dressing: Stir cooking oil into flour in small saucepan until smooth. Stir in pineapple juice, vinegar and brown sugar. Heat and stir on medium until boiling and thickened. Cool. Makes about 1/2 cup (125 mL) dressing.

Put next 5 ingredients into large bowl. Drizzle with dressing. Toss to coat. Chill until ready to serve.

Just before serving, add beets. Mix well.

Pile salad onto lettuce leaf-lined serving dish. Sprinkle with peanuts and sunflower seeds. Makes 8 1/2 cups (2.1 L).

3/4 cup (175 mL): 115 Calories; 2.7 g Total Fat; 55 mg Sodium; 2 g Protein; 23 g Carbohydrate; 2 g Dietary Fibre

Pictured above.

Variation: Add 2 medium bananas, sliced, to salad at same time as beets.

Variation: Add 1 pomegranate, peeled and membranes discarded, at same time as oranges, reserving 1/4 cup (60 mL). Sprinkle reserved pomegranate over top of finished salad.

Pineapple Coconut Curry

Lots of sauce with a mild curry flavour in this Asian dish. Serve with a variety of condiments, such as chopped cashew nuts, diced cucumber and chutney. Best to make the whole recipe the day before and reheat.

Beef inside round steak, cut into 3/4 inch (2 cm) cubes	2 lbs.	900 g
Lean boneless pork loin, cut into 3/4 inch (2 cm) cubes	2 lbs.	900 g
Cooking oil	2 tbsp.	30 mL
Sliced onion	1 1/2 cups	375 mL
Mild (or medium) curry paste	1 1/2 tbsp.	25 mL
Slivered crystallized ginger	1/4 cup	60 mL
Chopped fresh mint leaves (or 1 1/2 tsp., 7 mL, dried)	2 tbsp.	30 mL
Salt	1 tsp.	5 mL
Pepper	1/8 tsp.	0.5 mL
Ground cloves, just a pinch		
All-purpose flour	3 tbsp.	50 mL
Can of crushed pineapple, with juice	14 oz.	398 mL
Can of condensed beef consommé	10 oz.	284 mL
Coconut milk	1 cup	250 mL
Flake coconut	1 cup	250 mL
Lime juice	2 tbsp.	30 mL

Brown beef and pork, in batches, in cooking oil in large frying pan. Remove beef and pork, using slotted spoon, to ungreased 3 quart (3 L) casserole.

Add next 7 ingredients to drippings in same frying pan. Heat and stir for about 5 minutes until onion is soft. Remove from heat.

Sprinkle flour over onion mixture. Stir well. Slowly stir in pineapple with juice and beef consommé. Pour over beef and pork. Cover. Bake in 300°F (150°C) oven for about 1 3/4 hours until meat is very tender. Chill overnight to blend flavours. Skim fat from top if desired. Cook in 350°F (175°C) oven for 60 to 80 minutes, stirring once, until heated through.

Stir in coconut milk, coconut and lime juice. Makes 10 cups (2.5 L).

1 cup (250 mL): 499 Calories; 30.3 g Total Fat; 494 mg Sodium; 41 g Protein; 16 g Carbohydrate; 2 g Dietary Fibre

Pictured on page 170.

Shrimp Creole

This richly flavoured dish will remind you of Southern U.S.A. Serve over rice.

Chopped celery	1 cup	250 mL
Chopped onion	1 cup	250 mL
Green pepper, diced	1	1
Garlic clove, minced (or 1/4 tsp., 1 mL, powder)	1	1
Cooking oil	1 tbsp.	15 mL
Can of diced tomatoes, with juice	14 oz.	398 mL
Tomato paste	2 tbsp.	30 mL
Granulated sugar	2 tsp.	10 mL
Lemon juice	1 tbsp.	15 mL
Louisiana hot sauce (optional)	1 – 3 tsp.	5 – 15 mL
Bay leaf	1	1
Dried thyme	1/2 tsp.	2 mL
Salt	1/2 tsp.	2 mL
Pepper	1/4 tsp.	1 mL
Raw medium shrimp (about 60), peeled and deveined (or frozen, thawed)	2 lbs.	900 g

Sauté celery, onion, green pepper and garlic in cooking oil in large wok or Dutch oven until lightly browned.

Add next 9 ingredients. Stir. Bring to a boil. Reduce heat. Simmer, uncovered, for 10 minutes to blend flavours.

Add shrimp. Bring to a boil. Reduce heat. Simmer for 10 minutes, stirring occasionally, until shrimp are pink. Makes 6 3/4 cups (1.7 L). Serves 6.

1 serving: 226 Calories; 5.3 g Total Fat; 553 mg Sodium; 32 g Protein; 12 g Carbohydrate; 2 g Dietary Fibre

Pictured below.

Shrimp Creole, above

Varenyky With Onion Butter

This popular Ukrainian and Polish dish is also known as pyrohy, perogies or potato dumplings. Cheesy potato filling surrounded by a tender, almost non-existent, dough that melts in your mouth.

DOUGH

All-purpose flour	2 cups	500 mL
Baking powder	1/4 tsp.	1 mL
Salt	1 tsp.	5 mL
Cooking oil	2 tsp.	10 mL
Warm water, approximately	2/3 cup	150 mL

ONION BUTTER

Finely diced onion	1/2 cup	125 mL
Butter (not margarine)	1/4 cup	60 mL

TWO-CHEESE POTATO FILLING

Hot mashed potatoes (3 to 4 medium)	1 3/4 cups	425 mL
Grated sharp Cheddar cheese	3/4 cup	175 mL
Creamed cottage cheese, mashed with fork	1/3 cup	75 mL
Pepper	1/8 tsp.	0.5 mL
Boiling water	16 cups	4 L
Salt	1 tbsp.	15 mL

Dough: Combine flour, baking powder and salt in food processor. Process for 3 seconds.

With motor running, slowly add cooking oil and enough warm water through feed chute until a ball begins to form. Turn dough out onto lightly floured surface. Knead 3 to 4 times until smooth. Cover with plastic wrap. Let stand for 20 minutes.

Onion Butter: Sauté onion in butter in small saucepan on medium-low for about 10 minutes until onion is soft but not brown. Keep hot.

Two-Cheese Potato Filling: Mix first 4 ingredients in medium bowl until Cheddar cheese melts and mixture is evenly moist. Makes about 2 1/4 cups (550 mL) filling. Divide dough into 4 equal portions. Roll out 1 portion into a rope about 12 inches (30 cm) long. Keep other portions covered. Cut at 1 inch (2.5 cm) intervals. Press balls slightlyto flatten. Cover with plastic wrap. Stretch and press 1 ball to about 2 1/2 inches (6.4 cm) in diameter. Place in palm of hand. Place about 2 tsp. (10 mL) filling in centre.

Left & Bottom: Pineapple Coconut Curry, page 169
Top Right: Baccalà, page 172

Fold dough in half. With floured fingers, pinch edges firmly together to seal. Edges of dough may be moistened if desired. Arrange in single layer on lightly floured tea towel-lined baking sheet. Cover with tea towel to prevent drying. Repeat with remaining dough and filling.

Cook varenyky, in batches, in boiling water and salt in large pot or Dutch oven for 3 to 4 minutes, stirring occasionally, until varenyky float to top. Allow to bob for 1 minute. Remove using slotted spoon. Drain. Turn into large bowl. Drizzle some Onion Butter over each varenyky batch. Gently shake to mix and prevent sticking. Makes 4 dozen varenyky.

1 varenyky: 47 Calories; 2 g Total Fat; 104 mg Sodium; 1 g Protein; 6 g Carbohydrate; trace Dietary Fibre

Pictured on page 172/173.

Variation: Add 6 bacon slices, cooked crisp and crumbled, to Two-Cheese Potato Filling.

Variation: After varenyky are cooked, sauté, in batches, in 2 tsp. (10 mL) butter in frying pan until lightly browned.

To Make Ahead: Place filled varenyky (cooked or uncooked) on baking sheet, in layers between waxed paper or parchment paper. Cover. Freeze until solid. To remove varenyky, hit baking sheet on counter to pop them off. Store in resealable freezer bags in freezer. To cook from frozen, do not thaw. Boil, as above, increasing cooking time after they float to top.

Many Jewels Stir-Fry

The jewels are evident in the vibrant colours,
crisp texture and great shapes. Serve over rice vermicelli.

SAUCE

Water	1/3 cup	75 mL
Oyster sauce	1/3 cup	75 mL
Soy sauce	1/4 cup	60 mL
Sherry (or alcohol-free sherry)	1 tbsp.	15 mL
Cornstarch	2 tbsp.	30 mL
Brown sugar, packed	2 tsp.	10 mL
Cooking oil	2 tbsp.	30 mL
Garlic cloves, minced (or 3/4 tsp., 4 mL, powder)	3	3
Grated gingerroot (or 1/4 – 3/4 tsp., 1 – 4 mL, ground ginger)	1 – 3 tsp.	5 – 15 mL
Fresh small chili pepper, seeded and finely diced (see Note)	1	1
Medium carrot, decoratively cut	1	1
Small green pepper, cut into 3/4 inch (2 cm) diamond shapes	1	1
Small yellow pepper, cut into 3/4 inch (2 cm) diamond shapes	1	1
Small red pepper, cut into 3/4 inch (2 cm) diamond shapes	1	1
Medium zucchini, with peel, quartered lengthwise and sliced into 1/2 inch (12 mm) pieces	1	1
Quartered fresh mushrooms	1 1/2 cups	375 mL
Can of sliced water chestnuts, drained	8 oz.	227 mL
Sesame seeds, toasted (see Tip, page 100)	1 tbsp.	15 mL

Sauce: Stir first 6 ingredients together in small bowl. Set aside.

Heat cooking oil in wok or large frying pan on medium-high. Add garlic, ginger, chili pepper and carrot. Stir-fry for about 1 minute until fragrant. Add all 3 peppers. Stir-fry for 2 minutes.

Add zucchini, mushrooms and water chestnuts. Stir-fry for 2 to 3 minutes until zucchini is tender-crisp. Stir sauce. Add to vegetable mixture. Heat and stir until sauce is thickened and coats vegetables.

Sprinkle sesame seeds over vegetable mixture. Makes 6 1/2 cups (1.6 L).

1 cup (250 mL): 135 Calories; 5.4 g Total Fat; 1768 mg Sodium; 3 g Protein; 20 g Carbohydrate; 3 g Dietary Fibre

Pictured on page 172/173.

Note: Wear gloves when chopping chili peppers and avoid touching your eyes.

Greek Lemon Potatoes

A light lemon flavour with a hint of oregano
in these light golden potatoes.

Medium potatoes (about 2 lbs., 900 g), peeled and quartered	8	8
Olive (or cooking) oil	2 tbsp.	30 mL
Hard margarine (or butter), melted	2 tbsp.	30 mL
Freshly squeezed lemon juice	3 tbsp.	50 mL
Dried whole oregano	1 1/2 tsp.	7 mL
Salt	1 1/2 tsp.	7 mL
Pepper, generous sprinkle		
Hot water	2/3 cup	150 mL

Rinse potatoes. Turn into shallow roasting pan. Drizzle olive oil, margarine and lemon juice over potatoes. Sprinkle with oregano, salt and pepper. Stir to coat.

Carefully pour hot water down 1 side of pan, being sure not to rinse coating from potatoes. Roast, uncovered, in 400°F (205°C) oven for 45 to 60 minutes, shaking pan and adding more hot water as necessary to keep potatoes from sticking to bottom of pan, until golden brown. Serves 8.

1 serving: 147 Calories; 6.5 g Total Fat; 486 mg Sodium; 2 g Protein; 21 g Carbohydrate; 2 g Dietary Fibre

Pictured on page 173.

Baccalà

Pronounced bah-kah-LAH. An Italian dish made from salted cod, traditionally served as one of the many meatless dishes on Christmas Eve. We've adapted the very salty traditional recipe to suit most tastes by substituting regular cod for some of the salted cod that would normally be used.

Dried bone-in salted cod	10 1/2 oz.	300 g
Cold water, several changes		
Garlic clove, minced (or 1/4 tsp., 1 mL, powder)	1	1
Medium red peppers, cut into 3/4 inch (2 cm) pieces	3	3
Olive (or cooking) oil	1 tbsp.	15 mL
Can of roma (plum) tomatoes, with juice, chopped	19 oz.	540 mL
Dried sweet basil	2 tsp.	10 mL
Dried whole oregano	1 tsp.	5 mL
Pepper	1/4 tsp.	1 mL
Fresh (or frozen, thawed) cod fillets, cut bite size	16 oz.	500 g

Cut salted cod into large pieces. Put into large bowl. Cover with cold water. Soak for 24 hours, draining and changing water 3 to 4 times. Drain. Put into large saucepan. Cover with fresh water. Bring to a boil. Reduce heat. Simmer, uncovered, for 10 minutes. Drain. Let stand until cool enough to handle. Remove skin and bones from cod. Cut into bite-size pieces. Set aside.

Sauté garlic and red pepper in olive oil in large frying pan for about 4 minutes until red pepper is tender-crisp.

Add tomatoes with juice, basil, oregano and pepper. Bring to a boil. Reduce heat. Simmer, uncovered, for 30 minutes.

Stir in salted cod and fresh cod. Heat for 5 to 10 minutes until fresh cod flakes easily when tested with fork. Makes 8 1/2 cups (2.1 L). Serves 6 to 8.

1 serving: 292 Calories; 4.6 g Total Fat; 1954 mg Sodium; 48 g Protein; 14 g Carbohydrate; 3 g Dietary Fibre

Pictured on page 170.

Top Left: Maple Yams, page 151
Top Right: Greek Lemon Potatoes, page 171
Centre Left: Varenyky With Onion Butter, page 170
Bottom Right: Many Jewels Stir-Fry, page 171

Norwegian Almond Pastry

A very rich European pastry with crisp pastry and soft creamy filling. A bit fussy and time-consuming, so make in two or three stages and then have the rolls in the freezer to bake up fresh any time.

BUTTER PASTRY

All-purpose flour	4 cups	1 L
Baking powder	1 1/2 tsp.	7 mL
Salt	1/2 tsp.	2 mL
Cold butter (not margarine), cut into 16 pieces	1 lb.	454 g
Ice water	1 cup	250 mL

ALMOND FILLING

Blocks of almond paste (8 oz., 225 g, each), about 2 cups (500 mL), room temperature	2	2
Granulated sugar	2/3 cup	150 mL
All-purpose flour	1 tbsp.	15 mL
Water	1 tbsp.	15 mL
Large egg, fork-beaten	1	1
Ground almonds	1 cup	250 mL
Egg white (large), lightly fork-beaten	1	1
Granulated sugar, sprinkle		

Butter Pastry: Stir flour, baking powder and salt together in large bowl. Cut in butter until crumbly and consistency of small peas. Make a well in centre.

Pour ice water into well. Mix, bringing in flour from sides of bowl, until no flour remains and dough is wet and sticky. Press into ungreased waxed paper-lined 8 × 8 inch (20 × 20 cm) or 9 × 9 inch (22 × 22 cm) pan. Cover. Chill overnight. Store in refrigerator for up to 2 days.

Almond Filling: Crumble almond paste into medium bowl using hands. Microwave on high (100%) for 10 seconds if too hard to crumble. Add first amount of sugar, flour, water and egg. Beat until smooth. Add almonds. Stir. Cover. Chill overnight. Store in refrigerator for up to 2 days. Makes about 2 cups (500 mL) filling. Cut pastry in pan into 8 equal pieces. Roll out 1 pastry piece on floured surface to 8 × 10 inch (20 × 25 cm) rectangle. Turn filling out onto lightly floured surface. Form 1/4 cup (60 mL) filling into 9 inch (22 cm) long rope. Place rope down long side of pastry, about 1 inch (2.5 cm) in from long edge. Brush edges of pastry piece with water. Roll up, jelly roll-style, to enclose filling. Pinch to seal. Cover securely with plastic wrap. Repeat with remaining pastry and filling. Freeze until firm.

Arrange frozen rolls, seam-side down, on large ungreased baking sheet. Pierce each roll in several spots, through to filling, using wooden pick dipped in flour. Brush with egg white. Sprinkle second amount of sugar over top. Bake in 400°F (205°C) oven for 20 to 25 minutes until golden. Let stand until rolls are lukewarm. Cut, on diagonal, into 3/4 inch (2 cm) pieces. Makes 8 rolls, each roll cutting into about 12 pieces, for a total of about 96 pieces.

1 piece: 87 Calories; 5.7 g Total Fat; 59 mg Sodium; 1 g Protein; 8 g Carbohydrate; 1 g Dietary Fibre

Pictured on page 175.

Rice Pudding

This just might be the best rice pudding you'll ever eat. A Danish tradition at Christmastime gives an extra present to the lucky person finding the almond in their dish. Recipe reprinted from Dinners of the World, page 133.

Long grain white rice, uncooked	1 cup	250 mL
Water	2 cups	500 mL
Cinnamon stick (4 inch, 10 cm, length)	1	1
Milk	4 cups	1 L
Granulated sugar	1 cup	250 mL
Raisins	1/2 cup	125 mL
Salt	1/4 tsp.	1 mL
Egg yolks (large)	3	3
Vanilla	1 tsp.	5 mL
Whole blanched almond	1	1

Combine rice, water and cinnamon stick in medium saucepan. Cover. Bring to a boil. Reduce heat. Simmer for about 15 minutes until water is absorbed and rice is tender. Remove and discard cinnamon stick.

Heat milk in large heavy saucepan. Stir in sugar, raisins and salt. Add rice. Bring to a boil. Reduce heat. Gently simmer, uncovered, for about 15 minutes, stirring often, until thick but still soft.

Beat egg yolks in small bowl using fork. Stir in vanilla. Add about 1/2 cup (125 mL) hot rice mixture to egg yolk mixture. Mix well. Stir into hot rice mixture.

Add almond. Heat and stir for about 1 minute. Makes 6 cups (1.5 L).

3/4 cup (175 mL): 298 Calories; 3.5 g Total Fat; 144 mg Sodium; 7 g Protein; 60 g Carbohydrate; 1 g Dietary Fibre

Pictured on page 175.

Top Left: Rice Pudding, page 174   Bottom Left: Norwegian Almond Pastry, page 174   Right: Old Country Yogurt Slice, this page

Old Country Yogurt Slice

This dessert square, hailing from old Eastern Europe, is not very sweet, just very satisfying. Serve with fresh fruit.

DOUGH

Hard margarine (or butter), softened	1/2 cup	125 mL
Granulated sugar	1/2 cup	125 mL
Egg yolks (large)	4	4
Light sour cream	1 tbsp.	15 mL
All-purpose flour	2 1/2 cups	625 mL
Baking powder	1 tbsp.	15 mL

FILLING

Low-fat vanilla yogurt (not fat-free)	3 cups	750 mL
Light sour cream	1 2/3 cups	400 mL
Cream of wheat (unprepared)	1/2 cup	125 mL
All-purpose flour	1/2 cup	125 mL
Vanilla	2 tsp.	10 mL
Egg whites (large), room temperature	4	4
Icing (confectioner's) sugar	1/2 cup	125 mL

Dough: Cream margarine, sugar, egg yolks and sour cream together in medium bowl.

Mix in flour and baking powder until mixture is crumbly. Divide in half. Press 1 portion of dough into ungreased 9 x 13 inch (22 x 33 cm) pan. Set remaining dough aside.

Filling: Stir first 5 ingredients together in large bowl until well mixed.

Using clean beaters, beat egg whites in separate medium bowl until soft peaks form. Gradually beat in icing sugar until stiff peaks form. Gently fold into yogurt mixture. Spread evenly over dough in pan. Crumble remaining dough evenly over filling. Bake in 400°F (205°C) oven for 40 minutes. Cool. Cuts into 20 to 24 pieces.

1 piece: 225 Calories; 8.2 g Total Fat; 162 mg Sodium; 7 g Protein; 31 g Carbohydrate; 1 g Dietary Fibre

Pictured above.

Table
Decorations

Bring some true holiday glitter to the feast—enhance your
culinary efforts amidst these enchanting table decorations.
Here's a marvelous opportunity to show off
your creative side with stunning results!

Setting the Table

When you ask your family and guests to "please come and sit down" at the Christmas dinner table, you want their first impression to set the stage for the meal you have prepared. The art of creating can be quite simple—but with elegant and wowing results! Our creations for your Christmas dinner table couldn't be simpler. A beautiful red and gold table runner that doubles as the placemats, red and gold poinsettia centerpieces and red and green felt poinsettia napkin rings combine to present a gorgeous vision of Christmas splendor. No sewing or gluing is required for any of these ideas.

Woven Ribbon Runners

Take a plain, solid-coloured tablecloth and 2 or 3 colours of ribbon and you will transform your dining table setting from a conversation piece to a conversation topic for years to come. Build a colour scheme around your china by choosing ribbon of complementary or contrasting colours. Choose soft, heavier ribbon that will lie flat and straight throughout the course of the evening's meal. The ribbons can be of varying widths as well as texture and you can space them equal distance apart or with a pattern—the possibilities are endless! Use all one kind of ribbon for a less dramatic, but still effective, look. Each woven runner will make two "placemats" on opposites sides (or ends) of the table.

For our design for 8 place settings, you will need:
Silver ribbon (3 inches, 7.5 cm, wide), enough to cover
   2 lengths and 6 widths of table, plus additional
   48 inches (120 cm)
Red ribbon (2 inches, 5 cm, wide), enough to cover
   1 length and 3 widths of table, plus additional
   24 inches (60 cm)
Tape measure
Scissors

White table cloth

Cut 2 lengths of silver ribbon and 1 length of red ribbon to each measure length of table plus 6 inches (15 cm). Cut 6 lengths of silver ribbon and 3 lengths of red ribbon to each measure width of table plus 6 inches (15 cm).

Place table cloth over table. Place long red ribbon lengthwise down centre of table cloth. Lay long silver ribbons down either side, leaving about 1 inch (2.5 cm) in between. Take end of 1 short silver ribbon and feed it, across width of table, over, under and over the three longer ribbons about where the edge of the outside placemats would be. Pull ribbon through to hang about 3 inches (7.5 cm) over opposite side. Take end of 1 short red ribbon and feed it, about 1 inch (2.5 cm) beside first ribbon, under, over and under the same longer ribbons. Pull ribbon through to hang same as first ribbon.

Repeat with second silver ribbon to complete pattern. Repeat complete pattern two more times, moving down length of table.

Poinsettia Cups Centrepiece

This centrepiece can be used in a variety of ways. Make as many as you want for the centre of your dinner table, or place individual cups at each place setting. For a buffet meal, have a large arrangement of poinsettia cups in the back and a few placed randomly around the food. Although we have chosen a red poinsettia with red ribbon and a silver cup to complement our Woven Ribbon Runners, page 177, you can choose colours, ribbon and cups to match your china.

For 5 centrepieces, you will need:

White ribbon (1/4 inch, 6 mm, wide), cut into
　five 6 inch (15 cm) lengths
5 silver martini goblets
Small paring knife
5 small blocks of florist's (foam) oasis

Green florist's moss
Poinsettia bush with at least 5 flowers
　(or 5 individual poinsettia picks)
Wire cutters
20 to 30 Christmas picks (pine cones, evergreen,
　berries, holly, pine branches, etc.)

Place enough moss in goblet to cover oasis. Separate poinsettia bush using wire cutters. Push 1 flower through moss into centre of oasis. Push 3 or 4 Christmas picks in and around flower. Repeat with remaining supplies. (Note: Do not glue in place; goblets can then be used for their intended purpose at a later date.)

Tie 1 piece of ribbon around stem of 1 goblet. Cut and shape 1 oasis to fit down about 1 1/2 inches (3.8 cm) inside goblet.

Poinsettia Napkin Ring

Whether or not we use cloth napkins on a day-to-day basis, we can't seem to help but get them out for Christmas dinner. What table setting would be complete without them? And napkin rings add the final touch to the overall presentation. We have continued the poinsettia theme of the centrepiece with this napkin ring design.

For 1 napkin ring, you will need:
Piece of brown paper (or other heavier paper),
  6 × 12 inch (15 × 30 cm) size
Scissors

Piece of red felt (about 7 × 7 inch, 18 × 18 cm, size)
Piece of green felt (about 4 × 12 inch, 10 × 30 cm, size)

To enlarge pattern: Mark brown paper into 1 inch (2.5 cm) squares. Transfer above pattern to grid, matching lines within each square. Cut out patterns.

POINSETTIA PATTERN

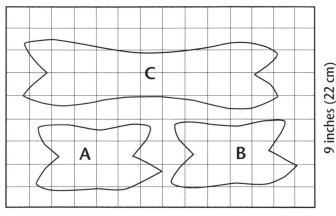

14 inches (35 cm)

9 inches (22 cm)

Bring folded ends of (A) together. Slip through slit in (B). Unfold to make flower.

Take long end of (C) and tuck back into itself. Leave loose to make ring for napkin.

Cut out both petals (A and B) from red felt and leaf (C) from green felt. Fold (A) in half lengthwise and insert halfway into slit in (C). Do not unfold (A).

Dessert Buffets

The dessert buffet is a pretty presentation for an afternoon tea, baby shower or engagement party. It provides a relaxing alternative after a more formal main course. After a play, ballet or concert, invite people back to your place for dessert and coffee with a flair.

Aprés Dinner Dessert Buffet

Mango Rum Fluff, page 96

Pineapple Cheese Pie, page 132

Dessert, served buffet-style after a formal sit-down dinner, is a pleasant way to get guests to move from the table to the sitting area to finish conversations and let the first course settle a bit longer. Dessert, in this case, would be a fork dessert such as a pie, layer cake or fancy dessert. It may already be cut and served on individual plates, ready to be picked up along with a cup of tea or coffee and perhaps a liqueur. Or it may be uncut with a serving utensil and stack of plates or bowls set beside it. In either case, guests can go over and serve themselves at their leisure. Sometimes a choice of two desserts is just as easy as making twice as much of just one dessert.

Dessert Buffet (After Main Course)

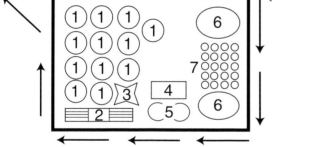

Dessert Buffet (Variety)

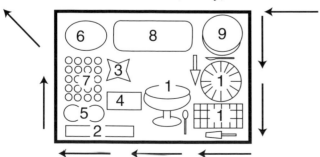

Chocolate Dessert Buffet

Chocolate-Coated Mint Patties, page 26

White Chocolate Fudge Truffles, page 83

Chocolate Orange Treats, page 84

Ragged Chocolate Drops, page 89

Chocolate Raspberry Biscotti, page 106

Brownie Cake Dessert, page 106

White Chocolate Cherry Cheesecake, page 110

Chilled Chocolate Cheesecake, page 96

Rocky Road Pie, page 133

As part of a cocktail party, a dessert buffet would be an assortment of pick-up-with-your-fingers treats such as squares, candies and confections or small cakes. But the truly sumptuous dessert offering is in the middle of the afternoon or later in the evening when an array of both fork and finger desserts are offered in an aesthetically picturesque way. The line should flow in one direction and towards the seating area so that if bottlenecks are going to occur, they won't interfere with people who have already gotten their food.

Buffet Table Legend
1. Dessert
2. Napkins, Cutlery
3. Mints
4. Coffee Spoons
5. Cream, Sugar
6. Coffee, Tea
7. Cups, Saucers
8. Centrepiece
9. Plates, Bowls

Measurement Tables

Throughout this book measurements are given in Conventional and Metric measure. To compensate for differences between the two measurements due to rounding, a full metric measure is not always used. The cup used is the standard 8 fluid ounce. Temperature is given in degrees Fahrenheit and Celsius. Baking pan measurements are in inches and centimetres as well as quarts and litres. An exact metric conversion is given on this page as well as the working equivalent (Metric Standard Measure).

Oven Temperatures

Fahrenheit (°F)	Celsius (°C)	Fahrenheit (°F)	Celsius (°C)
175°	80°	350°	175°
200°	95°	375°	190°
225°	110°	400°	205°
250°	120°	425°	220°
275°	140°	450°	230°
300°	150°	475°	240°
325°	160°	500°	260°

Spoons

Conventional Measure	Metric Exact Conversion Millilitre (mL)	Metric Standard Measure Millilitre (mL)
1/8 teaspoon (tsp.)	0.6 mL	0.5 mL
1/4 teaspoon (tsp.)	1.2 mL	1 mL
1/2 teaspoon (tsp.)	2.4 mL	2 mL
1 teaspoon (tsp.)	4.7 mL	5 mL
2 teaspoons (tsp.)	9.4 mL	10 mL
1 tablespoon (tbsp.)	14.2 mL	15 mL

Cups

1/4 cup (4 tbsp.)	56.8 mL	60 mL
1/3 cup (5 1/3 tbsp.)	75.6 mL	75 mL
1/2 cup (8 tbsp.)	113.7 mL	125 mL
2/3 cup (10 2/3 tbsp.)	151.2 mL	150 mL
3/4 cup (12 tbsp.)	170.5 mL	175 mL
1 cup (16 tbsp.)	227.3 mL	250 mL
4 1/2 cups	1022.9 mL	1000 mL (1 L)

Pans

Conventional - Inches	Metric - Centimeters
8x8 inch	20x20 cm
9x9 inch	22x22 cm
9x13 inch	22x33 cm
10x15 inch	25x38 cm
11x17 inch	28x43 cm
8x2 inch round	20x5 cm
9x2 inch round	22x5 cm
10x4 1/2 inch tube	25x11 cm
8x4x3 inch loaf	20x10x7.5 cm
9x5x3 inch loaf	22x12.5x7.5 cm

Dry Measurements

Conventional Measure Ounces (oz.)	Metric Exact Conversion Grams (g)	Metric Standard Measure Grams (g)
1 oz.	28.3 g	28 g
2 oz.	56.7 g	57 g
3 oz.	85.0 g	85 g
4 oz.	113.4 g	125 g
5 oz.	141.7 g	140 g
6 oz.	170.1 g	170 g
7 oz.	198.4 g	200 g
8 oz.	226.8 g	250 g
16 oz.	453.6 g	500 g
32 oz.	907.2 g	1000 g (1 kg)

Casseroles

Canada & Britain		United States	
Standard Size Casserole	Exact Metric Measure	Standard Size Casserole	Exact Metric Measure
1 qt. (5 cups)	1.13 L	1 qt. (4 cups)	900 mL
1 1/2 qts. (7 1/2 cups)	1.69 L	1 1/2 qts. (6 cups)	1.35 L
2 qts. (10 cups)	2.25 L	2 qts. (8 cups)	1.8 L
2 1/2 qts. (12 1/2 cups)	2.81 L	2 1/2 qts. (10 cups)	2.25 L
3 qts. (15 cups)	3.38 L	3 qts. (12 cups)	2.7 L
4 qts. (20 cups)	4.5 L	4 qts. (16 cups)	3.6 L
5 qts. (25 cups)	5.63 L	5 qts. (20 cups)	4.5 L

Tip Index

How-To Index

Recipe Index

DANIELLE
JACLYN
MARLENE
PETE
PATRICIA
STEPHE
MARGARET
MARY
LESLIE
BRENDA
DA
MARILYN
WENDY
ELIZABETH
LAURIE
SANDRA
SARAH
VICKI
TAMI
ALLISON
DOROTHY
BLAIR
DON
SHERRI
ROXANNE
JESSICA
PAT
RUTH
LEAH
DARLANE
AUDREY
KAREN
DERRICK
DEANNA
RICHARD
ELEANOR
JOHN
GEORGE
GRANT
AMANDA
SHELLY
SHEIL
DAWNA
LAUREL
CHARLENE
CONNIE
SUZANNE
PAULA
GAIL
PENNY
DANA
CINDY
CATHY
LOVONI
TEQUITA
NORA
DIANE
ROSE
SHELLEY
KATHY
JAMES
JODIE
BOB
STEPHANIE
GOD
LINDA
NETZUS
CARA
RENDI
VORI
NADINE
LYNDA
LORRAINE